100 THINGS PANTHERS FANS SHOULD KNOW & DO BEFORE THEY DIE

Scott Fowler

TRIUMPH
BOOKS

Library of Congress Cataloging-in-Publication Data

Fowler, Scott.
    100 things Panthers fans should know & do before they die / Scott Fowler.
        pages cm
    ISBN 978-1-60078-824-6 (pbk.)
    1. Carolina Panthers (Football team)—History. 2. Carolina Panthers (Football team)—Anecdotes. I. Title. II. Title: One hundred things Panthers fan should know & do before they die.
    GV956.C27F68 2013
    796.332'640975676—dc23
                                    2013031007
This book is available in quantity at special discounts for your group or organization. For further information, contact:
    Triumph Books LLC
    814 North Franklin Street
    Chicago, Illinois 60610
    (312) 337-0747
    www.triumphbooks.com

Printed in U.S.A.
ISBN: 978-1-60078-824-6
Design by Patricia Frey
Photos courtesy of AP Images unless otherwise indicated

To all the Carolina fans who have exulted in the Panthers' best times, suffered through their worst times, and maintained a sense of humor through all of it. And to my wonderful family and great friends— I am a lucky man to have you all.

Contents

Mike Minter spent his entire 10-year career with the Panthers.

Foreword

When the Panthers drafted me in the second round out of Nebraska in 1997, I hardly knew anything about North Carolina. I knew that it was the state where Michael Jordan had played basketball in college, and that was about it. All I knew about the Panthers themselves was that they were an expansion team and that they had just had a lot of success, going to the NFC Championship Game just before I got there, in 1996.

When I first flew in for a team minicamp in 1997, I remember seeing the trees before I saw anything else. I couldn't believe it. Where I was from, we just didn't have trees like that. I fell in love with all those trees right away, even before I started meeting the people and falling in love with the area.

North Carolina has been my home ever since, and the Panthers will always have a special place in my heart. I never left the Panthers for another team after I got there, and that's rare in the NFL. I played 10 years for Carolina and made a lot of lifelong friends in that locker room. We had some great times and some times that weren't so great, but we stuck together and I was proud to call the Panthers my team, then and now.

The first thing that comes to my mind when I think of all my years of being a Carolina Panther is "excellence." The second thing is "bring your lunch pail." The third thing is "loyalty."

In my mind, that's what the Panthers have been about for close to 20 years now. We are just a bunch of blue-collar guys, striving for excellence with a lunch-pail mentality. I think that has something to do with Jerry Richardson and the way he modeled his team after the Pittsburgh Steelers. He stands for excellence in everything he does.

When I got to that first minicamp way back then, Coach Dom Capers didn't have the veterans there, so I was just looking at the young guys. I was a little taken aback, like, *Wow. This is it?* That helped me gain some confidence that I could play there. This was before I saw what Sam Mills and the rest of those guys could do.

The first impression the other guys had about me was that I wasn't as big as they thought I was. They were saying, "Man, we thought we were getting this big old safety from Nebraska. You're a little guy. What's going on?"

I was thinking to myself, *When we put on the pads, you're going to find out what's going on.*

It was at my first training camp in Spartanburg where I began getting to know the veteran guys like Sam Mills and Eric Davis, who both showed me how to be a pro. Eric took me under his wing, since we were both playing in the secondary, and we became good friends.

I was in shock when I first saw Lamar Lathon. That was the first time I had ever seen a man who was that big, fast, and agile. Kerry Collins was our quarterback then, and it felt like a big deal to go against him in practice. "Rocket" Ismail was a really fast wide receiver who was a challenge to cover.

I made my first NFL start as a rookie in my sixth NFL game—Minnesota on the road. I was a little nervous at first. But then I thought, *Let's make it happen. You can do this.*

That year we played a game at St. Louis and Sam Mills and I were both going for a tackle. He got there before I did, and then I heard the loudest noise I'd ever heard. *BOOM!* I had never been in awe of someone who had hit someone else—not until that moment. I literally couldn't believe how hard Sam had hit that guy. It was so solid! I thought, *That's the way I want to hit people.*

My first two years for the Panthers were the last two years for Coach Capers. You talk about a perfectionist. With Dom, everything felt scripted from the moment we walked into the building to the moment we left. Everything had a purpose. There was a time and place for everything. Dom didn't joke around. He was kind of serious all the time. Very focused. I can see why he's still a great defensive coordinator in the NFL. Unfortunately, we didn't get it done as a football team for him. Once I got there, we were getting way too old way too quickly at significant positions.

Then I played for George Seifert during his three years there. George was a totally different guy than Dom. He was more laid back. I don't know if that came from his West Coast background or what. He had our respect from what he had done in San Francisco, winning Super Bowls there. But his thing was that he was already used to veteran guys, and he wanted that from us. But we were all young and trying to learn—he didn't have Joe Montana, Ronnie Lott, and Jerry Rice anymore. By the end, I thought George got to a point where he checked out and really didn't care much if we won or lost. I'm sure he actually did care, but that's what it felt like to us.

I do remember one time when it felt like he cared. We played Washington and they scored about 21 unanswered points on us by throwing the ball around. The next day he called all four of the starting DBs into his office and said to us, "If I could fire all of you, I would." He and I really didn't see eye to eye for a lot of reasons.

Then I played my final five years under John Fox, from 2002 to 2006, and that's when we had our greatest success. Now Foxy, he was a salesman—the greatest salesman I've ever known. And as a football coach, I feel like you have to be a salesman. That's part of the job. We didn't know anything about Coach Fox. He had to come in and win us over. And he did. I try to do that now with my own players.

By then, I was a veteran guy. I understood what the league was all about. I understood how to push my teammates. I was a captain. That first year with Fox, he had Jack Del Rio as his defensive coordinator, and that was the best one-two punch of coaches I've ever seen. He and Del Rio really complemented each other.

xi

It was Fox's second season when we had that run to the Super Bowl. That whole year was so special. We won so many games in the last minute. I remember both games against Tampa Bay—our defense against their defense. We showed them that we had to be taken into account, that we could play. And I remember the Arizona game when we won the NFC South. And all of the playoff games, one after another. It was so surreal. Dallas. St. Louis. Philadelphia. New England. If we only could have won that last one.

I made so many great friends during my time as a Panther. Eric Davis treated me like a little brother for those first few years. Then Mike Rucker came to us, also from Nebraska, in 1999. I was older than Ruck was by a couple of years and I hadn't hung out with him much at Nebraska—back then I thought he was kind of goofy. But he grew up. We became close in Charlotte, and our families became close. We lived down the street from each other for the final five or six years of my career. We went on vacations together, did business deals together. We are still very tight.

And there were other guys I became very close with. Muhsin Muhammad and I kind of grew up together with the Panthers—we came into the league just a year apart. John Kasay was the team's spiritual leader, and I spent a lot of time around him due to our common Christian faith. I've also had Bible studies with guys including Anthony Johnson and Winslow Oliver. All the DBs I played with for the Panthers were great fun—guys like Brent Alexander, Eugene Robinson, Doug Evans, Jimmy Hitchcock. And Reggie White—he was great.

When I finished playing, I decided I wanted to be a coach. I started in high school at Concord First Assembly, first helping to build the program and then coaching the team. We won two state championships there in my three years. I fell in love with the profession.

I stayed there three years and then thought I should try to move to college coaching. I went to Johnson C. Smith, a Division II school in Charlotte, and basically volunteered to become an assistant. I coached the secondary and was assistant defensive coordinator and the special teams coordinator. Then I went to Liberty, in Virginia, and was special teams coordinator there. Then in December 2012, I got hired by Campbell University for my first college head-coaching job.

As a coach, you have to prove yourself all over again. You can't say, "I was an NFL player" and just rest on your laurels. You have to work. You have to show your players that what you were has no effect on what you are going to try to do together. But I like that. I know how to work. The Panthers helped to teach me that. I'll always be grateful for everything the organization did for me, and I'll always be a Panther.

—Mike Minter

Mike Minter played his entire NFL career with the Panthers from 1997 to 2006 as a safety, starting 141 total games for three different Panthers head coaches. Minter remains the Panthers' all-time leader in tackles and interceptions returned for touchdowns. He now serves as the head football coach for Campbell University in Buies Creek, North Carolina.

Introduction

The Carolina Panthers made their official debut in 1995—playing their first exhibition game at the Hall of Fame preseason contest in Canton, Ohio, and then playing at Atlanta in their first regular-season game against the Falcons.

I was there for both, fortunate enough to attend those games as a sportswriter for the *Charlotte Observer*. And I've been able to go to almost every Carolina game in person since then for the same reason, covering more than 200 Panthers games on assignment for the newspaper and conducting thousands of interviews and informal conversations with Panthers players, coaches, and administrators over the past two decades for other stories, as well.

So when Triumph Books approached me about writing *100 Things Panthers Fans Should Know & Do Before They Die,* I gladly agreed to do so. I have a historical bent anyway, and the Panthers are now a worthy subject, for they are finally old enough to have an actual history.

People who were teenagers when the Panthers made their 1995 debut are now in their thirties. They have their own children, mortgages, and hopes. Just like their own fans, the Panthers have grown up. Think of it this way: If the Panthers were a person instead of an NFL team, they would now be old enough to vote (although not yet old enough to order a beer).

My primary hope is that this book will help you remember some of the best moments in Panthers history, from Sam Mills' interception return for a touchdown during Carolina's first win in 1995 at Clemson to Steve Smith's 69-yard touchdown catch to end the playoff game at St. Louis in double overtime in 2004 to Cam Newton's 72-yard touchdown run with a front flip into the end zone in 2012.

You don't have to read this book from number 1 to 100, either. Skip around. Flip through the pictures. Read about the people you care about the most. Each chapter is self-contained, so the book can be sampled like a table full of appetizers or devoured straight through from beginning to end.

As for the "top 100" order in which I have placed these men and events, put the blame solely on me if you don't like the rankings. Although I received input from some Panthers insiders whom I trust, the final decisions on where to rank No. 1 through No. 100 were made by me alone.

My rankings were based mostly on how significant (for better or for worse) the player or the particular event was or is to the Panthers. You can certainly debate every part of the list, and I hope you do. Football fans like to argue, and there's nothing wrong with that.

As for the "things to do" items, I hope even the most die-hard fan can find a couple of nuggets in those. Even with an expensive venture like the NFL, there are a surprising number of freebies on this list (going to training camp in Spartanburg, attending the team's annual draft party in April and scrimmage in August, following the players on Twitter, and so on).

More than anything else, I intend this book to be a celebration—as well as a thorough look at the people who made the Panthers' first 18 seasons noteworthy. Don't get the wrong idea, though. This is not an extremely serious book.

Football is ultimately a fun diversion, and this book is designed to entertain as much as to inform. You'll find out about the man who was briefly a Panther before becoming a reality TV star, the time team mascot Sir Purr drew a penalty by jumping on a live punt during a game, and the Panthers' remarkably bad run of losing coin flips in 2012.

The Panthers' future currently appears bright with Newton at quarterback, Luke Kuechly at middle linebacker, and a decided upswing in the talent level since the 2–14 season of 2010. But while we're waiting for the Panthers to win their first-ever Super Bowl, let's take a trip back in time now that the team has been around for close to 20 years.

You may have forgotten—or may have never known in the first place—what a long, strange trip it's been.

So come on, and enjoy the ride.

1 Sam Mills and "Keep Pounding"

When you think of the best the Carolina Panthers have been able to offer their fans in their first two decades of existence, one man and one motto come to mind first.

The man is Sam Mills.

The motto is "Keep Pounding"—a phrase Mills first used in 2004 in a speech to the team before a big home playoff win against Dallas. "Keep Pounding" has been widely adopted as the team's theme. The words are now sewn inside the collar in every one of the Panthers' jerseys.

Mills was many things to the Panthers: first, a Pro Bowl linebacker, who will always be the first player ever honored with his own statue outside of the team's home stadium. Then a valued assistant coach. Then a cancer victim who fought the disease valiantly, continuing to coach even as the disease wracked his body. And always a gentleman—a symbol of dignity and class who every Panthers player would do well to emulate. His No. 51 is the only Panthers jersey to have ever been retired.

Mills died of colon cancer in 2005, at age 45. But by then he had already established a legacy with the Panthers, even though he didn't get to Charlotte until the final decade of his life.

Mills and the Panthers first linked up in early 1995. Mills was 35, a time by which most NFL players have already been forced into retirement. But he had been the ultimate late bloomer, and Panthers head coach Dom Capers and defensive coordinator Vic Fangio wanted Mills to anchor their 3-4 defense at inside linebacker.

Mills didn't make the NFL at all until he was 27 years old. The first of his parents' 11 children to earn a college degree, he was a

Sam Mills, shown here in 1997, is one of the most inspirational figures in Panthers history. (Getty Images)

good player at Division III Montclair State in New Jersey—but not good enough to get drafted. With no pro prospects, his first job out of college was as a woodworking and photography teacher at a New Jersey high school. He made $13,600 a year.

But that didn't last long, because Mills made the old USFL at an open tryout in 1982 and became a standout in that short-lived league for the Philadelphia/Baltimore Stars. His prowess there earned him a spot with the New Orleans Saints (Jim Mora coached both teams), where Mills was a great linebacker for many years on a lot of average Saints teams.

Mills was only 5'9". Panthers coach Ron Rivera was also an NFL linebacker—although not as renowned as Mills—in Chicago, and respected Mills' work from afar. "They called him the field general," said Rivera, who also knew of the constant teasing Mills endured for his lack of height. "That or the field mouse."

But Mills was incredibly good at getting to the right place on the field. He was like a Peyton Manning on defense, diagnosing plays before they were ever run. And man, could he ever hit. Hall of Fame linebacker Lawrence Taylor once said of Mills, "Just once, I'd like to get a hit like he does. It has to be better than sex."

Mills liked to make fun of himself. He wore gold-rimmed glasses everywhere except on the field. He had a squat build and had lost almost all of his hair by the time he got to Charlotte. He sometimes referred to himself as a player who was "short, balding, and can't see very well."

Mills was an unrestricted free agent when the Panthers came into existence, in 1995. Carolina offered him a two-year, $2.8 million contract. New Orleans then matched the offer, but Mills was disappointed that it took Carolina's money to make the Saints ante up. As he told me once in an interview, "After all that I'd done playing in New Orleans, it kind of bothered me that they were only going to pay me the money because they *had* to pay it and not because they *wanted* to pay it. To me, it's almost like inviting somebody to

Sam Mills' Three Biggest Plays

The Shovel Pass. The Carolina Panthers were 0–5 in 1995, their first season, and trailing 12–6 in the second quarter of their sixth game, against the New York Jets. Mills was blitzing and came through the line untouched. Jets quarterback Bubby Brister was throwing a shovel pass and couldn't stop himself—he threw it right to Mills.

Mills would remember the play later like this: "The way it happened, it just kind of clicked. Right call, right place, right time. I intersected with where the Jets' back, Adrian Murrell, was supposed to be. I was never touched at all. I know I surprised Brister."

Mills then trundled toward the end zone, scoring from 36 yards out on what seemed like a slow-motion run. Noted then-Panthers quarterback Frank Reich, "I thought he was trying to do two things: score a TD and run out the clock."

Mills' teammates teased him about his speed for years afterward, but he would always say, "Hey, I got there."

The interception return was the key play in Carolina's first-ever win—a 26–15 victory over the Jets on October 15, 1995.

The Stop. On the opening day of the 1996 season, Carolina hosted Atlanta. On third-and-1 from the Carolina 14, Mills and Atlanta's bowling ball running back, Craig "Ironhead" Heyward, collided in the hole. The boom was like thunder—and Heyward fell

your party or to some special event because your mom says you've got to invite them. If I found out I was invited to an event because somebody forced you to invite me, I'd rather not be invited at all."

So Mills took Carolina's offer instead. He and his wife, Melanie, brought their three children to Charlotte (they would soon have a fourth). Sam III was the oldest and would eventually become a Panthers assistant coach himself, although back then he was a ball boy when the team went to their first training camp.

Mills immediately became the leader of a defense that had six starters over 30 and was nicknamed the "Grumpy Old Men." Teammates loved to tease Mills about his age—"What was it like to play with leather helmets?" wide receiver Willie Green would sometimes ask him—but they all respected his work ethic and his talent.

4

backward like an oak tree, losing a yard. Not only that, he hurt his shoulder and left the game for good.

"Sam Mills hit me right on the shoulder," Heyward told reporters afterward, "and it hurt really bad. I could have gone back in and played, but only if somebody had died."

The Falcons were forced to kick a field goal after that hit, which cornerback Eric Davis would later term his favorite play of the 1996 season. Carolina would go on to score 19 straight points for a 29–6 victory that kicked off their first-ever playoff season.

Sadly, both Mills and Heyward died early of cancer and its complications—Mills at age 45, Heyward at age 39.

The Playoff Interception. The Panthers' first-ever playoff game—and the Dallas Cowboys' 51st—wasn't decided for sure until Mills made a huge play. With Dallas trailing 26–17 but Troy Aikman trying to engineer a comeback in the final two minutes, Mills stepped in front of an Aikman pass at the Dallas 25. He thought about going to one knee but, with no one around him, started rumbling toward the goal line.

"I ran the whole time with two hands on the ball," Mills said. "So I wasn't going that fast—not that I have that many gears to work with anyway." He ended up making it inside the Dallas 5 to clinch the January 1997 victory.

It was Mills' interception of a shovel pass that keyed Carolina's first-ever win, in 1995.

His best season came in 1996, when the Panthers—in only their second year as a franchise—made a stunning run to the NFC Championship Game before losing to Green Bay. Mills had a late interception in Carolina's 26–17 home playoff win against Dallas that season that clinched the Panthers' first-ever playoff victory over a Cowboys team that included future Hall of Famers Troy Aikman, Emmitt Smith, Michael Irvin, and Deion Sanders.

Since I have covered the Panthers from the beginning, I had the great fortune to know Mills fairly well. In our last extensive interview—a three-hour lunch at a Charlotte restaurant in 2004—I asked him what his favorite game was in all his years as a player.

"The first Dallas playoff game," he said. "That was a real big moment. We knocked off the big kids on the block."

A five-time Pro Bowler, Mills retired after the 1997 season. Simply for his playing career with the Panthers, owner Jerry Richardson made Mills the first former Panthers player (and as of early 2013 still the only player) in the team's Hall of Honor. That led to the bronze statue of Mills being erected outside the stadium.

Mills was cut by the first two teams he tried out for in the pros—the NFL's Cleveland Browns and the Canadian Football League's Toronto Argonauts. When first told of his impending Hall of Honor induction in 1998, he said: "You're talking about a guy who was kicked out of one stadium in Cleveland, kicked out of another in Toronto, and now is going to be a permanent part of one right here in Charlotte. That's very special to me."

Mills then joined the Panthers as an assistant coach in 1999, becoming the linebackers coach and guiding players such as Dan Morgan and Will Witherspoon to fine seasons. But in August 2003 he was diagnosed with colon cancer. Doctors privately told him they weren't sure he would live to the new year.

That was the beginning of the Panthers' Super Bowl season, and Mills kept pounding at his job all the way through it. In a normal game week, he would have seven hours of chemotherapy on Monday, seven more on Tuesday, and then three more on Wednesday. His mind and body would ache. His black skin gradually lightened by several shades due to the chemicals. But he would go back to work Thursday, coach through the game on Sunday, and then start chemo all over again on Monday.

The Panthers players on that team knew of Mills' struggle with cancer, as well as the battle fought by linebacker Mark Fields. Fields missed that season with a more treatable form of cancer and later returned to play for one more season; he is still alive today.

But the players seemed almost afraid to ask Mills about the particulars of his disease, and while he didn't mind talking to them about it he also didn't go around volunteering about the daily details of his life. Then on January 2, 2004, John Fox, the team's head coach at the time, asked Mills to address the Panthers the night before the Dallas playoff game in a hotel meeting room.

In a calm, measured voice, Mills told the players about his cancer. He told them that they had to keep pounding—not just in football, but in life. That when things got tough, they had to remember to "Keep Pounding, keep pounding, keep pounding." The speech lasted no longer than 10 minutes, but it was so unforgettable that part of it is now plastered on the walls of the Panthers' weight room.

Steve Smith was one of the players in that room.

"His speech was so impactful to me," Smith told me in 2012. "Even nine years later, I remember it. You had a guy who had every opportunity to take pity on himself, to be like 'I don't feel like dealing with this.' And he opened up. And he made it about something else. Something bigger."

The Panthers won that home playoff game, 29–10, over Dallas—so Mills had a major impact on two different playoff victories over the Cowboys in Charlotte. He coached the rest of that season and the next as well, but passed away in April 2005.

Since Mills III still coaches for the Panthers—most of the rest of the family lives in the New Jersey area—he still hears lots of stories about his father.

"Fans will sometimes tell me their stories of meeting him," Mills III told me once. "A lot of the stories revolve around something like: 'Hey, one day I was shopping at T.J. Maxx and I ran into your dad. He sat there and talked to me about football for 20 minutes.'

"It's funny," Mills III continued. "I try to teach our young guys that they don't understand what it's like to be a fan. Sometimes your younger guys look at something like that almost like a nuisance. They need to take a step back and understand, you're that person's idol half the time. You taking five minutes out of your day just to chitchat—even if you're just talking about buying a belt—it can mean so much to them."

Smith has long kept Mills in his heart, too—and probably no other Panther has better personified the "Keep Pounding" motto. And Smith has another more personal reason for remember Mills.

"On April 18, 2005," Smith said, "my younger son, Boston, was born. And Sam died at almost the same time. Almost the same hour. As I was calling the team chaplain to tell him about the birth, he was calling me to tell me about Sam's passing. So as one part of the Panther family was born, another was passing away. Life moves like that sometimes in families, doesn't it?"

Mills' legacy threads through the Panthers today—on their jersey collars and in their team motto. When the going gets tough, you have to keep pounding. That was the message from an undrafted, undersized linebacker who was an NFL rookie at age 27 and made five Pro Bowls after that—a player who didn't play his first game as a Panther until age 36 and still became the most significant player in team history.

2 Steve Smith

The best player the Carolina Panthers have ever had is a complicated man. He can brim with fury or charm a child, spin a ball or snap at a perceived slight.

Steve Smith leads the Panthers' all-time list in touchdowns by a fair amount and in *"Did you just see that?"* moments by even more. No one has mesmerized Panthers fans more often. The Panthers drafted Smith out of Utah in the third round of the 2001 draft. Despite several bouts of serious rockiness, he has been at Carolina ever since.

Among the qualities that make No. 89 what he is: Extreme confidence. An incredible work ethic layered over enough ridiculous talent to compensate for his 5'9" height. A chip on his shoulder so wide his jersey should include extra material to cover it.

Ranked in the NFL's all-time top 35 in career receptions, receiving yards, and 100-yard receiving games (he's in the top 10 in that one), Smith is a possible Pro Football Hall of Famer and a Panthers player who will never be forgotten.

Before Smith ever played a single down for Carolina, the rookie sat in Marty Hurney's office. He hadn't liked Hurney's contract offer and wanted to make sure the future Panthers GM (Hurney didn't have the title yet) knew how important a player he was going to be to the team.

"Marty," Smith said, "I'm going to be the best player you're ever going to get here."

Stunned by the statement, Hurney didn't say much—just something like "I hope so."

But Smith's bravado was totally accurate. Some players have had great individual seasons and have made a similar number of Pro Bowls while at Carolina—players like Julius Peppers, Wesley Walls, and Michael Bates. Others—like Sam Mills and John Kasay—have carried themselves in a more consistently dignified manner.

But no one else has been as dazzling for so long. Smith has been an electric-blue live wire for more than a decade for Carolina. The first time he ever touched the ball in an NFL game, he went 93 yards for a touchdown against Minnesota.

Moments before that—and this isn't coincidental—Smith was disrespected for the first time just before a real NFL game. A Vikings player sidled up to him and cracked, "This ain't Utah no more, son."

Forgive that Viking. He knew not what he had done. Smith is fueled by such comments—and if he isn't currently being disrespected, he will make something up if necessary.

The Best of Steve Smith

Some highlights of Steve Smith's career at Carolina.

Best catch: The 69-yard touchdown pass from Jake Delhomme that won the 2003 playoff game against St. Louis on the first play of double overtime.

Best block: On Cam Newton's 72-yard touchdown run against Atlanta in 2012, Smith sprinted downfield to take out two Falcons defenders with one hit. He was awarded a game ball simply for the block.

Best single game: Smith's 218-yard receiving game on the road against Chicago in the 2005 playoffs.

Best touchdown celebration: Many to choose from (before the NFL reined in celebrations with 15-yard penalties), but I was always partial to Smith pretending the football was a baby and mimicking changing its diaper, even down to wiping the football's "bottom" in the end zone with a towel.

Best college receiver on other side: Chad Johnson—the future Ochocinco and Smith teamed together for a while at Santa Monica Junior College. Wouldn't you have liked to have been the quarterback?

Best pro receiver on other side: Muhsin Muhammad—who wasn't as fast as Smith but was a very physical player who helped mentor Smith and teach him how to block more effectively.

Best season: In 2005, Smith won the NFL's "triple crown" for wide receivers by leading the league in reception yards (1,563) and tying for first in receptions (103) and receiving TDs (12).

For instance, if you say something about the Panthers' 2003 Super Bowl team, Smith (depending on his mood) will sometimes believe you are implying he is a "loser" since the Panthers lost that game. Very few athletes actually play better when angered to the edge of self-control (John McEnroe was another exception) but Smith does.

In 2006, St. Louis cornerback Tye Hill supposedly said something to another Panther about shutting Smith out in a previous game. Ten months later, when the teams played again, Hill didn't remember what he said—or even saying anything.

It didn't matter. Smith had heard about it and—he told reporters before the game—had been "marinating" on it ever since. He toasted Hill for the 68-yard touchdown that was the key play in a win for Carolina.

Smith's anger has also hurt him. As he said in 2011, "You have to admit that pretty much I made an ass out of myself for a long time here by letting my emotions get the best of me."

As a Panther, Smith has struck a teammate in anger and was suspended by the team for it—not once, but twice. The second time he broke the nose of Panthers starting cornerback Ken Lucas at a training-camp practice. Later, Smith was remorseful, and Lucas accepted his apology. One of the moments I will always remember about Smith came weeks later, when I came upon Smith and Lucas peacefully playing dominoes in a team meeting room.

While Smith can be a hard pill to swallow—in the Panthers locker room, people check his many moods like meteorologists check the weather—he is at his best around children. He and his wife, Angie, have three kids, and Smith references them constantly in his conversation. He has coached some of his kids' soccer teams. They often join him in the locker room after games. He runs a football camp every summer in Charlotte that draws hundreds, and his touch-football games with those kids reveal Smith at his most joyous. He loves kids, he has said, partly because he knows they have no hidden agenda.

It's also true that few Panthers players have ever done more charity work than Smith. He is rooted deeply enough in the community to have taken underprivileged kids to Carowinds and to have played in a local flag-football league (in which he infamously broke his left forearm in 2010). He visited U.S. troops in the Middle East as part of an NFL-USO tour in 2013.

The ultimate reason Smith has stayed in the limelight for so long as a Panther, however, doesn't have to do with his behavior off the field, good or bad. It's because he has been one of the team's best players for so long—spinning the ball after first downs so that it twirls on its point like a top. Panthers coach Ron Rivera believes Smith could eventually make the Pro Football Hall of Fame and sometimes points out Smith's efforts—even at the tail end of blowout losses—to his younger players as something they should imitate.

"Kind of like that fine wine, he has most certainly improved with age," Rivera said.

Smith has always marched to the beat of his own drummer. Raised by a single mom in one of Los Angeles' roughest neighborhoods, he had little money growing up. His mother worked as a drug-abuse counselor for the county government. He didn't see his father much. One of his most vivid memories as a youngster was playing a basketball game in cleats because they were the only athletic shoes he had.

To get some spending money, Smith took a job at Taco Bell while in high school. The money he earned there paid for his prom. He was barely recruited at all—his grades weren't good, he quit the football team for a year as a junior, and he never even played wide receiver in high school. He ended up at Santa Monica Junior College, where he got his athletics and academics together and earned a scholarship to the University of Utah (where he would become a teammate of Jordan Gross).

For the Panthers, Smith was only a return man as a rookie in 2001, but was so good at it that he made the Pro Bowl. Then he won a starting job at receiver in 2002, John Fox's first year, and never looked back. He had his worst year in 2010, with Jimmy Clausen at quarterback, but bounced back with 1,000-yard receiving seasons in both 2011 and 2012 when Cam Newton became the QB.

Like all good NFL wide receivers, Smith constantly believes he is open. As Newton once noted about what Smith said to him about defensive coverages, "One man on him, 'I'm open.' Two men, 'Give me a chance.' Three men...'Throw it up and see what happens.'"

And usually, when the Panthers have thrown it up to Smith to see what would happen, it's been something good.

Shortly after he was drafted, Smith promised a "two- or three-second party" every time he scored. Through the years, there have been dozens of those brief but ebullient parties, as Smith celebrated in the end zone and thousands of Panthers fans celebrated everywhere else.

3 Jerry Richardson

Carolina owner Jerry Richardson founded the Panthers, dreaming them up from scratch and then putting so much money, muscle, and creativity behind them that they simply could not fail.

The only current NFL owner to have played in the league himself—and the first one since the late George Halas—Richardson has a unique standing in many ways. The Carolina Panthers literally would not exist without the man called "Mr. Richardson" by his employees and "Big Cat" by a few of his braver veteran players. No one else in franchise history can say that.

Given that, why is Richardson No. 3 on this list instead of No. 1? A good question. Richardson would make a very worthy No. 1. I ultimately put him behind Sam Mills and Steve Smith, however, because that's the way Richardson has seemingly preferred it for many years. He likes to be in the shadows. He wants other people to receive the credit.

Once Richardson's bid was awarded the NFL's 29th franchise on October 26, 1993, the owner almost immediately thrust the men he employed into the foreground and headed to the background himself. While still a hands-on owner who greatly enjoys interaction with players and coaches, Richardson never wanted to be like his friend Jerry Jones, the Dallas Cowboys' owner, and carry a permanently high profile.

Over the years, Richardson's press conferences have become so rare as to be almost nonexistent. In early 2011, when Richardson answered questions after parting ways with coach John Fox, it marked the first time in nine years he had held an actual press conference in Charlotte to answer questions. He still made appearances at notable hirings and retirements—usually starting with the line "Did you miss me?"—but then always thrust the current coach or general manager or player in question into the spotlight.

But to drop Richardson out of the top three entirely would be disingenuous, even if he might want it that way. Richardson made this franchise happen, beginning the process all the way back when he was a rookie catching passes (and a daily ride to training camp) from Baltimore Colts quarterback Johnny Unitas.

Born July 18, 1936, Richardson had been a standout, 6'4" wide receiver at Wofford College—the Panthers' future training-camp home in Spartanburg, South Carolina—in the late 1950s. He was not a highly regarded pro prospect, however, and beat considerable odds to make the Colts roster as a backup. As a rookie, Richardson caught a TD pass from Unitas in the 1959 championship game (the Super Bowl did not yet exist) when Unitas looked off Raymond Berry on the play and found Richardson instead. Grainy footage from that game still exists—Richardson scored standing up.

Richardson earned a $4,864 playoff check for his part in the Colts' title run that season. After another season, he was out of football and ready to start a career in business. He and a friend named Charlie Bradshaw opened the first Hardee's restaurant in 1961 in Spartanburg, serving cheap hamburgers to the masses. It was very successful, and they kept opening more of them. Richardson made many millions in the food business—running not only Hardee's restaurants, but also Denny's, Quincy's, and El Pollo Loco restaurants—before resigning as chairman in 1995 to concentrate on the family's new business of football.

Richardson got the idea that Charlotte—about 75 miles from Spartanburg—could work as an NFL market when he heard on the car radio while driving in April 1987 that owner George Shinn had convinced the NBA to put a team in Charlotte that would be called the Hornets. Richardson set to work, hiring PR genius Max Muhleman (who had helped Shinn get the Hornets).

He got Mike McCormack to work as a consultant—the former NFL player, coach, and executive who would give Richardson's bid an insider's credibility. He got former NFL commissioner Pete Rozelle as a mentor and confidant. He got financial backing from Charlotte mega-banker Hugh McColl Jr. He got his younger son, Mark, to do a little bit of everything. He even got a license plate that read PNTHERS.

What Richardson didn't get was a rent-free stadium to be paid for by public funds. All the other NFL expansion finalists at the time—St. Louis, Baltimore, Jacksonville, and Memphis had that. Richardson wanted to build and own the stadium himself.

That privately funded stadium concept seemed iffy, so much so that well-known oddsmaker Danny Sheridan listed Charlotte's odds of obtaining an NFL team in 1989 at 50 to 1. Those were the same odds as Montreal had then of getting a team, and much worse than odds for San Antonio and Sacramento—none of which ended up making the finals.

Even though the Panthers staged several successful NFL exhibitions to prove the viability of the Carolinas as a football market from 1989 to 1991—in Raleigh, Chapel Hill, and Columbia, at various college stadiums since there was no structure big enough to hold an exhibition in Charlotte—the stadium plan needed a boost. It came in the form of the permanent-seat license (PSL) concept created by Muhleman.

In order for fans to purchase season tickets at the proposed new stadium, they would first have to pay what amounted to a user fee—a "right" to the seat that cost anywhere from $600 to $5,400 per ticket. That was a onetime fee, but then the rights holder would be obligated to buy their season tickets every year or he would lose both his ticket rights and his original investment.

The PSL concept was a tremendous success, contributing more than $100 million toward the funding of a stadium that would eventually cost around $187 million. It was the last major roadblock. At an evening news conference when then–NFL commissioner Paul Tagliabue introduced Richardson as the league's newest owner, Richardson pointed to television cameras from the Carolinas and sent an exuberant "Thank you, thank you, thank you!" back home.

The next day Richardson would promise at a pep rally to thousands of fans in Charlotte that the Panthers would win a Super Bowl in 10 years—an unfulfilled promise he would be reminded of many times afterward.

Like all pro sports team owners, Richardson's popularity among Panthers fans goes up and down depending on whether his team is winning. He was extremely popular in the first few years of the franchise. Then he took a downturn in the George Seifert years and enjoyed another uptick during the best parts of the John Fox era. He purposely stayed out of the news for the most part, although he made big headlines in 2009 when his sons Mark and Jon both suddenly resigned their team presidencies.

The very public family split meant that the family business was no longer really a family business at all—Mark wouldn't take over as the team's primary owner and decision maker upon his father's death, as had been widely assumed. Now, in fact, it seems far more likely that the team will be sold within two years of Richardson's death. Richardson said in 2009 that he and his family owned 48 percent of the team, with the other 52 percent owned by a conglomeration of 14 minority partners.

Richardson has had some health problems—most seriously he underwent a heart transplant in February 2009. When a reporter asked him at his 2009 press conference about his health, Richardson said: "First, I've probably got a younger heart than you do. And I'm probably going to be here longer than maybe you think I am. I intend to own the team as long as I live."

The Panthers' future in Charlotte seems fairly assured—Richardson has repeatedly told people he is not interested in moving the team—but a new owner could always have a different objective once Richardson dies and the team is eventually sold.

That's why Charlotte officials were so interested in tethering the team to the city more completely in return for contributing money for a stadium renovation. After seven months of negotiations, they were able to complete a compromise deal in April 2013 that called for a six-year "hard tether" to keep the team in Charlotte in exchange for giving the Panthers $87.5 million to help renovate Bank of America Stadium. The Panthers will contribute $37.5 million to the stadium project and plan to install escalators and new video and ribbon boards with the money. But by around 2018, the politicians will undoubtedly have to start negotiating again to ensure that the Panthers stay in Charlotte for many more years, regardless of who owns the team.

While Richardson stays out of the shadows, it doesn't mean he's uninvolved. His first coach was Capers, who Richardson was so anxious to hire he ended up paying second- and sixth-round draft choices due to NFL anti-tampering regulations. Richardson used to meet with Capers just before each game to hear the coach's plan and what he thought the biggest challenges of the week had been. He now meets with head coach Ron Rivera regularly, too, although no longer on game days.

Richardson was the one who fired general manager Marty Hurney in 2012 after the Panthers started 1–5, and over the years the owner has called a number of players to his house to have a firm talk with them when they have done something wrong. He also was the one who decided Rivera could have a third season to prove himself after the coach directed his team to a 5–1 record in the final six games of 2012.

Blessed with a common touch, Richardson can be an intimidating presence and uses that to his advantage at times. But he also makes a point of being approachable to fans. He has for years answered letters and made the occasional phone call to fans who write him with problems and suggestions. He often circles the stadium in a golf cart before games, and now in this social-media age fans post pictures on Twitter of Richardson holding babies or shaking hands as evidence of these sojourns.

It is questionable whether the Panthers will win a Super Bowl while Richardson is alive, to fulfill his ultimate football dream. But it is unquestionable that without Richardson, the Panthers would never have existed in the first place.

4 Super Bowl XXXVIII

The most important game the Panthers ever played was also one of the most exciting—Super Bowl XXXVIII, played on February 1, 2004, at Reliant Stadium in Houston.

New England edged the Panthers 32–29 on a last-second field goal by Adam Vinatieri. The game was one of the most thrilling Super Bowls ever—especially in the fourth quarter, when the two teams combined to score touchdowns on six of their final seven possessions. The Panthers scored TDs the last three times they had the ball—all on Jake Delhomme touchdown passes—and they still lost.

"We had a shot," Panthers fullback Brad Hoover said. "They just happened to get the ball last."

The game that culminated the 2003 NFL postseason was easily the most-watched in Panthers history; Nielsen Media Research estimates that 143.6 million Americans saw at least part of it. And it was bizarre in a number of ways, including:

- The first 11 possessions ended with zero points. Neither team scored for the first almost 27 minutes. And neither scored at all in either the first or third quarters.

- Janet Jackson bared part of her breast during the halftime show in what was later famously referred to as a "wardrobe malfunction." For very casual NFL fans, this story and that phrase usurped the game itself within a few days.

- Both teams scored exactly four touchdowns and a field goal. The three-point difference was all about the two-point conversions: the Panthers were 0-for-2 on two-point tries, while New England was 1-for-1.

- John Kasay, who had only kicked one kickoff out of bounds the entire season, snap-hooked the Panthers' final kickoff out, giving New England possession on its own 40. (I believe, however, the Patriots would have scored even if they had started from their 10. They were just playing too well offensively.) Kasay would say later he "agonized" about his errant directional kick—a kick he had practiced for years.

- Delhomme threw for 211 yards in the fourth quarter alone—that's a pretty good full game by NFL standards.

- The Panthers scored exactly 29 points for the third time in their four playoff games of the 2003 postseason (the first two in wins over Dallas and St. Louis).

- The second-half was delayed when a streaker dressed up as a referee made it onto the field, undressed to a G-string, and started gyrating in front of Kasay. Security men were slow to get to him, which made the dance interminable. "It was like nobody would go get him," Panthers coach John Fox would say later. "But this big, fat, naked guy dancing around? Hey, I wasn't about to go get him either."

Any Panthers fan still remembers where he or she watched this Super Bowl. Although it ultimately is not a pleasant memory, it is a shared memory nonetheless.

And of course all of the Panthers players remember, too. They came so close, and in some ways they are haunted by the "what if" aspect of the game. If only this. If only that.

But the fact remains that New England quarterback Tom Brady absolutely savaged the Panthers defense, which allowed more first downs and yards than it ever had at that point in Fox's tenure. Brady was 32-for-48 for 354 yards. He made one mistake: an end-zone interception picked off by Carolina's Reggie Howard—and otherwise was nearly perfect. On the final drive for the winning field goal, he completed four passes for New England and overcame a first-and-20 situation to set up Vinatieri's 41-yarder.

The Panthers never could get to Brady. Julius Peppers, Kris Jenkins, and the rest of the Carolina pass rushers were shut out and seemed exhausted by game's end, as a no-name New England offensive line starting three backups due to injury handled everything the Panthers threw at them and allowed zero sacks. (The Patriots, in fact, allowed zero sacks throughout that entire postseason).

The retractable roof at Reliant Stadium was closed, which led to hot, humid conditions inside the dome in February. "I remember it being so hot that in the first quarter I was trying to catch my breath," Hoover said. "So muggy. It was kind of weird."

There were no points for the game's first 26:55. Delhomme started horribly for Carolina—at one point he was 1-for-9 for one yard, with three sacks. But then there were 24 points in the final 3:05 of the first half, as New England scored twice and the Panthers got a 39-yard touchdown on a fly pattern from Delhomme to Steve Smith and a 50-yard field goal from Kasay.

The rest of the scoring—37 of the game's 61 points—came in the fourth quarter. New England took a 21–10 lead on Antowain Smith's two-yard run. But the Panthers got a 33-yard run from DeShaun Foster to cut the lead to 21–16 with 12:39 to go and then missed on the two-point conversion.

Then, after Brady threw his interception, the Panthers took the lead for the first time in the game. It was also the first time New England had trailed since November. From his own 15, Delhomme took 6.2 seconds in a long-lasting pocket to fully survey the field and then throw it as far as he possibly could, to Muhsin Muhammad.

Muhammad hauled it in, stiff-armed a Patriot and scored on an 85-yard TD as Panthers fans everywhere jumped for joy. It was the longest TD pass in Super Bowl history and will always remain one of the best plays in Panthers history. The Panthers went for two again, trying to extend their lead to a field goal, but missed and instead led 22–21.

Following that play on the sideline, Smith pretended he had a microphone on the sideline and "interviewed" Muhammad in a bit that was captured by NFL Films.

"All right, Moose!" Smith said. "How do you feel about New England's corners? How do you feel now about how physical they are?"

Said Muhammad, pointing at his chest, "Well, they've been physical to Marvin Harrison and those little guys, but they don't want any of this!"

But the good vibes didn't last long. New England came right back, scoring on a one-yard pass from Brady to Mike Vrabel (a linebacker who was occasionally inserted as a tight end) and making the two-pointer to lead 29–22 with 2:51 left.

Carolina sped right back down the field, as Delhomme hit Ricky Proehl on third-and-8 with a 12-yard TD pass with 1:08 to go to beat an all-out Patriot blitz. The Panthers had TD drives of 81, 90, and 80 yards on their last three possessions.

But in a fourth quarter with very little defense, the Panthers couldn't hold off New England either. Carolina's best chance was one stop, forcing overtime, and then getting the overtime kickoff and scoring—because at that point the Patriots were tired and befuddled by Carolina's offense and probably couldn't have held the Panthers down either.

It never got that far, though, because of Vinatieri's kick.

Delhomme lingered on the field after the game, watching the Patriots celebrate and letting it hurt. He wanted to sear it into his mind as motivation for the next training camp, intent on getting the Panthers back there again.

But Delhomme is retired now, and the Panthers haven't been back since.

Not yet, anyway. For now, Panthers fans have only bittersweet memories of the team's lone Super Bowl, when Carolina played relatively well but fell just short of the game's biggest prize.

5 Jake Delhomme

He started eight of the Panthers' 10 playoff games at quarterback. He threw for 211 yards in a single quarter of the Super Bowl. He had a funny accent. He was one of the friendliest, most accessible, and downright nicest players Carolina has ever employed. He was the team's quarterback during almost all of their best times.

It's not surprising that Jake Delhomme remains one of the most popular players in Panthers history. The team's Carolina

"I'll always consider myself a Panther," quarterback Jake Delhomme once said.
We will too.

Cajun, a Louisiana native, is a fiery reminder of the best of the 2000s. In his Panthers heyday from 2003 to 2008, Delhomme was responsible for thousands of No. 17 jerseys being sold around the Carolinas. He was a bit undersized and definitely an underdog—an undrafted player who had to go to NFL Europe to prove himself, and even there was a backup for much of the time.

Delhomme won five playoff games as the Panthers' starting quarterback—three of them during his magical first season with the team, when he got Carolina all the way to the Super Bowl. Former Panthers offensive coordinator Dan Henning once compared Delhomme's quarterbacking style to a day trader—a high-risk, high-reward sort of player who liked taking chances far more than taking a sack.

"When I play, I like to sling it around," Delhomme would say.

That led to some remarkable comebacks. And it also had a downside—one that Panthers fans also became very familiar with.

The shorthand that fans started using after a while boiled down to this choice: Good Jake vs. Bad Jake. Which Delhomme would show up that Sunday?

Delhomme was 53–37 as a Panthers starter—by far the most games won by any Carolina quarterback. He was especially good in the fourth quarter when the game was tight. In 2003 alone, his first year as a starter, Delhomme led the NFL with eight game-winning drives in the fourth quarter, and the Panthers adopted the nickname "Cardiac Cats."

But sometimes Delhomme's early mistakes meant the game wasn't close in the fourth quarter. Bad Jake showed up twice at very key times—in the last two playoff games Delhomme started for Carolina. After beginning his career with an extraordinary 5–1 playoff record for the Panthers, Delhomme's final two postseason appearances were stunningly bad.

He threw three interceptions in a 20-point loss to Seattle in the 2005 postseason. Then, even worse, Delhomme had a six-turnover performance (five interceptions, one lost fumble) in Carolina's 20-point home loss to Arizona in the 2008 postseason.

"Inexcusable," Delhomme called the latter performance—just the sort of comment that endeared him to people. Delhomme was quick to both accept blame and deflect credit. Touchdown passes, in his opinion, were always because the receiver made a great catch (and sometimes Steve Smith had done just that). Interceptions, Delhomme would always say, were his fault.

After that Arizona playoff game, Delhomme never was the same quarterback. By that time he was 34 years old, and he never got back the mojo that he had for much of his Panthers career. This was unfortunate for both the Panthers and their leadership team, since general manager Marty Hurney and coach John Fox gave Delhomme a new five-year contract extension that included $19 million in guaranteed money three months after that last playoff debacle.

Delhomme never was able to justify that contract, having by far the worst of his seven Panthers seasons in 2009 with a career-high 18 interceptions. The Panthers then reversed course, deciding Matt Moore should be their starter at quarterback. They released Delhomme in March 2010, holding an emotional news conference during which both Fox and Hurney shed tears.

"We struggled with this one, a lot," Hurney said of the decision to fire Delhomme. "The guy, he's been so spectacular for us. He's a kind of player and person that we look for. So it's kind of hard not to get emotional when you talk about it. He just epitomizes everything we want."

Delhomme said in a separate press conference that day he was "blindsided" by the release. But he handled it gracefully, saying the Panthers had allowed him to morph from nobody to somebody in the NFL.

"Six out of my seven years here playing have been outstanding," he said, counting only his final season as an exception. "It's been a great run."

It wasn't quite the end of Delhomme's career, although it was close. He was supposed to start for Cleveland for all of 2010, but a high ankle sprain sidelined him for all but five games. One of those games, however, was a 24–23 Cleveland win over Carolina that Delhomme started and finished.

Delhomme also played briefly as a backup in Houston in 2011 to close out his 14-year career. Then he retired back to his horse farm in Louisiana, where he, his father and his older brother have long run a small stable and raised thoroughbreds to race.

Although he played for several other teams in his career and no longer lives in Charlotte, Delhomme said he will always harbor fond memories of his seven years at Carolina.

"It was fun," Delhomme said. "I'll always consider myself a Panther."

Delhomme Trivia

A handful of unusual facts about Jake Delhomme, the most successful quarterback the Carolina Panthers have ever had.

He chose No. 17 as his uniform number as a tribute to his firstborn daughter, Lauren, and his wife, Keri. Lauren was born on December 17 after Keri went through 17 hours of labor.

His hometown of Breaux Bridge, Louisiana, is the self-proclaimed "Crawfish Capital of the World."

At a Panther Christmas party that featured a karaoke machine, Delhomme once did an uncanny imitation of Vanilla Ice with "Ice Ice Baby," complete with dance moves.

He was an all-state high school football player in Lafayette, Louisiana, playing both ways for a small Catholic high school. He made all-state not as a quarterback, though, but as a defensive back.

His 85-yard throw to Muhsin Muhammad remains the longest touchdown pass in Super Bowl history.

Delhomme was an unabashed practical joker in the Panthers locker room, sometimes dumping buckets of ice water over the top of bathroom stalls and onto unsuspecting teammates. To avoid retribution, he occasionally took an umbrella into bathroom stalls with him.

6 Muhsin Muhammad

Muhsin Muhammad was always known as "Moose" around the Carolina Panthers locker room, and the nickname was fitting for a player who caught 860 passes in his 14-year NFL career but was just as well known for his punishing blocks. Muhammad was never the fastest wide receiver—although his speed was underrated, as the 85-yard touchdown pass he caught in the Super Bowl will attest. But tackling him was always like trying to get hold of a moose that wanted to get its antlers into you.

When Muhammad retired in 2009, his old quarterback Jake Delhomme said: "When I think of what a picture of a pro football player would look like, I think of Muhsin Muhammad."

Muhammad spent 11 of his 14 years in the NFL with the Panthers in two stints, sandwiching a three-year stint with the Chicago Bears from 2005 to 2007. He was sort of a Forrest Gump for Carolina, showing up for many of the team's biggest moments.

As a rookie he played on the Panthers' 1996 playoff team, and he was fast enough back then that linebacker Sam Mills called him "the Moose who runs like a deer."

In 2003, he was a standout for the Panthers' Super Bowl squad. And when he returned to Carolina in 2008, the Panthers made a run to the playoffs again before losing to Arizona. He played at a high level until age 36 and left the Panthers as the team's leader in both receptions and reception yards (both marks since surpassed by Steve Smith). Whenever he scored—and Moose had 50 TD receptions as a Panther, second only to Smith—he dropped to one knee and passed the ball back and forth through his legs a couple of times. That was about as fancy as this blue-collar player ever got.

There is no doubt Muhammad was the best blocking wide receiver the Panthers have ever employed. "There was no football player on the field he couldn't block," former Panthers quarterback Steve Beuerlein said.

The Panthers staged an elaborate retirement ceremony for Muhammad in June 2010, when he gracefully exited the game. He said that day he had decided that "I would walk away from the game on my own terms, while I still could, instead of crawling away later."

Muhammad noted then that when the Panthers made him a second-round draft choice in 1996 out of Michigan State, "When I came to Carolina in 1996, I had no kids and no stress. Fourteen years later, I have six children and a lot of stress."

Muhsin and Christa Muhammad's six children include two siblings they adopted from Ethiopia. As if that wasn't enough to handle, Muhammad also has founded a private equity firm (it made a substantial investment in the Wild Wing Café chain) and has dabbled in sports broadcasting as well.

Muhammad and team owner Jerry Richardson had a longtime bond. They each wore No. 87 as players. Before each game, they had this ritual in which they would stare at each other and then do something that both men claim was unprintable.

Muhammad played in two Super Bowls—one for Carolina and one for Chicago, losing both times. He bolted from the Panthers to Chicago after the 2004 season, which was his best as a pro (93 catches, 1,405 yards, and 16 touchdowns).

"You shouldn't have gone up there!" Richardson said jokingly to Muhammad at his retirement ceremony.

"Tell Marty Hurney," Muhammad joshed back, referring to the Panthers' then–general manager, who didn't offer Moose as much money as the Bears did at the time.

"We missed him," Panthers fullback Brad Hoover said of the Moose-less years from 2005 to 2007. "We never really replaced him."

All was well when Muhammad and the Panthers reconciled and he returned to Charlotte for the 2008 and '09 seasons. "Making up is so much better than breaking up," Muhammad said.

Muhammad had some of his best moments in the Panthers' biggest games. In the 2003 NFC Championship Game win at Philadelphia, he opened the scoring with a 24-yard touchdown catch in which he outfought two Eagles defenders. Then he dropped to one knee and made the "Shhh" gesture to the crowd—a pose that earned *Sports Illustrated's* cover the following week.

Muhammad's 85-yard, fourth-quarter catch from Delhomme in the 2004 Super Bowl remains one of the best plays in Panthers history, even though it ultimately came in a losing cause. At the time, it was the longest play from scrimmage in Super Bowl history.

On the play, Delhomme actually held the ball for an almost unheard-of 6.2 seconds and Muhammad just kept going, sneaking behind the New England secondary on a sideline takeoff route to give Carolina a short-lived 22–21 lead. "I saw Jake heave it up, and I was just smiling when it came down," Muhammad said. He caught the ball 51 yards downfield and stiff-armed Patriots safety Eugene Wilson at the 15 so brutally that Wilson suffered a torn groin.

"What was great about Moose is that he didn't quit," Delhomme later said of the play. "He just kept going. They lost him back there, but I saw him. I threw it as far as I could, and he just made a great play after that."

That was one of Muhammad's most visible highlights, but the invisible things he did were just as important, and part of the reason he lasted so long.

Said Delhomme, "He was someone who exemplified the qualities of being smart and tough. He was an unselfish player because of everything he did—film study, preparation, working out, and all of those things. He showed up to play every single week. He was a true pro."

7 Cam Newton

There is a moment as predictable as the sunrise when you walk up to Cam Newton for the first time. If you've ever seen him up close, you know what I'm talking about. If you haven't, keep this in mind when you do.

You get closer, and Newton starts to loom like a mountain over you. And you think something like, *My Lord—I didn't know he was* that *big!*

I have seen it happen over and over, and not just to fans, but also to other athletes who meet Newton. It's just not the same seeing Newton's listed height and weight of 6'5" and 245 pounds as it is seeing him in the flesh.

NFL quarterbacks generally are a couple of inches shorter than Newton and, more significantly, about 20 to 40 pounds lighter. He's as big as most of the linebackers who try to tackle him and larger than all of the defensive backs, some of whom have been known to try to shield their own bodies when Newton has a full head of steam and impact is imminent.

It's that build—combined with Newton's strong right arm and his surprising elusiveness and speed—that made him one of the most dynamic players in the NFL from the day he first jogged onto the field for Carolina in 2011.

In his first year with the Panthers, he set an NFL record for most rushing touchdowns by a quarterback (14) and was named the Associated Press Offensive Rookie of the Year after throwing for 4,051 yards. In his second year, he cut down significantly on his interceptions, setting a Panthers record with 176 straight throws without a pickoff. In 2012, he also became the first NFL quarterback to lead his team in rushing since Donovan McNabb did it for the Eagles in 2000.

Newton is the only player in NFL history with 30 or more passing touchdowns (40) and 20 or more rushing TDs (22) in his first two seasons. He also has established a cool tradition in Bank of America Stadium: after a Panthers touchdown he generally grabs the football and hands it off to a kid in the front row of the stands. "The Sunday giveaway—that's what we call it," Newton said.

What Newton has not done yet in the NFL is lead a winning team the way he did in college at Auburn, where the Tigers won a national championship and Newton won the Heisman Trophy in his only season there. That lack of winning is why Newton is on the top 10 on this list—the only current Panthers player to crack the top 10—but is not yet in the top five.

Newton can be a wondrous player, a staple of every NFL highlight show. But the fact remains that his first two teams at Carolina went 6–10 and 7–9. To be the elite NFL quarterback he aspires to be, the next step is to get to the playoffs, and the biggest and hardest step will be to eventually win a Super Bowl.

Can he do it? Absolutely.

In Newton, the Panthers have the sort of quarterback they've never had before. Steve Beuerlein was more accurate, yes. Jake Delhomme was a more natural leader, absolutely. But the Panthers have never had an athlete as otherworldly as Newton touching the ball on every single offensive play—a quarterback who threw for 400 yards in his first two NFL games in 2011 and ran for a 72-yard touchdown in 2012 during which he did a front flip into the end zone.

Newton is still learning the game, of course, and all that goes with it. He has admitted he was a "bad teammate" at times, especially as a rookie, when he was prone to occasional fits of immaturity—pouting after losses and brooding on the sideline when things weren't going well. In the Carolinas, the Gatorade towel Newton pulls over his head like a shroud while on the sideline has been the source of much debate.

His every word and action is analyzed, from the false step he took when he was the star attraction at a paid autograph session in Charlotte (signatures cost $125 and up) to the clothes he wears for his postgame press conferences (one comfy-looking brown sweater in particular drew comments for weeks) to his favorite phrase to emphasize a point ("simple and plain").

All that goes away, of course, when Newton quarterbacks a win. He knows that. He doesn't mind being a larger-than-life sports character but knows that it only works when he can pump out a string of victories to bolster his status.

"One thing that I'm not going to do is I'm not going to worry what people think of me in this setting," Newton said in 2012. "Because I guarantee you, if I was cussing everybody out and we're 6–0: 'Oh, that's just Cam being Cam.'

"You've got the likes of Mike Tyson, Dennis Rodman, Charles Barkley—guys who have gone on and had that M.O. (and were able to get away with it, because they won consistently). Dennis Rodman, they knew he was going to get all the boards and that was just his M.O. When he came in with green hair, that's Dennis. I guarantee if they were 0–82, he would have been out of the league way faster than he was. All the athletes I named were phenomenal athletes and they excelled at what they did."

Newton wouldn't mind being the Panthers' iconic star and Carolina wouldn't mind it, either. He oozes charisma, whether pretending to fly around like a jet airplane before each game, talking about the extensive clothing line he has launched with Belk department stores, or openly campaigning in a homemade YouTube video for the cover of the *Madden 13* video game (he lost, finishing second to Calvin Johnson).

Four Cam-tastic Performances

In only two years, Cam Newton has made it onto a lot of Panthers highlight films. Here are four of his most spectacular games:

September 11, 2011. Arizona 28, Carolina 21. Cam loses his opening-game debut, but opens eyes everywhere with a 422-yard passing day, including a 77-yard TD to Steve Smith.

December 24, 2011. Carolina 48, Tampa Bay 16. Newton sets a team record with a 91-yard TD pass to Brandon LaFell and runs for a 49-yard TD in a Panthers blowout.

November 26, 2012. Carolina 30, Philadelphia 22. Newton throws for 306 yards and two TDs and rushes for 52 yards and two more TDs as the Panthers beat the Eagles on *Monday Night Football*. He is named NFC Offensive Player of the Week.

December 9, 2012. Carolina 30, Atlanta 20. Newton becomes the first quarterback in NFL history to throw for more than 250 yards, run for more than 100 yards, and get at least one touchdown passing and running in a single game (the run was his aforementioned 72-yard TD).

Coach Ron Rivera and Newton came in the same season, and Rivera knows that his future is tethered in large part to how well Newton performs. Rivera has been strongly supportive of Newton in almost every instance, willing to ride the ups and downs of a young quarterback while looking out for the long-range good of the team.

When he was once asked to compare Newton's style of play to someone else, Rivera replied, "The only other player I've seen that has that kind of charisma or charm, in my opinion, was Walter Payton."

Then the coach went on, "I think there's something about guys like that that are special. They love practicing, they love meeting, they love just coming here and being here. Walter was the same way. He just loved being at the facility, loved to practice, loved his teammates. Treats everybody with the same type of respect. They both have this attitude about losing—they hate losing.

Everything they did was to win. They've always been winners....
It's infectious."

Rivera has talked to Newton about being a more positive influence on his teammates, however, when things aren't going well.
The coach once referred to Newton as "Mr. Mopeyhead" due to his dejected postgame demeanor after losses.

Newton's work ethic has impressed those around him. Since he went to three colleges (Florida, Blinn Junior College, and Auburn) and his father, Cecil, was involved in a scandal concerning his son's recruitment—Cam Newton was judged not to have known about it—Newton was thought by some to be an iffy prospect on the character scale before Carolina drafted him No. 1. But he impressed team owner Jerry Richardson with a handwritten thank-you letter and impressed key locker room leaders including Steve Smith and Jordan Gross early on with his competitive streak and willingness to put in extra work.

Newton remains close to his parents and his brothers—one older, one younger—and has bought a house near his family in Atlanta. He also owns a condominium in Charlotte, living uptown in the same building as Michael Jordan—who has had Newton as his guest at a couple of Charlotte Bobcats games.

Although Newton will occasionally say something he shouldn't, he is smart enough to have stayed off of Twitter—the social media phenomenon that so many athletes use to share their unfiltered opinions with fans. Newton doesn't need any more publicity—he already has done more national commercials than any Panther ever—and he realizes that a misstep in the Twitterverse could cost him.

Said Newton, "The social media world has turned into... they want to hear about Steve Smith or Jonathan Stewart drunk on North Tryon, rather than, 'He's on North Tryon giving away turkeys.' One wrong tweet to the wrong person could lead to so much. I think if you do 10 tweets, you do nine amazing tweets they still don't outweigh the one bad tweet a person may send off. You may send an ex-girlfriend your real feelings on how you feel and she sends it to TMZ or sends it to the *Charlotte Observer*."

Newton originally wanted to wear a No. 2 jersey for the Panthers as he had at Auburn. But when he got to Charlotte, quarterback Jimmy Clausen already had that number. He ended up with No. 1, which was fitting. Newton is the Panthers' most important player, and over the next few years they will go only as far as he can take them.

The Double OT Playoff Game vs. St. Louis

It was the longest game the Carolina Panthers have ever played. It was also the most thrilling.

Their 29–23 playoff win on the road at St. Louis on January 10, 2004, was an extraordinary contest. Whenever Panthers fans talk about the most exciting games in team history, this one generally gets the most votes for No. 1. If you can find an old videotape of the game or at least highlights from it online, it's worth your time.

The game wasn't decided until the first play of the *sixth* quarter, when quarterback Jake Delhomme found Steve Smith streaking down the middle of the field on a third-and-14 from Carolina's own 31. An untouched Smith took the ball 69 yards for a touchdown, spreading his arms wide as he sprinted into the end zone in St. Louis and throwing a blanket of silence over the crowd.

"I threw the ball, but it was really all Steve," Delhomme said later. "I just thought it would be a first down. He made the play. He made the catch. He made people miss. He made the touchdown. It was amazing."

But before that single play in double overtime—in what was at the time the fifth-longest game in NFL history—so much had already happened. That the game hadn't already been decided was somewhat remarkable. There were four overtime possessions before the Smith-Delhomme connection on a Panthers play called "X Clown"—two possessions for each team. On each of those four possessions, the ball was advanced inside the other team's 40.

And yet no one scored, over and over. The tension kept climbing until Smith's historic catch and run—on a play he later admitted he messed up in practice at least 10 times that week.

Let's set the scene first. St. Louis had not played the previous week due to a first-round playoff bye, while the Panthers had drilled Dallas 29–10 in a home playoff game.

The Rams featured their "Greatest Show on Turf" offense, directed by head coach Mike Martz and keyed by three speedy playmakers who looked even faster on artificial turf at the Edward Jones Dome—running back Marshall Faulk and receivers Torry Holt and Isaac Bruce. The Rams had averaged 33.6 points per game at home that season, had won 14 games in a row in their home stadium, and were favored by a touchdown.

There had never been two busier field-goal kickers in an NFL playoff game, as drives for both teams kept petering out just short of the goal line. Rams kicker Jeff Wilkins made five of them and barely missed a sixth in all. His first two gave St. Louis a 6–0 lead.

But in the second quarter, Panthers running back Stephen Davis burst through a hole and sprinted toward the end zone. At the end of his 64-yard run, though, Davis pulled up lame and was tackled at the St. Louis 4. He had an injured quadriceps, and he was done for the day.

Carolina still scored on that possession, but it was a weird play that foreshadowed this bizarrely dramatic game. On third-and-goal from the St. Louis 5, Delhomme tried to pitch the ball to DeShaun Foster. Rams defensive end Leonard Little blew up the

10 Other Interesting Game Facts

Every true Panthers fan knows something about Steve Smith's 69-yard catch to win the playoff game at St. Louis in double overtime, but how many of these other things about the Panthers' most exciting game ever played do you remember?

- Stephen Davis went 64 yards in the second quarter, but pulled up lame toward the end of the play with an injured quadriceps and didn't return. DeShaun Foster replaced him, running 21 times for 95 yards.
- The first time the Panthers ran X Clown, Jake Delhomme hit Smith for a 36-yard gain. The second time resulted in the game-winning TD.
- Ricky Manning Jr.'s acrobatic interception of a Marc Bulger pass in overtime kept the Rams from attempting a game-winning field goal.
- Muhsin Muhammad outwrestled a half-dozen other players to recover a fumble for the Panthers' first touchdown.
- Mike Minter and Deon Grant also both intercepted Bulger in the fourth quarter.
- Marshall Faulk carried the ball 19 times for St. Louis but never had a gain of more than eight yards.
- There were 11 field goals attempted in the game, which was an NFL playoff record. Carolina's John Kasay went 3-for-5 and St. Louis' Jeff Wilkins went 5-for-6. Oddly, Wilkins never attempted an extra point—the Rams went for two points and made it after their only touchdown.
- The game was so good that after losing, Faulk said this: "It was fun. It was one you love being a part of."
- The Panthers tried to surprise the Rams on their first series of the game by going against their own conservative tendencies. They ran a reverse to Smith, who threw a 25-yard pass downfield to Muhammad. It was a strike, but Moose dropped it.
- Holt, the former NC State star receiver who had led the NFL in catches and yards that season, was miked for the game by NFL Films. In the pregame huddle, he said, "We're going to dominate like we always do at home."

play, getting so far into the backfield that he actually tipped a pitch that Delhomme never should have made.

"If you look back at it, probably a pretty dumb play on my part, " Delhomme said later.

The ball bounced on the ground and—just when it looked like a Rams defender would swoop it up and go 95 yards the other way—Foster got a hand on it and it rolled toward the end zone. Then came a scrum of at least a half dozen players.

When they were all unstacked, Panthers wide receiver Muhsin Muhammad had the ball in the end zone, good for a score on a fumble recovery for a 7–6 Panthers lead.

The teams traded field goals after that, and Carolina led 10–9 at halftime. After Wilkins' fourth field goal, the Panthers scored the game's next 13 points—the last seven on Brad Hoover's seven-yard run in the fourth quarter and the ensuing point after, to give Carolina a 23–12 lead.

By then, the St. Louis crowd was growing restless. Carolina had the next scoring opportunity, too, but John Kasay's 53-yard field goal attempt hit the upright and bounced away. That miss came with 6:29 left to go, and the Panthers wouldn't see the ball for the rest of regulation.

The Panthers defense had held St. Louis' fantastic offense out of the end zone for more than 57 minutes but couldn't do it forever. The Rams scored on a one-yard run from Faulk with 2:39 to go, and a two-point conversion pass from quarterback Marc Bulger made it 23–20 Carolina.

The Rams then lined up for an onside kick, and Wilkins hit one of the most beautiful ones you will ever see. It actually had some backspin and totally fooled the Panthers as to where it was going—four Rams had the ball surrounded by the time it had gone the required 10 yards. Wilkins ultimately recovered his own kick.

The Rams quickly moved the ball to Carolina's 19, where they had one timeout left and 42 seconds to go. Surely Martz, known as a riverboat gambler, would take a couple of shots into the end zone. Right?

Wrong. Martz turned into a buttoned-down conservative instead, at the worst possible time for Rams fans. Bulger had thrown two fourth-quarter interceptions already. So the Rams ran just one play—a conservative pitchout to Faulk that gained four yards—and then let the clock run down to 0:03 before sending Wilkins out for the 33-yard field goal that would tie the game. (It also didn't hurt Carolina that given his lack of confidence in Bulger, Martz never went to the bench for former NFL MVP Kurt Warner, who had been hurt but was available for this game. Warner always gave the Panthers fits, as a playoff game five years later, with Warner starting for Arizona, would best attest.)

Said Fox-TV analyst Daryl Johnston on the game telecast, "I never thought I would see Mike Martz play for a field goal and go to overtime."

But that's what he did. "I felt I owed it to those players to give them the opportunity to continue playing," Martz said. "I just wanted to get it into overtime. I felt, if we could get it into overtime, we'd win the ballgame."

So Wilkins hit the field goal and the game continued into overtime, which at first looked like it would end quickly. The Panthers won the coin toss and moved efficiently down the field, getting inside the St. Louis 25. (This game was played in the days when a first-possession field goal would win a game—the NFL rule now requires a first-possession touchdown to end it outright).

On second down, John Fox sent out Kasay to win the game with a 40-yarder. And he did—almost. Kasay drilled the kick, but a flag for delay of game on Carolina nullified it. The Panthers had made a critical mistake. On the Panthers' radio network, the call came like this from play-by-play man Bill Rosinski:

"There it is. The placement. Kasay's kick is up, it's on the way… and the Panthers Are Going To The Nfc Championship!"

Then came the sad voice of analyst Jim Szoke, who had spotted the flag: "No, no, no."

The Panthers moved back five yards. Fox had them run the ball twice more, but they gained zero yards. After a Rams timeout, Kasay came out again—and this time missed the 45-yarder.

So the Rams got the ball. They drove down the field, stalled, and Wilkins came in to attempt a 53-yarder. He was 5-for-5 on the day and had also recovered his own onside kick. If he made this one, his day would go down as one of the great playoff performances by any kicker.

The kick arrowed straight toward the middle of the goalposts—and fell about six inches short.

And so it went. Carolina got inside the Rams 40 but had to punt after Delhomme was sacked. The Rams rolled past midfield, but Ricky Manning Jr. made an enormous play by intercepting a Bulger pass intended for Holt. Manning had only one hand on the ball and Holt had two, but Manning somehow wrested it away. Holt would have a terrible game by his standards, with just two catches for 21 yards.

So the Panthers got the ball for a third time in overtime. The fifth quarter ended with them facing third-and-14—and with Delhomme having been sacked on three of the past five offensive plays.

During the break for the teams to change sides, the call came in for X Clown with "max protection"—the Panthers would keep seven players in to block. St. Louis was playing Cover Two, with both its safeties lined up deep to protect against the big play.

Smith got a free release off the line, swiveled his hips, and got the St. Louis cornerback going the wrong way. Then he broke toward the middle, where safety Jason Sehorn was waiting but also stumbling a little. Delhomme hit Smith in stride with a perfect throw at the 50.

Quickly, Smith faked out the Rams cornerback, who started veering toward the sideline when Smith swiveled his hips that way.

Smith darted back toward the middle of the field and Sehorn. Smith, in his white No. 89 jersey, was a blur by then. Said Smith, "At first I was thinking, *Just catch it. Don't drop it. Don't be that guy....* I braced myself for the big hit, but it never came. And when I took off, I knew I was gone."

Said defensive tackle Brentson Buckner, "The defense was sitting over there saying, 'Smitty's gotta come through for us. We need one big play from Smitty.' And all I see is this little white streak running down the field."

On the radio, Rosinski got to say it again: "And we are going to the NFC championship!"

Rams fans filed mournfully out of their stadium, their dreams of a Super Bowl dashed. The Panthers formed a few small knots of celebrants on the field and in the stands. No extra point was attempted, so the game ended with Carolina winning, 29–23.

"I've never seen a game quite like that," Panthers coach John Fox said afterward.

No one else had either.

9 John Kasay

For years, placekicker John Kasay gracefully wore the title of "the Last Original Panther."

He kicked for the Panthers when they were an expansion team, in 1995, and for the next 15 years after that, suiting up far longer than any other player on Carolina's first team. Kasay (pronounced "Casey") outlasted three Panthers head coaches, overcame two significant injuries, and banked a lot of goodwill in the Charlotte community by becoming the team's leading scorer by a mile while also coaching youth baseball teams, speaking to churches about his Christian faith and signing autographs for hours.

After firing Kasay in 2011 in one of the most unpopular moves the franchise has ever made, the Panthers made a nice gesture by signing him to a one-day contract in May 2013 so he could officially retire as a Panther. Although he usually avoided the spotlight, Kasay decided to let it shine on him that day in the hope that he could use it to reflect his thanks to all the fans who watched him kick for the Panthers from 1995 to 2010.

"I told Mr. Richardson the reason I wanted to do this is I can't write 70,000 thank-you notes," Kasay said. "I wish that I could. But this is my feeble attempt to tell everybody thank you."

While kickers are often considered flaky, Kasay's persona on and off the field was one of calm strength. "John is a very thoughtful person," Panthers owner Jerry Richardson said. "He's not flighty."

Kasay developed a deep friendship with wide receiver Steve Smith, even though the two were polar opposites in playing styles. The left-footed kicker won 11 games for Carolina over the years with last-second field goals and ended up with 1,482 points as a Panther, more than a thousand more than anyone else.

Kasay couldn't outlast the fourth Panthers head coach, however—in fact, he never attempted a single field goal for Ron Rivera. In the summer of 2011, general manager Marty Hurney and Rivera made the controversial (and ultimately unsuccessful) move of replacing Kasay with Olindo Mare.

Their flawed reasoning was that Mare had a strong enough leg to also handle kickoffs, while Kasay had been limited to field goals only in the last few years of his career. Mare could kick off, but he turned out not to be nearly as clutch as Kasay on field goals. By 2013 the Panthers were on their third attempt at replacing Kasay.

While Kasay certainly could have been bitter after playing his heart out for 16 years for the same employer, he instead penned a gracious, 257-word thank-you note to Panthers fans in 2011, which he sent to me and entrusted me to publish it in the *Charlotte Observer.* I was honored to do so.

In the letter, Kasay took the high road, saying he would always root for the Panthers and hoped that the team's best days were ahead of them. The letter was dated, August 2, 2011. Here is its full text:

Dear Panthers fans,

I wanted to personally write this letter to every Carolina Panthers fan. Words cannot express how truly thankful my family and I are for the most wonderful 16 years of our lives.

We came to the Panthers as a young family with a 3-month-old baby. We leave with 4 children, 2 of whom are in high school. In between, you have loved and cheered and blessed us way more than we ever deserved. The only thing I could offer in return was the promise that I would try my best, every day, to make you proud.

Thank you for your encouragement when I failed. Thank you for the celebrations when we won. And most of all, thank you for letting me leave with a treasure trove of memories that time cannot erase.

It is my hope that the greatest years in Panthers history are still to come. A franchise decorated with numerous Lombardi Trophies. Dozens of Hall of Fame players. And a region that swells with pride whenever they speak of their beloved Panthers.

It has been a tremendous privilege to live in Charlotte, to play for the Carolina Panthers, and to be able to share my lifelong dream of playing in the NFL with all of you.

I pray that this will be a wonderful season and we will all get to watch the Panthers return to their rightful place as one of the most feared teams in the NFL.

May God bless you. Thank you again for the memories.

Blessings,

John Kasay

John Kasay (4) is the Panthers' original Captain Clutch—not to mention the team's all-time top scorer.

That letter unleashed a torrent of emotion among Panthers fans, many of whom were angry that Kasay had been fired in the first place.

Kasay did not stay unemployed for long. NFC South rival New Orleans hired him to kick for the entire 2011 season after the Saints' regular kicker went down with an injury. Because the New Orleans offense was so prolific, Kasay ended up No. 2 in the NFL in scoring that year and kicked three field goals in his return to Bank of America Stadium, where the Saints edged Carolina, 30–27.

In 2012, the Saints invited Kasay to training camp once again. But regular kicker Garrett Hartley was healthy by then and beat out Kasay for the starting job. At age 42, and ranked in the top 10 all-time in the NFL in points, total field goals, field goals over 50 yards, and games played, Kasay's career was finally over.

Kasay's three passions are ministry, coaching, and young people, and he decided to pursue all three by becoming the athletic director at a Christian high school in Charlotte in 2013. He is also a fine speaker who gave the commencement address at Wingate University in 2013. Kasay and his family have established deep roots in Charlotte, and he and his wife, Laura, have occasionally talked to groups about the principles of Christian marriages.

As Kasay mentioned in his letter to Panthers fans, he does have a "treasure trove" of good memories. Those who faced him don't have nearly as many. The Saints hired Kasay for 2011 in part because he went 37-for-42 against them over the years, beating them twice on last-second kicks.

Once, Tampa Bay coach Jon Gruden growled after Kasay had beaten Tampa Bay in 2006 with four field goals of more than 45 yards, including a last-second game-winner: "Let's not send him any Christmas cards this year…. I don't like that guy. I do not like John Kasay. He's killed me before, and he got me today."

In the Panthers' two home playoff wins, both against Dallas, Kasay kicked a total of nine field goals and was an instrumental part of each victory. His favorite field goal, he said, was a 32-yarder in the first Dallas playoff game that gave Carolina a nine-point lead with less than two minutes to go.

"I was so full of adrenalin," Kasay said of the kick. "I remember when I hit the ball, the ball went up over the net. We leave those nets high, so that doesn't happen very often. I hit that ball so hard. It was such a big day for everybody."

Almost every Kasay memory that Carolina fans have is positive, because he was so good in the clutch and made nearly 83 percent of his field-goal attempts as a Panther. There is one high-profile memory, however, that wasn't.

Kasay hooked a kickoff out of bounds in fourth quarter of the 2004 Super Bowl, with the game tied at 29-all and 1:08 left in regulation. Starting at his own 40 after the penalty due to the errant kick, quarterback Tom Brady got New England into field-goal range and the Panthers lost in the final seconds, 32–29.

Kasay said he "agonized" afterward about that kickoff. He had kept 77 of 78 of his kickoff inbounds during the regular season and all four in the Super Bowl before that one were in the field of play.

Regardless of field position, the Patriots were rolling. Brady had three timeouts and 68 seconds to get into field-goal range, after all. Carolina's defense was exhausted. The Patriots' previous average starting position after Kasay's four earlier kickoffs had been the 27-yard line. Kasay's bad kickoff, then, likely cost Carolina about 13 yards. It didn't lose the Super Bowl—it was just one of many factors.

"I had practiced that kick for years and years and years," said Kasay, who was trying to kick the ball toward the corner to give New England's return man fewer options. "You can try to kick it on a straight line over there. The other way is you can almost bend

John Kasay by the Numbers

A look at some of the most significant numbers in John Kasay's 16-year career with Carolina.

1—Pro Bowl appearance for Carolina (in 1996, when he led the NFL with 145 points).

2—Number of seasons Kasay missed most or all of which with Carolina due to injuries (2000 and 2002).

4—Years Kasay kicked in Seattle (he was originally a fourth-round pick in 1991 out of Georgia) before the Panthers signed him as one of their first free agents in 1995.

11—Game-winning field goals for Carolina.

50—Kasay's percentage with Carolina on field-goal attempts of 50-plus yards (34 of 68).

82.8—Career field-goal percentage with Carolina.

100—Consecutive games in which Kasay scored for Carolina from 2004 to 2010.

221—Kasay's total number of games played for Carolina, a team record.

1,482—Kasay's total number of points as a Panther, more than 1,000 more than any other Carolina player.

the ball like in golf. I did both at the same time...because I wanted it to be so perfect. If I had just given myself more of a margin of error...When my toe hit the ball I remember thinking, '*Oh no.*'"

What Kasay did do correctly for years for Carolina, though, was put the ball through the uprights. Kasay made 37 field goals in 1996, which was an NFL record at the time, to help the Panthers to their first playoff appearance. He is also the only Panthers player who has appeared in all 10 of the franchise's postseason games. He is a strong candidate to join the Panthers Hall of Honor, although by the team's "five-year-after-retirement" rule he can't be considered until 2018 for that honor.

"The role I play really doesn't change from week to week," he said. "My challenge is to try to kick a ball between two yellow posts."

He did that job so well that some Panthers fans literally wept when he was released. Because for years, No. 4 trotting onto the field meant almost sure points for Carolina.

10 Go to a Panthers Home Game

Every Carolina Panthers fan should make the trip to Bank of America Stadium in Charlotte at least once—and of course many Panthers fans have done so dozens or even hundreds of times. It is an addictive experience for many, especially those who sit in the same place year after year and get to know their seat neighbors well.

A typical Panthers Sunday for fans who haven't been to the stadium before includes at least a few pictures in front of the snarling Panthers statues—there are six of them, with a pair located at each of the three stadium entrances.

Because the stadium is on the southwestern edge of uptown Charlotte, there is no single, centralized parking lot where fans tailgate. Instead, the tailgate party spreads out all over the city in every direction, mostly in small parking lots and nearby restaurants. This natural dispersal of the crowd also gives the Panthers' stadium one feature that is seldom talked about but much admired among those like me who have visited the majority of NFL stadiums: it is easier to exit quickly from the parking lots than it is at almost any other stadium in the league.

Although all Panthers games officially sell out, tickets are actually much easier to come by than in some of the more traditional NFL cities, such as Green Bay or Chicago. While permanent seat license (PSL) holders officially control about 80 to 90 percent of the stadium, which opened in 1996, there is a significant secondary ticket market outside the stadium every Sunday (and also online at outlets such as StubHub.com or the Panthers' official ticket exchange, which is accessible from the team's website, Panthers.com).

Except for extremely high-profile games—or during seasons when the Panthers are very good—tickets can usually be purchased for face value on the street. The cheapest tickets are officially around $50, but occasionally you can find one for $20 outside the stadium from a fan desperate to get rid of some.

If you prefer to know where you're sitting before you reach the stadium but don't want to purchase a PSL—the Panthers always have some of those available—buy single-game tickets. You will likely have to sit in the upper-deck sections, which are numbered in the 500s, because most of the lower-deck seats are presold to PSL and suite ticketholders. In general, the lower the section number on the ticket, the better the seat. For example, Sections 131 and 132 are between the 40-yard lines on the lower level and command a hefty price.

Because the Panthers try to promote a family atmosphere, fans can't take their shirts off in the stands. Supporters who get too rowdy are also removed if there are numerous complaints. Usually, this isn't a problem unless the fan is obviously over-served.

Stadium concessions are overpriced, just as they are at every NFL stadium. So it's a good idea to eat lunch before you come inside (that's what tailgating is for, right?). Umbrellas are prohibited, so on rainy days you will need to either bring or buy a poncho. Backpacks also are not permitted. For a full list of items you can't bring inside, go to Panthers.com.

My favorite time of year to see a Panthers game from the stands is in the early fall, in October or November. Weather-wise, those are two of the best months of the year in North Carolina. September can be a little hot and December a little cold, but October and November are just right.

11 Julius Peppers

With apologies to Cam Newton, Steve Smith, Lamar Lathon, and Michael Bates, the best pure athlete the Carolina Panthers have ever employed is Julius Frazier Peppers.

Named jointly for basketball legend Julius Erving and boxing star Joe Frazier, Peppers became a two-sport star himself. The 6'6", 283-pound defensive end remains one of only two men to ever play in both an NCAA Final Four and a Super Bowl (the other is Donovan McNabb) and Peppers actually thought the Final Four was a bigger deal.

The Panthers have had many great athletes on their roster. Newton is also an athletic freak—huge for his position yet agile and strong. Smith is the absolute best player the Panthers have ever had, with an every-down motor that Peppers never matched. Bates was a somewhat limited football player—he was a great special-teamer, but couldn't contribute on offense—but was so fast he once won a bronze medal in the 200 meters in the Olympics.

But Peppers, by virtue of his eight Pro Bowl appearances, is the player who probably has the best shot of becoming the first Panther to make the NFL's Hall of Fame sporting a mostly Carolina pedigree. The late Reggie White is the only man who has ever played for Carolina and is currently in the hall, but he only played a year in Charlotte. White's best years were with Green Bay and Philadelphia.

Peppers played his first eight seasons with the Panthers, from 2002 to 2009, and made the Pro Bowl five times during that stretch. He remains Carolina's all-time sacks leader, with 81, and no one else is all that close. The Panthers drafted him No. 2 overall out of North Carolina in 2002—he was the first draft pick of the

John Fox era—and they knew very well what they had. They didn't want to lose him. On two different occasions, Carolina tried to sign Peppers to another long-term deal to make him the NFL's highest-paid defensive player.

But by the end of his tenure, Peppers wanted out of Charlotte. He was the rare NFL player who had grown up (in tiny Bailey, NC, raised by a single mother), gone to college, and played professionally for a team without ever leaving his home state. Quiet and introverted, Peppers had grown tired of his celebrity status in North Carolina. He was ready to try something new, preferably going to a bigger city where he would have a chance at anonymity.

The Panthers "rented" Peppers for one final year in 2009 by using their franchise tag on him, which ended up meaning they paid him slightly more than $1 million per game. They decided against doing that for a second year in a row in 2010—this time the price tag would have been more than $20 million for a 16-game season, and the Panthers were purposely shedding salary left and right that year. Peppers quickly left and signed a six-year, $91.5 million contract with the Chicago Bears. Peppers would later call the ending to his career in Carolina "a little sour"—and no one would argue with that, no matter what side you were on.

So Panthers fans' feelings about Peppers are mixed. Yes, they understand he was a great athlete and an important part of all three of Fox's teams that made the playoffs (in 2003, '05, and '08). But they also feel somewhat betrayed by him because he made no secret of wanting to leave toward the end of his time in Carolina. Those who had personal dealings with him in the Carolinas also got a mixed bag.

Peppers could be gracious. When the University of North Carolina accidentally posted his academic transcript online and the transcript was discovered in 2012, it was embarrassing to all concerned since the grade report showed that Peppers had made many bad grades in college and struggled mightily to stay eligible.

Peppers acknowledged he was "upset" (while also saying the transcript showed no academic fraud). But days later, he gave UNC $250,000 for a scholarship fund that supports African American students.

If you caught Peppers in the right mood, he would talk to you—thoughtfully, and without pretense. But he more often ducked away from crowds and autograph seekers, leaving the impression that he did not want to be bothered. The time he bought 25 bottles of champagne (at $350 apiece) at a Chicago nightclub to celebrate his new contract with the Bears was the exception, not the rule. Peppers generally didn't like to make a fuss.

But everyone who ever saw him play understands how great an athlete he was—a "larger Deacon Jones," as Dick Vermeil once called him while the head coach for the Kansas City Chiefs.

At Southern Nash High in Bailey, he was so good that both his football and basketball jerseys were retired. He excelled in track, too. One of the legendary Peppers stories is that after a three-hour football practice in high school, as his teammates lay on the ground catching their breath, Peppers did backflips. In full pads.

As a Panther, Peppers once had a 97-yard interception return. Another time, he took a Michael Vick fumble 60 yards for a touchdown. The Panthers let him dabble as a wide receiver near the goal line early on in his career. He never caught a pass, but he garnered so much respect from defenses that a couple of times he was actually double-teamed. He once basically won a game for Carolina during the Super Bowl season by submarining New Orleans running back Deuce McAllister on fourth-and-1 and stopping him short of a first down.

With all that athleticism, fans always wondered, *how is it that Peppers doesn't hold more records?* As great as Peppers has been, he has never seriously challenged the NFL single-season sack record.

The knock on him—which Peppers has long disputed, but which I do believe to an extent—is that he takes some plays off. If he is initially blocked on a play and the ball is going the other way or the quarterback looks like he's close to releasing it, Peppers tends to stay blocked. You sometimes forget about him being out there for whole quarters as a time and then—*boom!*—he does something magnificent.

While he has the talent to do so, Peppers has never been the NFL's Defensive Player of the Year. He has, in general, wreaked less havoc from his position (and far less in his personal life) than the other Tar Heel great to whom he is always compared—linebacker Lawrence Taylor.

So it is possible that Peppers would need a Super Bowl ring late in his career to ultimately make the Hall of Fame. And if he does become the first primarily Panthers player to make the hall, many Panthers fans will be clapping with one hand—admiring his talent, as always, but regretting the messy ending in Charlotte.

12 Home Playoff Win over Dallas No. 1

In terms of story lines, the Panthers have rarely been involved in a better one nationally than on January 5, 1997, when they got to host the Dallas Cowboys in Carolina's first-ever playoff game.

These were the Cowboys of legend. They had won three of the past four Super Bowls, including the most recent one. They had four players who would eventually make the Pro Football Hall of Fame on their team (at least so far)—quarterback Troy Aikman, running back Emmitt Smith, wide receiver Michael Irvin, and cornerback-and-punt returner Deion Sanders. And they had played 50 playoff games as a franchise. Carolina had played zero.

Given that, the Cowboys were installed as a three-point favorite over a Carolina team that was seeded higher, had earned a first-round playoff bye, and was playing at home in Charlotte.

But the Panthers provided three of the best hours in team history that Sunday afternoon, edging the Cowboys 26–17 before a delirious home crowd. John Kasay had four field goals, Kerry Collins threw two touchdown passes, and the Carolina defense was inspired—stopping Dallas on three separate possessions inside the Panthers 5-yard line and intercepting Aikman three times.

It was a glorious afternoon in many respects. The temperature was an unseasonably warm 67 degrees and the crowd was louder and larger than it had ever been for a Panthers home game. Ericsson Stadium (now called Bank of America Stadium) had only opened in 1996, and the Panthers had yet to lose a single game there. They went 8–0 in the regular season and allowed only three fourth-quarter points at home all season, riding a 3-4 defense stacked with three linebackers in Kevin Greene, Lamar Lathon, and Sam Mills—all of whom would make the Pro Bowl that year.

Until the Super Bowl run of 2003, this game was the peak of Panthers football experience from a fan's point of view. The Panthers gave blue towels to everyone who attended, and it turned the stadium blue. (The Cowboys were also wearing a darker shade of blue—as the home team, the Panthers had chosen to wear white jerseys to make Dallas wear its "unlucky" blue ones.)

Pat Summerall and John Madden did the game on TV, and Madden bubbled with enthusiasm as he introduced the game like this: "I think this is the greatest. Carolina gets its glory today…and it's something. You get the Carolina Panthers. Who would have thought? Here's a team that wasn't even a team three years ago and they are just two games away from the Super Bowl."

By the time the game was 17 minutes old, the upset was well in progress. By then, the Panthers led 14–3 on Collins' two TD throws—a one-yarder to Wesley Walls that the tight end had to dive for because Collins threw it short—and a 10-yarder to Willie Green that was an absolute strike. Lathon had also made a huge play, fracturing Irvin's shoulder on a legal tackle after the wide receiver's first and only catch of the game.

Irvin would later reappear on the sideline in a gold six-button suit and sunglasses, but he couldn't play again that day. Without him, the Dallas passing offense fell into disarray, as Aikman (11–1 in the playoffs entering the game) badly missed his preferred target.

Dallas did cut the lead to 14–11 later in the second quarter on an Aikman pass to Daryl Johnston and a safety when Panthers long snapper Mark Rodenhauser accidentally rifled the ball out of the end zone and over punter Rohn Stark's head.

After that, the last six scores were all field goals—four for Kasay, two for Dallas' Chris Boniol. The Panthers defense was a rock in the fourth quarter. First, it knocked Sanders out of the game when four Carolina players hit him following a reverse (Sanders broke a small bone just below his eye). Fourth-quarter interceptions of Aikman by safety Pat Terrell and linebacker Sam Mills in the game's final four minutes then sealed the win. Anthony Johnson ended up outrushing Smith 104 to 80.

Following the game, veteran Panthers wide receivers Green and Mark Carrier decided they should get the team to leave the locker room and return for an encore victory lap around the stadium. The team did so, in various stages of undress (Lathon no longer had a shirt on, and many players wore only T-shirts). This impromptu but well-loved gesture would be copied seven years later by a mostly different group of Panthers when they again beat Dallas at home in the playoffs.

As the final seconds ticked off, Panthers play-by-play announcer Bill Rosinski proclaimed, "The Panthers have done it! The king is dead! The king is dead!"

But the quote that most Panthers fans remember about this playoff game came from Lathon, who like several other players had taken offense at Dallas coach Barry Switzer's seeming to not realize exactly where Charlotte was. Once the Cowboys were guaranteed to be going to Charlotte to play, Switzer had said that Dallas had never traveled so far south for a playoff game.

Since Charlotte is actually northeast of Dallas, some Panthers players (and fans) took that to mean that Switzer didn't know where Charlotte was. Long after the game, Switzer would say he misspoke, that he had given coaching clinics in Charlotte and that he knew where it was. His sense of geography was just off.

But as he was coming off the field, Lathon didn't know all of that and probably wouldn't have cared, anyway. The linebacker waited until a semicircle of TV cameras had gathered around him and then yelled, "So now I propose a question for you, Barry Switzer! While you're sitting at home next week, do you know where Charlotte, North Carolina, is now, *baby*?!"

13 Home Playoff Win over Dallas No. 2

When you talk to Carolina Panthers fans about their favorite home-game memory, the words "Dallas" and "playoffs" often come up. But that's not enough to narrow down what game they are talking about, since the only two home playoff wins in Carolina franchise history both came against the Cowboys and were separated by a seven-year span.

Which win was better? That's a matter of taste. Both ended with the Panthers players taking a slow victory lap around the stadium (the 2003 team taking its cue from the 1996 squad).

The Panthers' first-ever playoff game, against Dallas in 1996, was closer for longer (a 26–17 Carolina victory) and also was

Six Strange Similarities

The Panthers' two home playoff wins over Dallas—after the 1996 and 2003 seasons—occurred almost exactly seven years apart. Here are a half dozen other similarities between the two games.

- In the first game, Anthony Johnson rushed for 104 yards on 26 carries for Carolina. In the second, Stephen Davis rushed for 104 yards on 26 carries for Carolina.
- Both games were played in unseasonably warm weather, with temperatures of at least 63 degrees.
- John Kasay was a major factor in both games, kicking four field goals in the first for the Panthers and five in the second.
- Sam Mills had a huge role in both games. Mills had a key interception in the first one as a player and gave the famous "Keep Pounding" speech as a coach on the eve of the second.
- Muhsin Muhammad played in both games as well—he was a reserve wide receiver who didn't have a catch in the first one and a starter who had 103 yards in receptions in the second. For Dallas, guard Larry Allen and safety Darren Woodson were the only holdovers.
- John Madden was the color analyst for both games. He worked with Pat Summerall for the first game and Al Michaels for the second.

played against a Cowboys team that had far more future Hall of Famers.

The 2003 game, however, was a more dominant Carolina performance and also foreshadowed the Super Bowl run, as the Panthers whipped Dallas 29–10 in a "Saturday Night Live" first-round playoff contest broadcast by the announcing team of Al Michaels and John Madden. The Panthers played about as close to an error-free game as you can in the playoffs, committing no penalties and no turnovers. They were only the second team ever to do so in the playoffs (Pittsburgh did it in the Super Bowl following the 1975 season).

"We picked a good time to start clicking," Panthers coach John Fox would say after the game.

The game actually started at 8:00 p.m. on January 3, 2004. Yet the weather was a balmy 63 degrees in Charlotte. It was a good omen. The Panthers gave out white towels at the gate and the stadium turned into a sea of white on every good Panthers play.

The Cowboys were coached by Bill Parcells, who had been hired to turn around a Dallas team that had fallen on hard times after dominating much of the 1990s. Dallas had already beaten the Panthers earlier in the season, 24–20, in Texas. In that game, Parcells and his staff had outmaneuvered John Fox and his staff, as the Cowboys' very average NFL quarterback (Quincy Carter) set a career high for completions (29). The Panthers let Carter get comfortable in the pocket, didn't blitz much, and allowed one chains-moving completion after another. For the rematch, the Panthers got after Carter much more effectively.

The game began auspiciously for Carolina. After a Dallas punt, Jake Delhomme dropped back on third-and-3 and threw a flanker screen to Steve Smith that was simply designed to get a first down. But Smith split two Cowboys defenders and burst down the sideline after the catch, getting all the way to the Dallas 1 before getting caught. It was a 70-yard gain, which ultimately set up a field goal and established the lead that the Panthers held the whole game.

This was a game in which almost everything worked for Carolina. Fox was famous (or infamous, depending on your point of view) for running third-and-long draw plays because of his innate conservatism. But this time, with the Panthers already leading 6–0 and facing a third-and-10 at the Dallas 23, the draw worked perfectly. Behind great blocking, Stephen Davis scored on the play, and Carolina suddenly led 13–0 in the second quarter.

It was 16–3 at halftime and 23–3 at the end of the third quarter after Delhomme connected with Smith on a 32-yard TD pass. John Kasay would end up kicking five field goals in the game, as the Panthers thoroughly dominated the Cowboys. The Cowboys never borrowed one of those white towels that waved in the stands throughout the game, but they could have by the time the fourth quarter began—by then, they had all but surrendered. Julius Peppers had a late interception and 34-yard return to set up one of Kasay's field goals.

Although the Dallas defense came into the game ranked No. 1 in the NFL, Davis ran for 104 yards and both Smith (135 yards) and Muhsin Muhammad (103 yards) went over the century mark, too. Smith had gotten sick in a sideline garbage can shortly after his 70-yard play, but came back strongly and had nearly half of Delhomme's passing yardage (273).

The Panthers defense also played extremely well, led by Peppers, defensive tackle Kris Jenkins (Parcells believed he was the best DT in the NFL at the time), and safety Mike Minter (who had a huge fumble recovery in the red zone).

The Panthers left the field to cheers when the game ended and then Fox—well aware of what the 1996 team had done—asked the players to run back out there for that victory lap.

"Those fans had been waiting for something good like that to happen for a long time," defensive tackle Brentson Buckner said. "We owed them that lap."

Someone in the stands slipped a Mardi Gras–style necklace around Delhomme's neck during the celebration. A Louisiana native, Delhomme liked the festive feel of it.

"I don't even know who it was who gave me the beads," Delhomme said, "but I liked them and I wore them proudly."

During the game, Michaels noted on TV that he and Madden both lived on the West Coast and that many people in California still didn't know in what city the "Carolina Panthers" played (apparently, the Lamar Lathon / Barry Switzer dustup from the 1996 Carolina-Dallas playoff game ad failed to make an impact on the West Coast). After this game, though, a few million more did.

The win advanced the Panthers to a road playoff game at St. Louis the following weekend, in a stadium where the Rams had won 14 games in a row. That game would ultimately be the only six-quarter game in Panthers history—but that's another story.

14 John Fox

The most successful coach in Carolina Panthers history, John Fox was hired in 2002 after George Seifert was fired. Fox left in 2010 after a 2–14 season, his expiration date literally and metaphorically up (Jerry Richardson didn't want to renew his contract). Most Panthers fans were ready to see him go at that point, tired of a philosophy of coaching conservatism that could be summed up with one of Fox's favorite football maxims: "A punt is not a bad play."

In between, though, came most of the Panthers' landmark victories. Fox won five playoff games as Carolina's coach—three in 2003 on the way to the Super Bowl and two more in 2005 on the way to the NFC Championship Game. His Panthers also made the playoffs in 2008 after an impressive 12–4 season that secured a first-round bye, but then faltered badly in the divisional playoff round at home against Arizona.

Fox was purposely boring when the cameras were on him, coming off as unapproachable and condescending in most of his press conferences. But when reporters weren't around, he was an earthy storyteller. Players and coaches both liked working for him. Constantly chewing gum on the sideline and exhorting his players, he remained true to his system through thick and thin—always wanting to run the ball, rarely going for it on fourth down, and playing good defense.

No Panthers coach has ever posted consecutive winning seasons in the team's history, and Fox was no exception. But in his nine

Fox's Bests and Worsts

The three best wins and three worst losses under Panthers coach John Fox (2002–10):

Best Wins

Carolina 29, St. Louis 23 (double overtime), 2003 playoffs. Fox's Panthers upset the heavily favored Rams when Jake Delhomme hit Steve Smith with a 69-yard touchdown pass on the first play of double OT.

Carolina 23, New York Giants 0, 2005 playoffs. Fox's defense totally dominated Eli Manning and company, as the Panthers allowed only 132 total net yards to a Giants team that had ranked fourth in the NFL in total offense in the regular season.

Carolina 14, Philadelphia 3, 2003 playoffs. Another defensive-oriented win in which the Panthers didn't allow a touchdown and rookie cornerback Ricky Manning Jr. had a startling three interceptions.

Worst Losses

Arizona 33, Carolina 13, 2008 playoffs. Jake Delhomme was awful and the Panthers seemed totally unprepared for wide receiver Larry Fitzgerald, as the Cardinals led 27–7 at halftime in Bank of America Stadium. Fox said after the game that his team had picked "a bad day to have a bad day," which struck many as too flippant of a comment.

Seattle 34, Carolina 14, 2005 playoffs. A slightly more understandable loss than the above, since it happened on the road. The script was similar, down to the same 20-point margin. The Panthers fell way behind early—17–0 early in the second quarter—and never made a run.

Atlanta 41, Carolina 0, 2002 regular season. The Panthers had already lost 30–0 to Atlanta on the road earlier in the season—with Michael Vick at the height of his powers. A month later at home the result was even worse.

seasons, the Panthers finished worse than 7–9 only once—in that final 2–14 year, when the team went young, started Jimmy Clausen at quarterback, and tried to purge a lot of big salaries.

Most of the time, Fox's teams were competitive. And occasionally, they had moments of brilliance. His handling of the 2003

Super Bowl team was exemplary, as he had to integrate a new quarterback (Jake Delhomme) and deal with an assistant coach and a standout linebacker who were both fighting cancer (Sam Mills and Mark Fields, respectively).

Fox had made his reputation as the New York Giants defensive coordinator before he got to Carolina. He was enthusiastic on the sideline, which the Panthers happily played up by showing him on billboards before the 2002 season in the heat of a passionate sideline moment. Seifert had had very few of those displays—they just weren't in his nature, as his sideline persona was one of aloofness.

Fox knew at the time that his differences with Seifert were part of the reason why he was hired. "I know how it goes in this league," Fox said. "If you had a fat guy, you hire a skinny guy."

While Seifert's most famous analogy as a Panthers coach concerned a wildebeest, the analogies Fox used often involved

Head coach John Fox exhibits a typical sideline reaction during the playoff contest against St. Louis following the 2003 season.

something one of his four kids had done. He had three boys and a girl with his wife, Robin—although like most NFL coaches he rarely saw them during the season. He worked what he called the "7–11 schedule" Monday through Thursday during every game week: in by 7:00 A.M., out by 11:00 P.M.

Fox was raised in Virginia Beach and San Diego, mostly by his mother. Because he was near the ocean in both places, he had learned to surf by the time he was 10. The father figure in his life was actually his stepfather, a former Navy SEAL officer who did three tours of duty in Vietnam. (Fox never knew his own biological father as a child.) He played football in college at San Diego State—he was a safety nicknamed "Crash"—but wasn't good enough to make the NFL.

He bounced around as an assistant coach until landing the Giants defensive coordinator job and then the Panthers' head post. In his first meeting with his full Carolina team, he went on the offensive—questioning the players' manhood and saying they weren't tough enough. Remember, this was a Carolina team that had just gone 1–15 under Seifert.

The players didn't like it much, but it worked. Fox got the Panthers to 7–9 in his first season, and to the Super Bowl in his second. Along the way, he became known as something as a cliché factory in the locker room—uttering phrases like "Don't be afraid to be great" or "Keep chopping wood" in every conversation. His most well known was "It is what it is," a phrase which didn't originate with Fox but which he adopted as his own.

"It is what it is" means, basically, that although you can wish your life was different, this is what you're stuck with, so get on with it. As Fox explained it to me once, talking about players complaining about having to come in the day after a game to lift weights, "Maybe they'd come in and say, 'I'm sore.' And I'd say, 'Hey, it is what it is.' You're sore, but you've still got to do the freakin' work."

Once Fox finally fell out of favor with owner Jerry Richardson, it took him hardly any time to find another job. John Elway hired him to coach the Denver Broncos, and Fox quickly made the playoffs the first two years he was there—first with Tim Tebow as his quarterback and then with Peyton Manning. He underwent some criticism for his conservative style in Denver, too, especially when the No. 1–seeded Broncos were upset in double overtime at home by Baltimore, 38–35, in the 2012 playoffs. With the game tied at 35, 31 seconds still on the clock and Manning in the huddle with two timeouts on his own 20, Fox had Manning take a knee and played for overtime instead of trying to win the game in regulation.

But that was Fox, staying true to his conservative roots. He won a lot of games that way in Carolina—and lost a number of them, too. The best way to describe his nine-year tenure? It was what it was.

15 The First-Ever Win in 1995

No matter how many games the Carolina Panthers win, those who were there will always remember the team's first-ever victory.

It came in Clemson, South Carolina, in 1995—the year the expansion Panthers played in Clemson University while their new stadium was being built in Charlotte. Carolina beat the New York Jets 26–15, improving their record to 1–5 after beginning the year with five straight losses.

The play everyone remembers is Sam Mills' 36-yard return of Bubby Brister's ill-fated shovel pass—a play Mills would eventually recall as the most memorable of his entire career. But there was far more to the game than that—most of it defensively-oriented, as both Brister and Carolina rookie quarterback Kerry Collins struggled mightily on what was a gorgeous, 65-degree afternoon at kickoff.

When the game ended, team owner Jerry Richardson let out a growl in the locker room. Richardson said afterward the win felt "pretty terrific." Running back Derrick Moore, who ran for 93 yards on 21 carries, supplied the most colorful quote, saying, "We finally grabbed the chicken by the jugular."

Although more people than this like to say they were there, only 52,613 actually attended in Clemson's "Death Valley" Memorial Stadium, which was about 25,000 fans short of a sellout. They saw some ugly football early—at least if you like offense.

The Panthers' Bubba McDowell blocked a Jets punt in the first quarter, and that led to the first of John Kasay's four field goals. Then the Jets scored the game's next 12 points, and almost all of them were due to Collins' mistakes. The rookie quarterback allowed a safety when he was tackled in the end zone. One interception set the Jets up for a field goal and another was returned for the Jets' only touchdown of the day by linebacker Mo Lewis.

That made it 12–3 Jets. A field goal for Carolina cut the margin to 12–6 when, with 22 seconds left in the half, the Jets behind backup quarterback Bubby Brister (starter Boomer Esiason stayed home with a concussion) tried for more points.

On the play, Mills blitzed up the middle and was supposed to be picked up by Jets guard Roger Duffy. But Duffy got too concerned with another rusher and left Mills with a free path toward Brister, who had rolled left and already started his forward pitch to Adrian Murrell before he even saw No. 51.

"I flicked it right to him," Brister said afterward. "I've never seen anything like it."

Mills caught the ball and started juking. "The way he was bobbing and weaving out there, he looked like a running back," Moore said.

"Maybe an older running back," added linebacker Carlton Bailey.

"I told him he looked like he was 25 again," Capers said.

Mills ultimately scored, giving the Panthers a 13–12 lead just before halftime. They extended that to 20–12 on a five-yard run from little-used running back Vince Workman in the third quarter, then got two late field goals from Kasay to seal it. Brister managed to throw another interception that banged off Bailey's helmet and caromed into the hands of Panthers safety Brett Maxie. Bailey said after the game in the giddy locker room that he was—you guessed it—just using his head.

The Panthers defense was most responsible for the win, and it would key the team for most of the 1995 and '96 seasons. The Panthers used their first win as a catapult—they went 19–9 over their next 28 games following the victory.

The Jets, who had entered the game 1–5, would end the season 3–13. They were coached by Rich Kotite, who had been under heavy consideration for the Panthers' head job before Capers beat him out for it. The Jets only gained 138 yards and earned seven first downs the entire game against Carolina.

"The heat was on Bubby all day," Kotite said. "He couldn't establish a rhythm. That's very distressing. Losing the way we lost is extremely discouraging, to say the least. It's a downer for everyone."

It was an upper for the Panthers. As the final seconds rolled off the clock, linebacker Lamar Lathon and safety Pat Terrell gave Capers the first NFL victory shower in team history, dumping a cooler of Gatorade over the coach's head. In the locker room, center Curtis Whitley passed out cigars in celebration of the victory and of becoming a father two days earlier.

16 Get Your Picture Taken with the Panthers Statues

You see it at every Panthers home game. Hundreds of fans pose in front of the six snarling black panther statues that ring Bank of America Stadium. With their smart phones, their tablets, and their digital cameras, fans take pictures of each other in front of the most famous landmark at the stadium.

There are two panther statues guarding each of the three entrances to the stadium. They are 22 feet long, eight feet high, and stand on 16-foot-tall pedestals. Their eyes are emerald green and their mouths are open, baring their teeth. Their claws grip their pedestals as if ready to spring.

Each pedestal contains thousands of names of the fans who originally bought permanent seat licenses. Another popular hobby for fans who have PSLs is to find their name on the relevant pedestal and take a picture beside it.

The panthers were created by California sculptor Todd Andrews, who posed them as if they are ready to leap off their perches and snatch their next meal from the pedestrian walkways below. It took him two years to make them all. The statues have been known to scare small children, although the Panthers lend a humorous touch to the statues every year by placing huge Christmas wreaths around their necks for December home games.

The statues debuted along with the stadium in 1996. Team owner Jerry Richardson told the Panthers players that season that if they ever need a reminder of what the team is about to take a look at the statues. At the public unveiling, Richardson said: "I've got goose bumps all over. We think these set the tone for what's going to happen. It's stately and it's strong. We feel like it is just perfect for us."

Other Great Stadium Photo Ops

There are several other frequent photo spots utilized by fans on game days. They include:

The Sam Mills statue by the north gate. Mills had a posing session with Andrews, so the sculptor was able to include a number of real-life details, including the scratches on Mills' helmet and a biblical scripture.

The Top Cats. The Panthers' popular cheerleaders sometimes are outside the stadium, particularly by the north gate, and will gladly pose for pictures with fans.

Jerry Richardson and his golf cart. Richardson, the team owner, frequently cruises the stadium for an hour or so during pregame and sometimes surprises fans by stopping by their tailgate parties. There's no telling where he will turn up next, but if you ever catch him, he is very much the Southern gentleman and will pose for pictures and sign autographs.

The players have liked the bronze monuments from the beginning, especially their fierce look. Linebacker Kevin Greene joked when the statues debuted that he was going to have a late night "mind meld" with the panthers at midnight, bringing his own wood for a small bonfire. Linebacker Carlton Bailey said: "When another team comes into the stadium and sees those statues, they'll be thinking, *Man, we're coming into the house of doom.*"

Quarterback Kerry Collins said: "They're a good thing to have on your doorstep. They're ominous—very ominous."

The monuments were named "the Indomitable Spirit" by Andrews, and they were so well received that the Panthers later commissioned Andrews to make statues of their first two Hall of Honor members—team president Mike McCormack and linebacker Sam Mills.

Andrews, originally selected from more than 40 artists, studied a zoo leopard in California for hours to make the model for the sculpture. He said at the unveiling in 1996 that the leopard "actually crouched down like this when [it] was feeding," with its muscles tensed. While the amount the panther sculptures cost was never publicly revealed, Andrews said in 1996 that the contract was for more than $500,000.

The sculptures were brought to Charlotte from California on trucks and hoisted onto the pedestals with a crane. In part because their pedestals aren't easy to scale and fans can't actually touch them, cutting down on wear and tear, they look today almost exactly the same as they did when they were first revealed to the public.

17 Visit Panthers Training Camp in Spartanburg

There are a couple of pilgrimages every Panthers fan must make no matter where they live. Going to at least one home game at Bank of America Stadium in Charlotte is the first. Going to Spartanburg for at least one day of Panther training camp is the second.

The second one is a lot cheaper than the first. Panthers training camp practices are all free and open to the public, and some players (although not all of them) sign autographs after each workout. The training camp schedule is published several weeks in advance on Panthers.com, the team's official website—although be warned that practice times can occasionally be adjusted. Generally, the team practices once or twice on most days between the end of July and mid-August in Spartanburg.

The best time to visit and to get autographs are usually the night practices. Players aren't as tired afterward and the temperatures are a lot more comfortable. Long periods of 90-degree days are a feature of every Panthers training camp—the coaches like it

Training camp in Spartanburg gives fans an up-close-and personal—and free— look at the Panthers team. Keep an eye out for owner Jerry Richardson cruising the grounds on his golf cart too.

because it gets the players in better shape—but the temperatures usually cool off into the 70s at night.

Wofford—the alma mater of Panthers owner Jerry Richardson— is the only place the Panthers have ever used for training camp since their birth in 1995. The school is small and compactly built—its enrollment is about 1,600—which allows players to get almost everywhere on campus by walking. During training camp, however, fans can't go near the player dorms or their cafeteria.

At night, players stay in the dorm and have a strictly enforced curfew. Fans, however, can do whatever they want. If they spend an entire day and night in Spartanburg, a trip to the Beacon drive-in restaurant for burgers, onion rings, and sweet tea is a good bet for an inexpensive meal and a frequent stop for Panthers supporters.

Checking out VisitSpartanburg.com for other restaurant and hotel recommendations is a good idea before you go.

Nestled in the foothills of the Blue Ridge Mountains, Spartanburg is about three hours from Atlanta, 75 minutes from Charlotte, and one hour from Asheville, NC. Summer is also the peak of peach season, and the area is famous for its homegrown peaches. If you like that delectable fruit, you can buy some of the best cheaply at one of the many roadside farms just off Interstate 85.

18 Dom Capers

The first coach in Carolina Panthers history was Dom Capers, a man so meticulous that he used to edge his family's small-town Ohio lawn with a fork to make it look exactly right.

The Panthers hired Capers after former Washington Redskins coach Joe Gibbs turned them down to coach the team starting with the 1995 season. Capers was Pittsburgh's defensive coordinator at the time and had helped devise the zone-blitz package that fooled offenses repeatedly and helped give the Steelers' defense the nickname of "Blitzburgh."

At Carolina, Capers was famous for his consistency, his tenacious work habits, and his notebooks. Since 1982, he had kept thousands of pages of notes about everything football-related, planning out the Panthers' practice schedules down to the minute months in advance and writing down nearly every word he ever said to the team and every meal he ever ate. He slept two to three nights a week during the season in a small room inside the stadium that he jokingly called "the Cell," on a small fold-out couch with a green bedspread he would crisply fold up each morning.

Capers lasted four years with the Panthers, going 31–35 (including playoffs) before Carolina owner Jerry Richardson fired him following a 4–12 season in 1998. A well-respected tactician throughout the league, Capers turned out to be best suited as an NFL defensive coordinator. After the Panthers, he became Jacksonville's defensive coordinator and then had one more head-coaching stint with the expansion Houston Texans. But Capers never had a winning season there and got fired again after four years and a record of 18–46. Then he became Green Bay's defensive coordinator, and he directed the defense for the Packers when they won the Super Bowl following the 2011 season over Pittsburgh.

Richardson has probably never been as close to a Panthers head coach as he was to Capers. When he fired Capers following the 1998 season, Richardson was obviously upset, calling Capers an "extraordinary person" and "as nice a person as I've ever met."

"He had heartache just like I had heartache," Richardson said that day shortly after the firing of Capers was announced.

Capers' greatest hits at Carolina all came in his first two years. His first team was 7–9, far better than expected for an expansion squad. Those 1995 Panthers beat the San Francisco 49ers, the defending Super Bowl champions, the first time they ever played them and won five of the eight games they played at "home" in Clemson's Memorial Stadium, popularly known as "Death Valley" and 140 miles from Charlotte. Capers' obsessiveness and dedication were seen as great characteristics—in Pittsburgh, he had been two hours late for his first date with his future wife because Bill Cowher had stepped into his office and wanted to talk defense; Capers was never about to cut a conversation short with a head coach to go on a date.

In 1996, Capers' second Panthers team went 12–4 in the regular season, won a home playoff game against Dallas and advanced to the NFC title game, which they lost to Green Bay at Lambeau Field. That squad, paced by a trio of Pro Bowl linebackers in Sam

Five Facts You Didn't Know About Dom Capers

- He wore crisply ironed dress pants every day to high school.
- He didn't vote in the 1996 presidential election because he was too busy devising the Panthers' game plan for the week.
- During the O.J. Simpson trial, his assistant coaches delayed a meeting so they could hear the verdict. Capers, oblivious to the trial, wondered if everyone had quit.
- Close observers of Capers noticed that he had far more hair later in his Panthers career than he did in his first season. Capers denied that he had altered his hair in any way other than combing it differently.
- When Capers met with Packers coach Mike McCarthy to interview for Green Bay defensive coordinator, he broke out 900 pages of handwritten notes from the era when he was part of the Pittsburgh staff that installed the zone blitz. McCarthy was so impressed he hired Capers and they later won a Super Bowl together.

Mills, Kevin Greene, and Lamar Lathon, sacked the quarterback 60 times, a team record that still stands. Second-year quarterback Kerry Collins led the conservative offense.

But it started to come undone in 1997, when the Panthers were picked by some pundits to go to the Super Bowl but instead went 7–9. Carolina had based its early teams on veteran players, especially the defense, and the Panthers started to look old all of a sudden.

And then 1998 was a disaster. Capers, who had gained final authority over personnel matters after Bill Polian left for Indianapolis, made a controversial trade to get defensive tackle Sean Gilbert from the Redskins in April 1998 in exchange for two No. 1 draft picks. Perhaps having a GM with a strong personality would have saved Capers from himself, but Gilbert was signed to a contract that made him the NFL's highest-paid defensive player. He underperformed from the beginning, and the personnel move became Capers' albatross. The Panthers ended up ranked dead last in the NFL in yards allowed in 1998, as Gilbert seemed to make no difference at all.

Then, after the fourth game of the 1998 season following a 51–23 loss to Atlanta, Collins met with Capers. The coach told the media soon afterward that the quarterback had told him his heart was no longer in the game and he didn't want to start for the Panthers anymore. Soon, Capers had waived Collins outright, getting nothing for a player who would wind up being in the league for more than another decade. Certainly, Collins had his problems and was no prince at the time, but he had been the No. 5 draft pick only three years earlier. He certainly still had some value that was cast into the wind when the Panthers released him.

So Richardson fired Capers following the 1998 season. Capers, always a model of graciousness, was classy even on the day he got canned.

"I understood at the time I took the job that our responsibility was to win football games," Capers said at the time. "This year, we did not win enough football games. So I'm sorry to say that's the reason the Carolina Panthers will have a new football coach next year. I'm not angry. I know the business."

Capers never varied from the 3-4 zone-blitzing system that got him the job at Carolina, however. Its concepts—which involved defensive linemen occasionally dropping into pass coverage and overloading one side with rushers—and his legendary preparedness served him well in the Super Bowl with Green Bay. When star cornerback Charles Woodson went out in the second quarter with a broken collarbone, Capers was able to make adjustments and contain Pittsburgh quarterback Ben Roethlisberger. After 25 years in the NFL, Capers finally reached the peak and earned a Super Bowl ring.

Many in the Carolinas were happy for him. Although the decisions to sign Gilbert and release Collins will always haunt Capers' four-year tenure in Carolina, his first two years were a fine honeymoon, and Capers is still remembered fondly by most everyone who had personal contact with him.

19 Ron Rivera

The fourth head coach in Panthers history is a testament to the power of perseverance.

Ron Rivera interviewed unsuccessfully for eight other NFL head-coaching jobs before the Panthers chose him in January 2011 to replace John Fox.

That was not the first time Rivera had had to wait. As a Chicago Bears linebacker, he played under Mike Ditka and didn't become a starter until his fifth season—although he did win a Super Bowl ring early in his career on the ferocious 1985 Bears team.

It was the same thing growing up in California for Rivera. He was the third of Eugenio and Dolores Rivera's four sons, which meant when the boys had to clean up the yard every Saturday morning. His older brothers always got the plum jobs and made him do whatever they didn't want to.

Eugenio Rivera was a Puerto Rican–born, commissioned Army officer. The Rivera sons understood the concept of a chain of command early. After successful stints as a defensive coordinator in Chicago and San Diego, Ron Rivera got his chance at the top of the chain with Carolina—with mixed results in the first two seasons.

Rivera inherited a team that had gone 2–14 in 2010. In his first year, the Panthers tripled their win total to six and rookie quarterback Cam Newton had a spectacular season. In their second, though, the Panthers began the season 1–6. Newton was struggling. General manager Marty Hurney got fired. Owner Jerry Richardson told

Five Signature Games From Rivera's First Two Seasons

September 11, 2011—Arizona 28, Carolina 21. In Rivera's first game as a head coach, rookie quarterback Cam Newton throws for a staggering 422 yards—but the Panthers lose a close one in what will become a recurring theme.

October 2, 2011—Chicago 34, Carolina 29. The Panthers set a franchise record with 543 total yards, but allow Matt Forte to rush for 205 yards and make the mistake of kicking to Devin Hester, who returns a punt 69 yards for a TD.

December 24, 2011—Carolina 48, Tampa Bay 16. Newton throws for three touchdowns and runs for a 49-yard TD as the Panthers eviscerate the Buccaneers in the feel-good home win of Rivera's first season.

September 30, 2012—Atlanta 30, Carolina 28. A heartbreaking loss. Rather than go for fourth-and-short, Rivera punts to the Falcons. The punt is downed at the 1, but Panthers safety Haruki Nakamura allows a 59-yard pass over the top of his head and the Falcons kick the game-winning field goal.

December 30, 2012—Carolina 44, New Orleans 38. Needing to "trend upward" to save Rivera's job, the Panthers respond with a four-game win streak that includes this season-ending win at New Orleans to close the season at 7–9. Rivera is presented with a game ball by defensive coordinator Sean McDermott and gets choked up with emotion. Six days later, owner Jerry Richardson tells Rivera he will return to coach the Panthers in 2013.

Rivera that the team had to "trend upward" in the last two months of the season or his job was in serious jeopardy as well.

The Panthers went 6–3 in their final nine games, however, which saved Rivera's job for at least one more year. The 2013 season will be critical for the coach, however, as Richardson is getting impatient with a Panthers team that hasn't earned a winning record or a playoff berth since 2008.

Rivera's main fault as a head coach at Carolina thus far has been an inability to get his team to close out games. The Panthers were 2–12 in games decided by seven points or fewer in Rivera's first two seasons. They rarely got blown out, but they often lost in the last two minutes.

Rivera doesn't mind the pressure, though—he's used to it. He was never a star in the NFL, playing nine years for the Bears as a middle-class grinder. "I always feel like I'm coaching for my job," he said in 2012. "It's just like when I was a player. I was drafted in the second round in 1984. For nine years, I came into that facility in Chicago, wondering if I was going to get cut. This is no different. I come to work like I did as a player, and that's to do the best I can."

Rivera was an All-American linebacker at the University of California before going to the Bears, and much of his football history after college centered on Chicago. After his nine seasons as a player, Rivera worked as a television analyst from 1993 to 1996. He got the itch to return to football, however, and talked Bears coach Dave Wannstedt into letting him volunteer as an unpaid defensive assistant. Wannstedt was impressed enough that it turned into a paying job. Rivera then was an assistant with the Philadelphia Eagles for five years before returning to the Bears as the defensive coordinator from 2004 to 2006. In his last season there, the Bears made it to the Super Bowl but lost.

Although that Bears defense had fine success, head coach Lovie Smith did not rehire Rivera for the 2007 season. Rivera landed in San Diego, first as a linebackers coach and then as the defensive coordinator from 2008 to 2010. His 2010 Chargers unit was ranked No. 1 in the NFL in total defense, and Hurney hired him shortly after that season ended.

Rivera is not the only coach in his family. His wife, Stephanie, is a former WNBA assistant basketball coach and has also coached some high school teams. They have two grown children—a daughter and a son.

Although Rivera can be intense, he is universally regarded as a nice guy—and one who is much more open about his team with reporters (and thus Panthers fans) than Fox ever was. While

Fox's tendency in press conferences was to purposely bore reporters until they threw up their hands and stopped asking questions, Rivera answers questions thoroughly and honestly. In many ways Rivera's personality and demeanor are reminiscent of Dom Capers, the Panthers' first head coach, who also got his first head job in Carolina after making his name as a defensive coordinator.

Capers ultimately lasted four years in Carolina before being fired, and Rivera would certainly like his tenure to be longer. Rivera signed a four-year, $11.2-million contract in 2011 to begin his time in Carolina.

To fulfill all of that deal—and to get an extension—he will have to make the playoffs soon. His perseverance has gotten him this far, but his next step for the Panthers is to achieve the same sort of excellence he was part of on those great Bears teams of the 1980s.

20 The 1996 Playoff Season

The first Panthers team that was truly embraced by the entire Carolinas was the 1996 squad, which won 13 games and made it to the NFL's final four in only the Panthers' second year of existence.

This was the team that gave Panthers fans a false sense of security. They thought, *How hard can this really be?* after the Panthers went 7–9 as an expansion team in 1995 and followed that with a 13–5 mark in 1996.

Very hard, it turned out. The team went on a six-year streak of non-winning seasons after 1996, with the defense getting old in a hurry, quarterback Kerry Collins imploding, and both Dom Capers and George Seifert getting fired.

But in 1996, ignorance was bliss. The Panthers really did make it look easy that year, paced by a fearsome defense that still holds

Nicknamed "Salt," linebacker Kevin Greene recorded 14.5 sacks during the 1996 season. (Getty Images)

the team record for sacks in a season (60). That mark led the NFL in 1996, and the Panthers' 3-4, zone-blitzing defense was at the forefront of what was new and cool in the league.

Three of that team's four linebackers—Sam Mills, Lamar Lathon, and Kevin Greene—made the Pro Bowl that year. Greene (14.5 sacks) and Lathon (13.5), who were nicknamed "Salt and Pepper," seasoned the squad with the best combined sack performance the Panthers have ever had. (Lathon lost a $2,000 bet to Greene that year as to which one of them would have the most sacks.) The Panthers were incredible in the second half, outscoring opponents 191–56 in the final two quarters.

Second-year quarterback Kerry Collins played the most mistake-free football of his relatively brief Panthers career, throwing only nine interceptions all season (with 14 touchdown passes). Steve Beuerlein was a more-than-capable backup, winning several key games when Collins was hurt.

It was also the team's first season in Charlotte after playing its inaugural year in Clemson. The Panthers opened their new

Home Sweet Home in 1996

The Panthers could literally have not started out any better playing at home in what was then known as Ericsson Stadium in 1996, as they went 9–0 in Charlotte that year. Those nine wins were:

Date	Opponent	Score
September 1	Atlanta	29–6
September 22	San Francisco	23–7
October 13	St. Louis	45–13
October 20	New Orleans	19–7
November 10	NY Giants	27–17
December 1	Tampa Bay	24–0
December 15	Baltimore	27–16
December 22	Pittsburgh	18–14
January 5, 1997	Dallas*	26–17

* playoff game

stadium—then called Ericsson Stadium—by going 9–0 at home (8–0 in the regular season and then 1–0 in the playoffs with a 26–17 win over Dallas). They allowed only three fourth-quarter points at home all season. Evangelist Billy Graham dedicated the stadium in one appearance and then held a four-night crusade there in September 1996. Running back Anthony Johnson not only rushed for more than 1,000 yards but also played a significant role on many of the special teams. Tight end Wesley Walls seemingly caught everything in sight, scoring a team-high 10 times.

In other words, 1996 was a season that included about four seasons' worth of memorable moments. The Panthers dethroned San Francisco to win the NFC West division by beating the 49ers twice. After the playoff win against Dallas—which is covered in greater detail earlier in this book—they finally lost 30–13 to Green Bay at Lambeau Field in the NFC Championship. In that game, Carolina briefly led 7–0 before a Packers team led by Brett Favre and Reggie White started to dominate.

Every home game was a different highlight that season, which is part of the reason it is remembered so fondly. The Panthers opened the season with a 29–6 drubbing of Atlanta in Charlotte and followed that with a 23–7 whipping of the 49ers. On and on it went, until Carolina closed out the regular season with a goal-line stand to beat Pittsburgh on Chad Cota's interception, 18–14, and then whipped a Cowboys team featuring Troy Aikman, Emmitt Smith, Michael Irvin, and Deion Sanders in the playoffs. The Panthers even went all the way to the White House, where a Cabinet meeting was once postponed so that Erskine Bowles—Bill Clinton's chief of staff at the time and also a Charlotte investment banker—could watch the team in the playoffs.

It couldn't last forever, and it didn't. Since that first season in Charlotte, the Panthers' home record has been decidedly mediocre. But in 1996 it was truly magic.

21 Steve Beuerlein and "the Draw"

In five years with Carolina, Steve Beuerlein was a consummate professional. He was a fine leader in good times and bad—making the Pro Bowl in 1999 with the best year of his 17-year NFL career and also serving as unofficial team spokesman during the Rae Carruth saga.

Beuerlein started 51 games for Carolina during his five years with the team and threw 86 touchdown passes—second only to Jake Delhomme on the all-time Panthers list. He was a steadying influence and an extremely accurate passer, although his mobility was roughly equivalent to that of an elephant. Cornerback Eric Davis once said he thought there were a number of third-graders who could outrun Beuerlein.

It was that lack of mobility, however, that was part of the backstory for the play Beuerlein is most noted for as a Panther. It was not a throw at all, but one of only three rushing TDs he ever scored for the Panthers.

On December 12, 1999, Beuerlein earned what he later would call the "crown jewel" of his pro career, beating the Green Bay Packers in Lambeau Field on the final play of the game with a five-yard quarterback draw for a touchdown. That play remains one of the most famous Panthers plays in history. Beuerlein—who entered into a broadcasting career calling NFL and college games for CBS after he retired in 2004—still gets asked about it every week.

In one of the most entertaining games the Panthers have ever played, Beuerlein and Green Bay quarterback Brett Favre engaged in a shootout that had nine lead changes. Beuerlein ended up throwing for 373 yards and Favre for 302.

With the Panthers down 31–27, Beuerlein got the team to fourth-and-goal from the Green Bay 5 with five seconds left. Carolina called its last timeout, and the three Panthers quarterbacks—Beuerlein, Jeff Lewis, and veteran Steve Bono—formed a small circle around head coach George Seifert.

"I remember looking at George Seifert on the sideline," Beuerlein would recall years later. "I couldn't tell if he was looking back at me—you never knew because he always wore those sunglasses. And then, out of the blue, he said, 'What do you think about the quarterback draw?' And Steve Bono almost fell down laughing."

The Panthers had actually run the play in practice that week, also fooling their own defense. Everyone knew Beuerlein couldn't run. His body was a mess. The fourth-round pick out of Notre Dame eventually had more than 20 surgeries in his NFL career due to various injuries.

But that was the point. The Panthers had only rushed for eight yards all day. No one would expect a run from Beuerlein (pronounced BURR-line).

Beuerlein ran back onto the field, knowing he first had to sell his teammates on the fact that the play would work. "I gave them the play while the timeout was still going on, so they could get their minds right," Beuerlein said. "I said, 'Well, you're not going to believe this, but we're running the quarterback draw.' They all busted out laughing. It was just like Bono. "

Seifert had actually sent Beuerlein back out onto the field with two options. If Green Bay looked like it was blitzing, he would throw to his favorite target—tight end Wesley Walls. If the Packers weren't, however, he was to run straight up the middle.

The Packers rushed only three men on the play, leaving eight to cover. The Panthers motioned fullback William Floyd outside, leaving the backfield empty behind Beuerlein. He took three steps back, counseling himself not to give the play away too early, and then took off for the end zone.

The play was so beautifully designed that only one Packer had a shot at Beuerlein. Green Bay safety Rodney Artmore came flying up to make the stop.

"He could have hit me in the chest and I'd have never made it," Beuerlein said. "Instead, he dove at my legs, and he hit my left knee with his helmet. I was jumping—soaring, I like to say—into the end zone."

Beuerlein scored, but the pleasure of the TD was leavened by the pain of what he thought was a blown-out knee (it wasn't) from Artmore's hit and of about 1,500 pounds of humanity piling on top him in jubilation. "I really thought I was going to die," Beuerlein said.

It was the high point of Beuerlein's career with the Panthers. He ended up leading the NFL in passing yardage in 1999 with 4,436 and making the Pro Bowl. Beuerlein also played an important backup role for Carolina during the 1996 season when he went 3–1 as a starter after Kerry Collins was sidelined due to injury.

Although Seifert and Beuerlein teamed up perfectly on that day in Green Bay, Beuerlein would be left with a bitter taste in his mouth when Seifert abruptly released the quarterback prior to the 2001 season. Beuerlein was expected to be the starter again; instead, Seifert wanted to play Lewis, who was nowhere close to NFL quarterback material. Even team owner Jerry Richardson was "taken aback" by Seifert's decision to part ways with Beuerlein, although the owner didn't block the move. Seifert's decision to fire Beuerlein led in part to the 1–15 season of 2001, which in turn led to Seifert getting fired.

Beuerlein finished his career with three years as a backup quarterback in Denver and then became an entrepreneur and a TV broadcaster. He signed a one-day contract with Carolina in 2004 so he could retire as a Panther.

22 Talk to Someone Who Went to the Clemson "Home" Games

There is a badge of honor among longtime Carolina fans, and you can invoke it with just one word: Clemson.

More recent additions to the Panthers fan family should make it a point to ask someone older who was actually there how it was to travel hundreds of miles every weekend to "home" games in 1995—if you lived in Charlotte, the round trip was 280 miles to "Death Valley."

The Panthers knew going in that their new stadium in downtown Charlotte wouldn't be ready until 1996, so they would need to play home games during their expansion season in a temporary facility. The obvious choices were Clemson or the University of South Carolina—the two largest stadiums in the Carolinas—and the Panthers ended up in Clemson. (It didn't hurt that team owner Jerry Richardson's son, Mark, had gone to school and played football there.)

So 1995 was a grand adventure in a lot of ways. The Panthers were on the road for 21 consecutive games—five exhibitions and then their 16 regular-season contests. Although this was well before smart phones were invented—and so not a single text was sent on these trips, if you young people can believe that—players kept busy on the 2½ hour bus trips to Clemson by watching movies, playing cards, talking, and eating. The rookies were usually responsible for paying for the grub and linebacker Carlton Bailey often arranged for it to get to the right place at the right time. There was normally a "fried-chicken bus" and a "pizza bus," and as a veteran you chose your bus based on what you wanted to eat.

Most of the time, players and coaches got to ride back home after games in their own cars from Clemson—if they had a family

Notable Non-Clemson Games in the 1995 Season

The Panthers' first-ever game was the Hall of Fame Game against Jacksonville, which was played on July 29, 1995, in Canton, Ohio. The Panthers beat their expansion rivals 20–14.

The Panthers' first regular-season game played in Atlanta. Carolina gave early evidence that it wouldn't be a traditional expansion powder puff, playing the Falcons close all the way. Willie Green caught a late 44-yard touchdown pass from Frank Reich to cut Atlanta's lead to 20–19 with just 26 seconds remaining, and coach Dom Capers wanted to go for two points and the win. But as the Panthers set up for the play, offensive lineman Derrick Graham false-started. Capers had to kick an extra point instead, and the Falcons quickly got a field goal in overtime to win, 23–20.

The Panthers' first-ever road win came in at Foxboro Stadium against the New England Patriots, who weren't very good back then. The Panthers won 20–17 in overtime on a 29-yard John Kasay field goal.

The Panthers' biggest win of their inaugural season came against the defending Super Bowl champions, the San Francisco 49ers. They upset the 49ers 13–7 the first time they ever played them—in San Francisco.

Carolina ended its first season on Christmas Eve 1995 at Washington, trying to get to 8–8. They lost 20–17, as the Redskins got two touchdowns from running back Terry Allen.

member who had driven the car down in the first place. Or they could have their families ride the bus back to Charlotte with them.

The bus rides in 1995 were long enough that the Panthers team later felt that they were as important to the bonding experience as anything the players did all year. Remember, these players didn't have the breadth of knowledge about each other that normal athletic teams have—these guys had been spread out all over the football universe less than a year before. Said Sam Mills, looking back at the time: "We had food, old movies playing, friendship forming—it was just so much fun."

It wasn't quite as much fun for the fans at first, who got a rude awakening on the very first Clemson trip—an otherwise forgettable exhibition game played on August 12, 1995. Because of road construction and lane closures near Gastonia, North Carolina, many Panthers fans experienced backups that stretched for hours on the interstate and made them fume. It was not uncommon to hear after that first game that it took somebody five or six hours to make what should have been a trip that took half that time.

That first-game traffic nightmare scared some people off, but not the heartiest ones. The North Carolina governor decreed no more lane closures on the days the Panthers played, and fans came by the thousands to Clemson, over and over.

The way the stadium was configured for Panthers games, a sellout was approximately 76,000 fans. The Panthers have a sellout streak of more than 100 games in a row now in Bank of America Stadium, but they certainly didn't have one in their first year. They sold out only a single one of their eight games—a contest against the defending Super Bowl–champion San Francisco 49ers, who had Steve Young throwing and Jerry Rice catching.

Carolina lost that game, but overall was very good for a first-year team in Clemson. The Panthers went 5–3 at home (but only 2–6 on the road) that year. Their Clemson victims, in order, were: the New York Jets (in their first-ever franchise win), New Orleans, Arizona, Indianapolis, and Atlanta.

It was a memorable season in many ways, and the "road trip" aspect added to the experience. Everyone has to come from somewhere to get to Clemson—you don't get there by accident unless you are a college student on campus—and so weekends stretched longer and tailgate parties seemed more festive. The games were fun, too. Behind a very good defense directed by Mills and a decent offense led by rookie quarterback Kerry Collins, the Panthers were only blown out twice.

The crowds weren't large, but they were loud. The Panthers had attendance in the 49,000 to 56,000 range—at least 20,000 seats short of a sellout—for every game except the one against San Francisco on a chilly December day that drew 76,136.

A lot of the Panthers fans who went to Clemson have kept right on coming ever since. The Panthers are still young enough that thousands of fans have been able to attend most of their home games in the past two decades. And it all started with Clemson—a long drive for everyone, to a place named Death Valley that was full of life.

23 Wesley Walls

A self-proclaimed "redneck from Mississippi," Wesley Walls didn't become a full-time NFL starter until age 30 with the Panthers. He proceeded to set all of the team's records for tight ends, using hands softer than a fat man's belly to engulf one pass after the next while making the Pro Bowl five times for Carolina.

The Panthers signed Walls as a free agent before the 1996 season, and it took Kerry Collins only a few practices to realize that Walls was about to make his life a lot easier. Collins and quarterback Steve Beuerlein would constantly target Walls over the next seven years, with Walls using his 6'5", 240-pound frame to nimbly grab balls like they were defensive rebounds.

Unabashedly egotistical, Walls always believed he was open and wasn't hesitant to let his quarterbacks know that. "Selfishly competitive," George Seifert called Walls once, and he meant it as a compliment. In that way, Walls was similar to many of the NFL's top wide receivers, and he had the ability to occasionally stretch the field like they did as well. Walls also fumbled the ball only three times in 15 NFL seasons.

Walls was famously insecure in the locker room, however. "I'm one play away from being put out to pasture," he started saying late in his NFL career. Said Beuerlein once of Walls, "Wesley has the unique ability to make a mountain out of a molehill. It's almost like he needs something to think about, to worry about... He never lets himself get comfortable."

Walls grew up in Mississippi, attended a daycare center named after Elvis Presley, and liked to hunt. He paid homage to the former hobby when he would score in the end zone and occasionally pretend to shoot a dove out of the sky. He played both ways for part of his time at Ole Miss, catching passes and also attacking quarterbacks at outside linebacker. The "redneck" act sometimes made people think he was dumb, but he was far from it. He got his college degree at Mississippi and sported a 3.3 grade-point average.

San Francisco drafted him in the second round and then buried him on the bench behind Pro Bowler Brent Jones, twice putting him on injured reserve for the entire year. Walls would develop a particular dislike for Seifert during those seasons as a bench-warmer—ironic since some of Walls' best years at Carolina would end up coming under Seifert once the veteran coach changed teams.

Walls caught only 11 passes in his first five years with the 49ers, but he caught hundreds more on a practice field from Joe Montana, himself trying to rehabilitate an injury. Montana could barely lob the ball 10 yards when he started, but he got his arm back with Walls on the receiving end. (Walls would later be miffed many years later when Montana didn't invite him to his retirement party.)

Walls left for New Orleans after those unfulfilling five years ended—he at least did get a Super Bowl ring from his rookie season—and he was a part-time starter with the Saints before Panthers general manager Bill Polian signed him prior to the 1996 season.

As a Panther, Walls blossomed. He scored 44 of his 54 career touchdowns in Charlotte. Former Panthers tight end coach Don Breaux once said that Walls' tombstone should read GREAT CATCH.

Before Seifert got to Carolina, Walls took extra delight in scoring against San Francisco. He said once that after scoring against the 49ers, "On a couple of those touchdown spikes, if I was strong enough I would have made them bounce all the way to his [Seifert's] sideline."

Seifert then took over in Carolina before the 1999 season and Walls promptly had his best season ever, with 822 receiving yards and 12 touchdowns. The 12 TDs tied an NFL record for most scores by a tight end in a single season.

Always a good storyteller, I still remember Walls telling me one about the time he and NASCAR legend Dale Earnhardt were the featured attractions at an autograph session in his home state of Mississippi. "There were 2,000 people in his line," Walls said. "There were four of my cousins in mine."

The Panthers finally released Walls prior to their Super Bowl season in 2003—firing him on his 37th birthday. Panthers coach John Fox placed far less emphasis on the tight end as a receiver than his predecessors had, using the position almost as a sixth offensive lineman for blocking purposes. Blocking had never been Walls' specialty, and by then he had a big contract and some bad knees. But Walls managed to play one more season, for Green Bay, before retiring.

Ultimately, Walls had a career that went far longer than most, even though he was quite a late bloomer. He once said, "Your football career is kind of like life. It doesn't go perfect. Goodness gracious. It'd be great to be able to play 15 years, never have an injury, never have a setback. But that's not the way it happens."

For Walls, though, it was plenty good.

Kerry Collins

Kerry Collins was called a lot of things during his stormy tenure with the Panthers. A rifle-armed star in the making. A No. 1 draft pick. A rookie starter. A playoff quarterback by his second season. And then: A racist. A drunk. A quitter.

Eventually, Collins would mature and stick around for 17 years in the NFL, throwing for more than 40,000 yards and leading three different teams to the playoffs and one to the Super Bowl. He had the sort of career, ultimately, that thousands of young kids dream about.

But in Carolina, Collins was still a kid—a hard-partying, introspective, take-no-junk-from-anyone sort of kid. The majority of his off-field mistakes were made from 1995 to 1998, when the Panthers employed him until his tenure ended in a sudden and bizarre way.

Collins was the Panthers' first-ever draft pick; he was taken with the No. 5 overall selection in the 1995 draft after general manager Bill Polian traded down from No. 1. By the fourth game of Carolina's first season, coach Dom Capers had installed Collins as the team's starting quarterback. He had the best arm of any Panthers quarterback until Cam Newton came along in 2011. And at 6'5", 240 pounds, Collins was difficult to bring down in the pocket when defenders were flying around him.

As a rookie, he was an impressive 7–6 as a starter. In his second season he was even better, as the Panthers went all the way to the NFC Championship Game. That was a defense-first team, but Collins made a lot of big throws when it counted. After the Panthers lost to Green Bay in the NFC Championship Game, Collins told the 3,000 fans who met the team back in Charlotte, "What you've witnessed is the beginning of a dynasty."

Off the field, though, Collins' life was starting to unravel. He bought a big home in Charlotte, christened it "Club Kerry," and turned it into a party house. He was drinking a lot and teammates were beginning to notice.

During training camp in 1997, he used a racial slur in front of several teammates after a night of partying. He would apologize many times for that and say he meant it only as a joke. Collins would end up having a very poor season for the Panthers, throwing a league-high 21 interceptions as the Panthers slumped to 7–9.

Then the Panthers got off to an 0–4 start in 1998. Collins was reeling after the last of those losses—a 51–23 defeat against Atlanta. He went in to see Capers, and what happened next is a matter of dispute.

Capers said Collins told him his heart "wasn't in it anymore." To Capers, this was tantamount to quitting the team.

Collins would later say he didn't mean it that way—he just thought he should be benched and wanted to take himself out of the starting lineup. But Capers stood firm, saying that once Collins said something like that he couldn't take it back. Within days, Collins was released. Capers himself was fired a few months later.

New Orleans picked up Collins on waivers, and he became a backup there. He returned to Charlotte later that season for a Saints-Panthers game and then asked permission to stay the night after a game in which he didn't play. He was then arrested for driving under the influence of alcohol. When released shortly after his arrest, he came out of jail with a cigar dangling jauntily from his mouth. That jarring image was captured by a TV cameraman and is still remembered by many longtime Panthers fans.

That was the lowest point. New Orleans released him shortly after that. But Collins went to alcohol rehabilitation, dried out, and became a far better person and player. He would eventually turn into a starter for Oakland, Tennessee, and the New York

Kerry Collins by the Numbers

A few significant numbers about Kerry Collins, the Panthers' primary starting quarterback for their first 3¼ seasons:

1—Pro Bowl appearance. Collins was the NFC's second alternate after the 1996 season, but played in the game in Honolulu when injuries kept Steve Young and Troy Aikman out.

1–1—Playoff record. Collins was the Panthers' quarterback for the playoff win over Dallas and the loss at Green Bay following the 1996 season.

7–6—Collins' record as a starter in his rookie season of 1995. He was the first rookie NFL quarterback with at least nine starts to post a winning record since Dan Marino in 1983.

23–21—Collins' overall record as a starter for Carolina.

55.7—Collins' quarterback rating during the 1997 season, when he had an NFL-high 21 interceptions. This was actually lower than the widely derided Jimmy Clausen's QB efficiency during the 2–14 season of 2010 (which was 58.4).

327—Collins' yardage total in an upset win over San Francisco in 1996, when he threw three touchdown passes, had zero interceptions, and played his best game as a Panther.

Giants, leading both the Titans and the Giants to the playoffs and the Giants to the 2001 Super Bowl. His high point with the Giants came in the 2000 NFC Championship Game, in which the underdog New York team destroyed Minnesota 41–0, with Collins throwing five touchdown passes.

Befitting Collins' rocky career, that game was immediately followed by one of his worst, as he threw four interceptions in the Super Bowl against Baltimore in a decisive loss to the Ravens.

Even after he left the Panthers, Collins kept returning to North Carolina. He met his future wife at a George Strait concert at Charlotte Motor Speedway. He eventually bought a 1,580-acre working cattle ranch in Troy, North Carolina, and named it Blue Q. The *Q* stands for "quarterback" and the "Blue" refers to the fact that Collins' three primary NFL teams—Carolina, Tennessee, and the Giants—all wore some shade of blue.

Collins' final season was 2011, when he was briefly brought back by Polian to try and rescue an Indianapolis team that was floundering after losing Peyton Manning for the season to a neck injury. Collins lasted only three games before sustaining a concussion and being placed on injured reserve after suffering post-concussion symptoms. He ultimately retired for good.

Along with his cattle, Collins has another business interest: music. He has written or co-written dozens of country songs and started a music publishing business. He and his wife and daughter split time between their homes in Nashville and the North Carolina ranch.

As a man, Collins is a long way from the kid Charlotte got to know in his early twenties. Although his time as a Panther was tumultuous, he understands that much of that was his own fault. And he will always be the Panthers' first-ever playoff quarterback.

"My memories of Charlotte are mostly pleasant ones," Collins told me once. "I don't think there's anything that went on in Charlotte that I harbor any resentment about. I made my share of mistakes, for sure, when I was there."

25 George Seifert

The most unusual hire the Carolina Panthers ever made at head coach was also the most unsuccessful. George Seifert—an aloof, intellectual man who had won two Super Bowls as the head coach of the San Francisco 49ers—was hired by the Panthers in 1999 after team owner Jerry Richardson fired Dom Capers.

Seifert lasted only three seasons and had an overall record of 16–32, the worst winning percentage among the four men who have served as Panther head coaches. The other three—Dom Capers, John Fox, and Ron Rivera—were all NFL defensive coordinators who had never been head coaches before when Richardson hired them.

Seifert was different—in a lot of ways. He had previously been a head coach who had a lot of success. While the other three Panthers head coaches all got fairly close to their players, engaging them in conversations about their families, Seifert was extremely business-like and did not traffic in personal chatter. He wasn't unfair, but he didn't mind players being uneasy around him either. He wore sunglasses almost all the time on the field, making it hard to read his eyes. He liked to go for it on fourth down and didn't care much about running the ball. He didn't wear headphones on the sideline and sometimes liked to isolate himself so he could think better.

All of that had worked in San Francisco, where Seifert replaced Bill Walsh as head coach and won two Super Bowls and made it to five NFC Championship Games in eight years (1989–96). He won one Super Bowl each with Joe Montana and Steve Young at quarterback. He reached 50, 75, and 100 victories faster than any NFL coach ever, and he left the 49ers with the best winning percentage (.755) in league history. Interestingly, the Panthers went 3–1 against Seifert teams in 1995 and '96, which the coach once said helped lead to his "demise" as the 49ers' head coach.

But without players of the caliber of Montana, Young, and Jerry Rice, Seifert never could duplicate the magic at Carolina. His three seasons went like this: 8–8, 7–9, and 1–15 in 2001, whereupon Richardson fired him with two years still remaining on a five-year contract—even though he would have to pay Seifert $5 million to do so.

Although his winning-percentage record was long gone by the time he went back to the West Coast, Seifert was not a total failure. He had a few moments of brilliance.

Three Important Late-Season Games Under Seifert

Here are three of the most important games the Panthers played under George Seifert. All came very late in the year, and the final one provided the epitaph of Seifert's rocky three-year career in Charlotte.

December 12, 1999—Steve Beuerlein scored on a surprising quarterback draw from five yards out as time expired, giving Carolina a 33–31 win at Green Bay. Seifert made the draw call, which completely flummoxed the Packers. Carolina finished a decent 8–8 in its first season under Seifert, who had taken over a 4–12 team.

December 24, 2000—Oakland thrashed the Panthers 52–9 in what remains one of the most lopsided losses in team history. The Panthers fell to 7–9 in Seifert's second season with the loss.

January 6, 2002—The skimpiest crowd ever for a Panthers game—21,070 in the 73,000-seat Charlotte stadium—watched New England cream Carolina 38–6. By the end, there were only a few thousand fans left, and most of them were Patriots supporters. The same two teams would play two years later in the Super Bowl. It was the last game in the Seifert era and it was quite a bomb, with Chris Weinke throwing two pick-sixes for Patriots TDs.

It was Seifert who made the draw-play call that ended up with Steve Beuerlein winning a game at Green Bay on a last-play touchdown. The Panthers had no official general manager during Seifert's time at Carolina, so Seifert had heavy input into personnel decisions and presided over the fantastic 2001 draft that netted Carolina Dan Morgan, Kris Jenkins, and Steve Smith—three future Pro Bowlers—in the first three rounds, all of whom would contribute heavily to the Panthers' 2003 Super Bowl run.

But he set the stage for his own downfall in March 2001, when he suddenly released Beuerlein—a fan favorite who had made the Pro Bowl in 1999 and played decently as a starter in 2000. Seifert wanted his team to get younger and had the idea that Jeff Lewis—whom he had traded a third- and fourth-round pick to Denver to get and to whom he had given a three-year contract extension before he took a snap—would be the mobile quarterback he wanted.

Instead, Lewis was a complete bust. After two straight horrid preseason games in August 2001, Seifert reversed field on himself, sticking Lewis on the fourth team and then cutting him a few days later. He instead went with rookie Chris Weinke as his starting quarterback. The Panthers weren't ready for that, and to make matters worse, their defense was going through one of its down periods. What resulted was a first-game upset win for Weinke at Minnesota, followed by 15 straight losses—the most consecutive games any NFL team had ever lost in a single season (a record broken in 2008 when Detroit went 0–16). It remains the worst season in Carolina history.

After that season, Richardson felt as if he had no choice but to fire Seifert. As he said at the time, "The energy has been sucked out of our organization and our fan base. In my opinion, we had no alternative. We had lost 15 consecutive games. We were 0–4 against Atlanta and we were 0–4 against New Orleans the last two years. We were 31st in the league in offense. We were 31st in the league in defense. It couldn't continue."

In Seifert's final two home games, the Panthers drew the two smallest crowds in franchise history. "When we go through a situation like we went through this past season, [it] sucks the energy out of coaches, players, fans," Richardson said. "What we've got to do starting today, we've got to start pumping the energy back in. That's what we intend to do."

Seifert, a zoology major in college, occasionally reached back into his past for analogies to use in team meetings. In his first training camp with the Panthers, in 1999, he told the team it couldn't be "wildebeests."

"The story he gave is when the wildebeest gets caught by a lion, and [the lion] grabs his neck, the wildebeest kind of gives up and gets wide-eyed," safety Mike Minter said at the time. "So what coach Seifert was saying was, 'Guys, don't be that wildebeest. Don't give up.'"

Later, though, Seifert's speeches to the team grew shorter and shorter and players on the team sometimes said he looked "spent." After the club's 14th straight loss in 2001, Seifert gave a one-sentence speech to the team—saying something like he didn't have the team ready to play—and quickly left the locker room.

While former coaches Capers and John Fox both resurfaced quickly after Richardson fired them and went on to success with other NFL teams, Seifert was older (61) at the time of his dismissal and never worked in the NFL again. Instead, he retired back to California to fish. The occasional interview request from Carolinas-areas reporters went unanswered, as Seifert decided to live out his life in the low-profile way he preferred.

"I have no real regrets as far as getting back into coaching," Seifert said the day he was fired in January 2002. "My only regret is that we weren't successful during my tenure here with the Carolina Panthers."

26 The Playoff Win at Philadelphia

The Carolina Panthers have gotten to three NFC Championship Games in their history—following the 1996, 2003, and 2005 seasons. In each case, they've been on the road, and in only one case have they won: a 14–3 whipping of Philadelphia on January 18, 2004.

This was a game the Panthers didn't particularly want to play. They had lost to Philadelphia by nine points just two months before. And if Green Bay had beaten the Eagles in the playoffs—they were about to until Philadelphia converted a fourth-and-26 late in the game—the Panthers could have hosted the NFC championship for the first (and so far only) time in team history.

But Philadelphia won, and the Panthers had to go back to one of the nastiest places to play in the NFL, a stadium so inhospitable that some of the Carolina fans who went to the game were pelted with snowballs and had beer dumped on them. Knowing the reputation of Eagles fans, a number of Panthers players told their families not to go to the game.

Those who did go witnessed one of the Panthers' most dominating defensive performances ever. The Panthers had five sacks, made four interceptions, and allowed only three points. They knocked Philadelphia quarterback Donovan McNabb out of the game with a rib injury. It had snowed earlier in the day before the game, and it was a cold night when kickoff came at 6:50 P.M.—the temperature was 33 degrees and, with the wind chill, 22.

The game came a week after Carolina had edged St. Louis 29–23 in double overtime, in what remains the most exciting game in franchise history. This win was much more workmanlike, as the Panthers simply ground the Eagles into oblivion. Carolina ran the ball 40 times and threw it only 14, as the Panthers grabbed an early lead and then froze the Eagles out.

The game's first touchdown came on a classic Jake Delhomme throw—a jump-ball heave into double coverage targeted for Muhsin Muhammad. The Panthers had a first-and-10 from the Eagles 24 and Delhomme was blasted by a linebacker blitz just after he threw the ball. It didn't look like much, but Muhammad judged the ball better than two Eagles defenders, outleaped them, and came down with it. Suddenly it was 7–0. Muhammad then dropped to one knee and made a "shhh" motion by holding his finger to his lips that landed him the cover of *Sports Illustrated* the following week.

"I trust Moose," Delhomme said later. "That's what he does. He fights for a ball and he goes and gets it."

In the second quarter, defensive end Mike Rucker got a great jump on a snap and disrupted an Eagles play. McNabb fell while trying to avoid the sack and was then belted in the ribs by Panthers linebacker Greg Favors—legally, since he had not yet been touched down.

From then on, McNabb continued to play, but he wasn't the same quarterback. He would say later that "it hurt to breathe" and he stopped trying to run at all—and he was a major threat to run

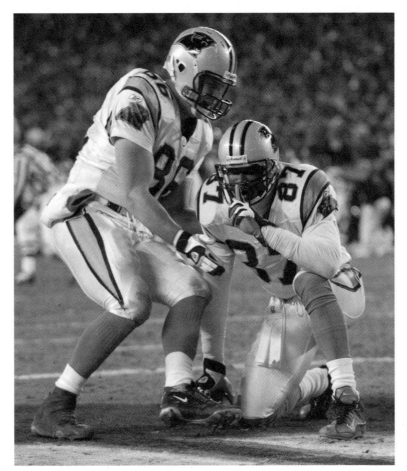

Muhsin Muhammad (87) hushes the Philadelphia crowd after scoring a touchdown in the NFC Championship Game following the 2003 season.

at the time, having rushed for 107 yards the week before against Green Bay.

Instead, McNabb kept forcing throws toward the Eagles' well-covered receivers, who really didn't have the speed to break away from anyone. Rookie cornerback Ricky Manning Jr. intercepted McNabb three times—easily the best game he ever had as a Panther. Philadelphia coach Andy Reid eventually took McNabb out in the fourth quarter, more for his own protection than anything else.

Manning had criticized the Eagles' starting receivers—James Thrash and Todd Pinkston—before the game on a Charlotte radio station, saying they didn't impress him. What seemed like a rookie mistake turned out to be the unvarnished truth. As Manning would explain later, "They didn't seem that fast to me and they weren't that physical."

The Eagles could have been in better shape had they had Brian Westbrook, who had often outrun the Panthers defense in Philadelphia's 25–16 win over Carolina two months before, but Westbrook was out for the playoffs with a torn triceps. Once McNabb was hurt, too, there was really no one on the Eagles offense who scared anyone on the Panthers sideline.

When Reid ultimately pulled McNabb, the quarterback had completed only 10 for 22 passes for 100 yards with three interceptions. His quarterback rating was 19.3. He also wasn't helped by the fact Eagles receivers dropped six passes.

Leading 7–3, the Panthers basically clinched the game on one of the most famous one-yard runs in team history. Second-year back DeShaun Foster had yet to score in his NFL career—running back Stephen Davis was the starter and usually got the short-yardage carries. But Foster got the ball on a pitchout from the Eagles 1 with Carolina leading 7–3 late in the third quarter.

The Eagles got good penetration and the play looked like it was going nowhere. But Foster then proceeded to bounce, sidestep, and juke his way out of five—yes, *five*—tackles. And still he was running parallel to the goal line. But then he held the ball out in his right hand, just over the goal-line pylon, and got the touchdown while dragging the last tackler along with him. It was a remarkable effort, and it pushed the Panthers ahead, 14–3.

The Panthers nursed that lead the rest of the game. Reid substituted Koy Detmer in for the injured McNabb, and he threw the Eagles' final interception to linebacker Dan Morgan. Delhomme knelt three times at midfield to end the game. The Panthers had won the right to go to their first—and still their only—Super Bowl.

27 Buy Your Favorite Player's Jersey

To have the full-scale Panthers fan experience on Sundays—whether you are watching from the stadium, from home, or from a sports bar—it sometimes helps to own and wear a jersey of your favorite Carolina player. They can generally be had for around $100 at various sporting goods stores or online, although bargains can sometimes be obtained. After the Panthers waived Jake Delhomme, there were a slew of No. 17 jerseys on sale around the Carolinas for $5, and you still see some of those at Carolina games today.

While there are no exact figures available, the dozen jerseys that have been spotted most often in the Panthers' stadium over the team's history in no particular order are: Sam Mills (No. 51), Steve Smith (No. 89), Cam Newton (No. 1), Muhsin Muhammad (No. 87), Delhomme (No. 17), Julius Peppers (No. 90), DeAngelo Williams (No. 34), Jonathan Stewart (No. 28), Mike Minter (No. 30), Jon Beason (No. 52), Lamar Lathon (No. 57), and Kevin Greene (No. 91).

By virtue of Smith's longevity, it seems you see more of his No. 89 jerseys than any other Panther. But Newton made a huge push in his rookie year of 2011, and before the 2011 Christmas season there was a shortage of No. 1 jerseys at many stores around Charlotte. Of course, Newton had originally wanted No. 2 when he came to Charlotte, because that was the number he had worn during his Heisman Trophy season at Auburn.

Since Jimmy Clausen had No. 2 at the time and didn't want to part with it, longtime Panthers team equipment manager Jackie Miles assigned Newton No. 1. Miles in general had steered away from giving Panther players No. 1, thinking the number because of its "I'm No. 1" double meaning might put too much pressure on a player. But since Newton was the first No. 1 draft pick in Panthers history, not to mention the team's field general, Miles made an exception.

Newton grew accustomed to the number. And when Clausen switched to No. 7 before the 2012 season and No. 2 became available, Newton said thanks but no thanks—he was set with No. 1. That was good news for the thousands who had bought his jersey during his rookie year.

Many players switch jerseys at some point in their career. Delhomme was another who changed numbers, only to end up in one that he will always be associated with at Carolina. Delhomme had worn No. 12 in both college and as a backup at New Orleans. But when he came to Carolina in 2003, reserve quarterback Randy Fasani had the number. Delhomme needed to choose a new number and chose 17 in tribute to his wife and daughter. Eventually, Delhomme's No. 17 would be worn by thousands each Sunday. And then the quarterback's time at Carolina would end and it would be sold for $5 on clearance racks—part of the circle of life in the land of NFL jerseys.

Jon Beason

Before Luke Kuechly, there was Jon Beason.

Beason, nicknamed "the Beast," preceded Kuechly by five years as a Carolina Panther. Like Kuechly, Beason was a first-round draft pick from an ACC school who began his NFL career as an outside linebacker but who was quickly inserted into the middle once the starter at that position got a significant injury. Then, like Kuechly, Beason immediately flourished in the middle as a rookie, winning recognition for his speed and tackling ability.

The difference is that Beason replaced Dan Morgan at middle linebacker. Kuechly replaced Beason, whose four-year run of durability ended with a thud in 2011 and 2012. In those years, Beason missed 27 of a possible 32 games—first with a torn Achilles' tendon in 2011, then with shoulder and knee injuries in 2012 that both required surgery.

The timing wasn't good. Beason had signed a five-year, $51.5 million contract extension, with $25 million guaranteed, before the 2011 season. But the Panthers believe in Beason's versatility and his ability to make a comeback, which is why they released James Anderson and kept Beason in the 2013 off-season. The thought is that Kuechly will continue to play middle linebacker but that Beason will play one of the outside spots (although Beason would prefer the middle, he is okay with playing outside and better suited for that than Kuechly, coach Ron Rivera believes).

Up until his injuries, Beason has been quite a success story. He grew up in south Florida, the son of a poor but resolute single mother who would take him and his older brother, Adrian, to the local Barnes & Noble bookstore on most Saturday mornings to read.

Terry Beason banned the words "stupid," "dumb," and "can't" from her house and sacrificed constantly for her two boys. Originally, she wouldn't let them play football due to the risk of getting hurt, but relented when Jon Beason brought home a book from the library extolling the virtues of team sports.

Beason became a high school star in Fort Lauderdale, Florida, and didn't have to go far for college, accepting a scholarship at the University of Miami. He was recruited as an athlete and at first Hurricanes coaches were unsure where to put him, having him play fullback before switching him to linebacker. He found his niche there and by the end of his redshirt junior year was a sure first-round NFL pick. He declared eligibility a year early.

In the private workouts that followed, Beason developed strong opinions about several teams. One he didn't like was New England—he felt coach Bill Belichick wasn't that loyal to his veterans, plus he didn't want to play in that cold weather or in Belichick's 3-4. He gently tried to sabotage a workout with Belichick, asking for a water break during a key part of one drill because he knew the coach wouldn't like it.

Ultimately, New England picked 24th in the 2007 draft and passed on Beason. Carolina picked 25th and took him. Beason—watching on TV—later said he "cried like a baby." He led the Panthers in tackles as a rookie (as Kuechly did). Then he made the Pro Bowl three years in a row, from 2008 to 2010. That led to the big contract. Not long after, unfortunately, came the big injuries.

What the Panthers desperately hope for is that their "Beast" returns to his beastly form. When healthy—and Beason played in 64 straight games from 2007 to 2010—he is one of the Panthers' best players. When he's not healthy, they are diminished.

29 Kevin Greene

Although he played only 20 percent of his 15-year NFL career with the Carolina Panthers, Kevin Greene remains one of the players who is most strongly identified with the team.

In his three seasons as a Panther—1996, 1998, and 1999—Greene collected 41.5 sacks, or almost one sack per game on average. On a sacks-per-game basis, the Panthers have never had a player better than No. 91 at getting to the quarterback.

They have rarely had a player who was more controversial, either. Greene made two major errors in the eyes of most Panthers fans, and some of them still have not forgiven him. He held out before the 1997 season, wanting more money, and ended up playing for San Francisco, the Panthers' fierce rival at the time. And a few months after he returned in 1998, he angrily grabbed assistant coach Kevin Steele by the collar during a sideline altercation. Head coach Dom Capers allowed Greene to keep playing in that game, and the lack of an immediate punishment became a source of discontent in the locker room, as some players believed Greene had gotten special treatment. Capers then suspended Greene for the next game.

"I lost my composure," Greene said in the locker room after the incident. "What I did was wrong."

But when Greene had his composure and was at his best—which was most of the time—he was a magnetic player. He had the personality of a pro wrestler, which was fitting because he dabbled in that sport and once shared the ring with Ric Flair. He was an entertainer who made sure to dance after sacks, but he also studied far more videotape than most NFL players.

Blessed with a body that never required a single knee surgery (his battery mate, Lamar Lathon, had 15 surgeries on his knees alone) Greene maximized his career to the point where he has barely missed making the Pro Football Hall of Fame numerous times—and may one day get in there. He had 160 sacks in his career—slightly more than 10 per year—and retired as the NFL's third-leading sacker in history, behind only Reggie White and Bruce Smith (though the NFL did not make sacks an official statistic until 1982).

Capers once said of Greene, "He made a lot of plays over the years, led the league in sacks with two different teams, and a lot of that was because he outworked his opponent. His combination of strength, power, quickness, and very good technique was special, but I've never been around a player who studied more tape. Kevin had a plan ready for whatever happened on the field."

Greene said when he retired following the 1999 season that he most closely identified with the then-L.A. Rams, whom he played for in Los Angeles for his first eight seasons. The Panthers did not get hold of him until 1996, in his 12th season, when he joined the team to rush the quarterback for Capers and quickly dubbed himself and Lathon "Salt and Pepper." He was an integral part of that team's run to the NFC Championship Game. His wife, Tara, also was considered a good luck charm for the team for a while, since the Panthers ended up winning most of the games at which she sang the national anthem beforehand.

Greene played in six AFC or NFC Championship Games in his career but made it to only one Super Bowl—following the 1995 season, when he played on a Pittsburgh team that lost to Dallas. The Super Bowl ring that eluded him throughout his playing career came to him later, though, when he coached Green Bay's defensive ends. Under Capers, who by then was the Packers defensive coordinator, Greene helped the Packers' Clay Matthews have a great season that ended up with Green Bay edging Pittsburgh in the Super Bowl following the 2010 season.

Although Greene's knees always supported him well, the repeated blows that he took for 15 years to his head are a concern. He once estimated to the *Charlotte Observer* that he had had 20 to 30 concussions all told in his 15-year career, and revealed that late in his career that he routinely played through periods of partial blindness that lasted up to 40 minutes. He could only see with his right eye during those periods, which meant that he asked teammates to warn him of blockers approaching him on his left.

Greene's first sack came against Dallas quarterback Danny White. The last two sacks of Greene's career came against Jake Delhomme. In the Panthers' 45–13 rout of a New Orleans squad quarterbacked by Delhomme in 1999, Greene sacked Delhomme twice and helped force an interception. Several of his teammates, cognizant of the fact that it was probably Greene's final game, carried him off the field after the final gun.

30 Lamar Lathon

If you were going to use any current or former player as a model for the six panther statues that surround Bank of America Stadium, linebacker Lamar Lathon would be your best choice.

Like the statues, Lathon at his best was all tightly bunched muscle and coiled fury. His 6'3", 260-pound body was nearly perfect for the NFL—as long as you overlooked all the scars on his knees, evidence of 15 separate surgeries that prematurely ended his pro career.

In the Panthers' first two seasons, Lathon was a tremendous force—a relentless pass-rushing linebacker whose moodiness and talent could not be ignored. His best year came in 1996, when he and fellow linebacker Kevin Greene formed what Greene dubbed the "Salt and Pepper" duo, terrorizing opposing quarterbacks. Greene had 14.5 sacks in that playoff year and Lathon had 13.5—still the best dual performance in team history—as they crashed in from opposite sides on passing downs.

Although the two eventually became close friends, Lathon resented Greene at the beginning of their time together as teammates. Lathon was the Panthers' highest-paid player in 1996, having signed a five-year, $13.5-million contract in 1995 with the idea he would be the team's first premier pass rusher.

Lathon did lead the team in sacks in 1995, with eight. Then Capers—who had coached Greene in Pittsburgh—got Greene to come to Carolina to join Lathon.

"There was something about Kevin I didn't like at first, " Lathon told the *Charlotte Observer* in 1996. "He was loud and obnoxious. I was like, *Man, I know what he's thinking. He's thinking he's going to come in here and be the Show. But that's not going to happen.* My mind-set was, *I'm going to be the man.* I used that energy inside of me to make myself better."

In their first game together, Lathon had three sacks to set a team record and Greene had two. But Greene got far more attention on ESPN and on other media outlets, in large part because his post-sack dances were so entertaining. An angry Lathon barely spoke to the media for weeks.

But Lathon made his peace with Greene after the two ate at each other's homes and they eventually became close friends. In December 1996 they posed for a picture for the *Charlotte Observer* wearing Santa Claus costumes. (Sixteen years later, Greg Hardy and Charles Johnson would duplicate the pose for the same newspaper.) Years afterward, Lathon and Greene kept in touch, and in 2007 went on a trip together to Iraq to visit with U.S. troops.

Lathon's star burned brightly for Carolina in 1996, but it dimmed rather suddenly after that. His knees simply couldn't hold up.

He had only two more sacks in his career following that 13.5-sack Pro Bowl season, and one of George Seifert's first personnel moves in 1999 was to release Lathon to clear salary-cap room. Although Lathon wanted to play elsewhere, his body wouldn't let him. A Texas native, he went back home to Houston—where he had gone to college and also played for the Oilers.

Many years later, Lathon remains one of the most colorful players in team history. He was known for brash predictions. He said the Panthers would win 10 games as an expansion team in 1995 (they didn't) and that they would make the playoffs in 1996 (they did).

Lathon was also known for his conspicuous consumption. No Panthers player has ever driven more sleek sports cars into the players' parking lot than Lathon did. Mercedes, Ferrari... you name it, Lathon at one point owned it. He also was exceedingly generous at times, buying friends their own cars and once hearing a tale of distress in an airport and buying a stranger a plane ticket because of it.

"You only live once," Lathon would say sometimes. And although his time as a Panther was relatively brief, he lived it to the fullest.

31 Eric Davis

The Panthers' best-ever cover cornerback was Eric Davis. Cocksure and consistent, Davis played five seasons for Carolina and posted exactly five interceptions in each one of them.

Those 25 career interceptions as a Panther rank Davis second on the team's all-time list, behind only Chris Gamble. But Gamble took nine years to get his 27 career interceptions as a Panther, averaging a modest (by comparison) three interceptions per year.

Davis played for Carolina from 1996 to 2000, signing with the Panthers after a fine six years in San Francisco during which he started and won a Super Bowl. Deion Sanders and Davis played together for a season with the 49ers, and Neon Deion later called Davis the best cornerback he had ever played alongside. In practice, Davis got to guard Jerry Rice thousands of times, and he was one of the few players who ever had a shot at staying with Rice.

The key to Davis' success was twofold: his footwork and his confidence. He wasn't the biggest or the fastest cornerback in the league, but his sense of balance was extraordinary. He seemingly could have played the game in cowboy boots and never slipped despite the frequent changes of direction a cornerback must make. And when he did get burned—inevitable for any cornerback—he had the short-term memory lapse that all good defensive backs need.

For much of his time at Carolina, Davis drove a Mercedes with a license plate that read BMPNRUN. That was his preferred method of coverage, bumping a wide receiver legally in the first five yards of a pass route rather than hanging back eight to 10 yards and allowing the receiver to launch off the line unimpeded.

Panther Pickoffs

A list of all the Panthers players with at least 10 career interceptions (through the 2012 season). The number of interceptions refers only to the interceptions the player had while at Carolina:
1. Chris Gamble (2004–12): 27
2. Eric Davis (1996–2000): 25
3. Mike Minter (1997–2006): 17
4. (tie) Doug Evans (1998–2001): 14
4. (tie) Richard Marshall (2006–10): 14
6. Ken Lucas (2005–08): 13
7. (tie) Deon Grant (2000–03): 11
7. (tie) Charles Godfrey (2008–12): 11

"If I've got a wide receiver out there running a 4.2 40, I can't run a 4.2 40," Davis said once. "So why am I going to stand back there and let him run? I'm going to see how fast he can run with my hand in his face. Okay, so you run a 4.2 by yourself? Let's see how fast you run dragging me along."

Davis joined the Panthers before the 1996 off-season. Before he ever played a game, his wife had triplets. So he rarely had a peaceful night's sleep during his first season with Carolina, when the Panthers advanced to the NFC Championship Game.

Quotable and authoritative, Davis had all sorts of theories about the NFL. Once he said that the ideal NFL defense should include "a couple of guys who—if they weren't playing football—might be out stealing your car. Then you need a couple of guys who you wouldn't mind coming home with your daughter." Although Davis had an infectious, gap-toothed smile, he counted himself in the "stealing your car" group.

Davis made himself into quite a respectable citizen, however. The Panthers released him in a salary-cap move after five years, but he played for two more seasons (one each in Denver and Detroit) before retiring following a 13-year NFL career after the 2002 season.

After that, Davis and his family moved back to California and he began a broadcasting career. It was a natural fit. In 2011, he became the 49ers' primary radio analyst and got to do the radio broadcast of his former team in the Super Bowl following the 2012 season. Earlier in 2012, he also added some NFL Network broadcasting duties to his plate. Davis and Steve Beuerlein—who has worked as a CBS television analyst for years—are the two former Panthers players who most frequently show up talking about pro football on national TV.

Bill Polian

The first Panthers architect was Bill Polian, who built the 1996 NFC championship team from scratch but then didn't leave a whole lot in the Carolina cupboard when he left for Indianapolis following the 1997 season.

Polian was the Panthers' first general manager and became one of the most successful personnel men in league history, winning the NFL Executive of the Year award six times (including his first two years with the Panthers).

Besides his success with Carolina, he built the core of the Buffalo teams that got to the Super Bowl four times and the Indianapolis teams with Peyton Manning that constantly seemed to win 12 or more games in the regular season and once won a Super Bowl. For all that, one day Polian may end up in the Pro Football Hall of Fame.

Fiery, smart, and opinionated, Polian was a bit of an odd hire for owner Jerry Richardson. The first man outside his own family that Richardson put in place very high on his leadership team was

Mike McCormack, a former Hall of Fame offensive tackle who had since been an NFL head coach in Philadelphia and team president with Seattle.

McCormack was a genial, sharp consensus builder who was well liked by pretty much everyone. In general, that sort of personality has been Richardson's preference with his top people (current team president Danny Morrison, PSL creator Max Muhleman, longtime ticket director Phil Youtsey, media relations director Charlie Dayton, equipment guru Jackie Miles, and many others fall into this category).

Polian—who had worked his way into some of the NFL's top jobs from the bottom up, scouting players at small colleges around the United States and Canada—was more confrontational. For instance, he considered sports agents a necessary evil and had been known to bark at a particularly stubborn one with whom he was trying to negotiate, "I'm going to come through this telephone and tear your tonsils out!"

Another time, before the Panthers' playoff game against Dallas after the 1996 season, Polian found a Cowboys helmet on the field where the Panthers were going to warm up. He slung it back toward the Dallas sideline. It turned out to belong to Michael Irvin, and that fact delighted the Panthers who saw Polian's throw.

It was McCormack who actually wanted to hire Polian as his long-term replacement and did so with Richardson's okay in 1994. McCormack was actually the Panthers' general manager, but then was promoted to president; Polian assumed the GM title and the day-to-day personnel responsibilities.

At first, it all went beautifully. The Panthers were 7–9 in their first season in 1995—the best record ever by an expansion team. With a blank slate to work with, Polian signed linebackers Sam Mills and Lamar Lathon and kicker John Kasay for that first team. He drafted Kerry Collins, and Collins was the team's starter at quarterback by Week 4 of his rookie season.

In his second season in Charlotte, Polian did even better in free agency, grabbing tight end Wesley Walls, cornerback Eric Davis, special-teams specialist Michael Bates, and linebacker Kevin Greene. All four would make the Pro Bowl the very next year on a Panthers team that made it to the NFC championship in 1996.

At his peak at Carolina, Polian was on his telephone headset for five hours a day, drinking Diet Coke, chewing gum, eating lunch at his desk, and rewarding himself with a jog at the end of a long day. He said he did some of his best thinking while running.

Those were the best parts of the Polian era. But it was hardly all wine and roses. The Panthers got extra draft picks in each of their first two NFL drafts, as did Jacksonville, per the expansion rules of 1995. But Polian missed on a lot of those picks. For every Chad Cota—a nice late-round find at safety—there seemed to be a Shawn King (a second-round pick who never worked out).

Polian did draft Muhsin Muhammad, a longtime Panthers star, in his final draft for Carolina in 1997. But he also gave the team Tshimanga Biakabutuka, who never was the standout running back Polian had envisioned.

The Panthers also didn't like the fact that Polian seemed to be rumored for every open GM or team president job throughout his time at Carolina even though he already had a job—and worse, that he didn't seem in a hurry to squelch the rumors.

And then there was Polian's legendary temper. Sometimes Richardson would write c-a-l-m on a note and pass it to Polian when the two were sitting in a meeting and the GM's temper started to flare.

Sometimes it worked; sometimes it didn't. The two proud men were at odds some of the time. And the issue was also complicated by the fact that both Polian and Richardson had sons who were in the family football business at that time.

After McCormack retired in 1997, according to a lengthy *Charlotte Observer* story written by Panthers beat writer Charles

Chandler in late 1998, "Polian wanted to succeed McCormack as team president, but Richardson gave the job to his son Mark. Polian wanted to give his son, Chris, a top job in the personnel/scouting department, but Richardson objected. That infuriated Polian and created a debate about nepotism."

Eventually, Polian left for Indianapolis following the 1997 NFL season. With the Colts, he got more money and more power. His son, Chris, also became a more highly valued part of the organization than he had been in Charlotte.

The Colts thrived after Polian selected Peyton Manning with the No. 1 pick in 1998, winning the Super Bowl following the 2006 season against Chicago and making the playoffs 11 times.

The Polians' time with the Colts ended following the 2011 season, when owner Jim Irsay fired both of them following a 2–14 season in which Manning was out due to a neck injury (Bill Polian had tried, unsuccessfully, to replace him with his old favorite Collins). Polian then became a regular presence on ESPN as an NFL studio analyst and drew a number of rave reviews for his honesty, which translated well to TV.

The Panthers did not thrive for many years after Polian departed, and they did not thrive in his final Carolina season of 1997. Too many of the draft picks weren't panning out, and the Carolina defense suddenly looked old.

"I wish I had brought in more youth on the squad," Polian would admit later in an interview. For all his free-agent home runs in 1996, he also struck out a lot in the free-agent market in 1997 (anyone remember Ray Seals and Ernie Mills?).

Polian also did not endear himself to the Panthers when, following the 1997 draft, he convinced former colleague Dom Anile to join him with the Colts. Anile was a close associate of Polian's but had been retained by the Panthers following Polian's departure as player personnel director. The Panthers expected him to fulfill his contract, but Polian hired him as his director of football operations. Carolina then immediately fired three young NFL scouts who had worked closely with Polian and Anile and had them escorted out of the stadium by security guards.

So it was something of a messy ending for Polian with the Panthers, although he went out of his way a number of times to praise Richardson after being hired in Indianapolis and kept a home in Charlotte for years.

Polian's legacy with the Panthers? A mixed bag. He deserves credit for getting the Panthers off to the incredibly fast start they had in 1995 and 1996, but he also deserves blame for some of the freefall that occurred for several years after that. Had he been persuaded to stay longer, though, given his admirable NFL track record over many decades, it is almost impossible to imagine that the Panthers would have gone through the six-year playoff drought they did between 1997 to 2002.

33 Panthers' Overtime History

When the Carolina Panthers have gone into overtime, their fans have ended up disappointed more often than not.

The Panthers are 5–10 overall in overtime games. The one exception to this general lack of OT productivity was in the Super Bowl season of 2003. In that one splendid season, the Panthers played an astonishing number of overtime games—five. (Over their history, they average less than one OT game per year.) And they won four of those five in 2003, including the famous double overtime playoff win at St. Louis. Here's a look at the six most important overtime games in team history, as well as what happened in the other nine OT games involving the Panthers.

The Huge Half-Dozen

In order of importance, these OT games either had playoff implications or changed the team's momentum at a key point in a season.

Carolina 29, St. Louis 23—January 10, 2004. Not to belabor the point, since this game is well-covered in its own entry in this book, but this was the most exciting win in Panthers history. Steve Smith's 69-yard TD reception from Jake Delhomme on the first play of the second overtime suddenly ended an astonishing game.

NY Giants 34, Carolina 28—December 21, 2008. DeAngelo Williams scored all four of the Panthers' touchdowns, but John Kasay missed a 50-yarder at the end of regulation that would have won it and likely given the Panthers the No. 1 seed in the playoffs. Instead, the Giants' Derrick Ward rushed for 215 yards—the most ever against Carolina, with 87 coming in overtime—and Brandon Jacobs won the game on a two-yard TD run after a Ward burst for 51 yards.

Carolina 12, Tampa Bay 9—September 14, 2003. This game appeared over when the Buccaneers scored on the final play of regulation to tie the game at 9. But Kris Jenkins made the rarest of plays—blocking the extra point, which replays showed he actually did with his elbow. Carolina won on a 47-yard Kasay field goal following a 52-yard Smith punt return.

Atlanta 34, Carolina 31—December 18, 2004. The Panthers seemed ready to make the playoffs after a 1–7 start, winning five games in a row. But this loss at Atlanta broke their momentum when Delhomme threw a key interception and it set up a Falcons field goal.

Carolina 23, Indianapolis 20—October 12, 2003. The Panthers beat Peyton Manning in Indianapolis behind DeShaun

Foster's 26 overtime rushing yards and Kasay's 47-yard field goal. The game was rock-concert loud the entire way, but the crowd fell totally silent when Kasay's field goal went through.

Atlanta 23, Carolina 20—September 3, 1995. In the Panthers' first-ever game, they scored on their first-ever drive and played well for most of the game. After getting to within 20–19 late, coach Dom Capers was about to go for two points and a 21–20 win. But the Panthers' Derrick Graham false-started, putting the ball back five yards and causing Capers to reevaluate and take the extra point instead. In overtime, Frank Reich lost the ball on a sack and Atlanta won with a field goal.

The Other Overtime Nine

In chronological order, here are the other times the Panthers have played in overtime games that weren't quite as significant and what happened in each:

Carolina 20, New England 17—October 29, 1995. The Panthers' first-ever OT win (in their first season, back when the Patriots were a bad team) came on a 29-yard John Kasay field goal.

San Francisco 31, Carolina 28—December 6, 1998. The Panthers stormed all the way back from 28–7 down vs. a 49ers team quarterbacked by Steve Young, but lost in OT.

Dallas 16, Carolina 13—October 1, 2000. The Cowboys won the coin toss, Troy Aikman drove the team 68 yards, and Dallas got a field goal. (By today's rules, the Panthers would also be allowed a possession, since OT games can no longer end on a first-possession field goal.)

Washington 17, Carolina 14—October 21, 2001. A 47-yard pass from Tony Banks to Rod Gardner set up a Redskins field goal and ended this overtime game less than two minutes after it started.

San Francisco 25, Carolina 22—November 18, 2001. The 1–15 Panthers team lost two games in overtime that season, this one when Jose Cortez kicked a 26-yard field goal.

Carolina 23, New Orleans 20—October 26, 2003. Julius Peppers made a marvelous submarine tackle of Deuce McAllister on a fourth-down play, causing a loss and also a fumble recovered by Jenkins. The Panthers then drove for a field goal behind Stephen Davis.

Atlanta 20, Carolina 14—December 7, 2003. The Panthers went 4–1 in overtime games in 2003; this was the loss. Kevin Mathis intercepted Delhomme's pass and went 32 yards for a touchdown just 90 seconds into OT.

Minnesota 16, Carolina 13—September 17, 2006. The Panthers punted on their first possession and Ryan Longwell won it with a short field goal for Minnesota.

Tampa Bay 27, Carolina 21—November 18, 2012. Up 21–13 with 1:02 left, the Panthers gave up an 80-yard TD drive even though the Bucs had no timeouts and then allowed the tying two-point conversion. After that demoralizing comeback, the Bucs' overtime TD came relatively easily.

34 DeAngelo Williams

The Panthers' all-time leading rusher, DeAngelo Williams is known for the burst of speed that sometimes turns a 10-yard run into a 50-yarder. Although he has shared carries at running back for virtually his entire career, he owns three of the top five single-game rushing performances in team history.

Williams has a gregarious personality. He doesn't mind singing karaoke, sharing his love of horror movies, or attending whatever pro wrestling event he can get to. Half of the "Double Trouble" tandem, Williams is the one who came up with the nickname for

Cream of the Crop

DeAngelo Williams ranked No. 1 in most of the key categories for Panthers running backs all-time through the 2012 season, including these two:

Panthers Career Leaders In Rushing Yards

Player	Yards
DeAngelo Williams	5,784
Jonathan Stewart	3,836
DeShaun Foster	3,336

Panthers Career Leaders In Rushing Touchdowns

Player	TDs
DeAngelo Williams	43
Jonathan Stewart	27
Cam Newton	22

himself and Jonathan Stewart and made sure to publicize it. He admittedly treats Stewart like a little brother sometimes—Williams was a first-round draft choice for Carolina in 2006, Stewart was a first-round pick in 2008. The two have long had a healthy relationship, though, and developed a "slow motion" touchdown dance that they do whenever either one of them scores.

Williams has been the one who scores most frequently. Although known primarily as a speed back, he also has a gift for finding the end zone. In 2008, his best season, and one in which he should have made the Pro Bowl, he rushed for a franchise-high 1,515 yards for Carolina, scored 18 rushing TDs—and didn't fumble the ball a single time.

That was the year that Williams' No. 34 jersey started popping up more and more often in the stands in Charlotte. It was early the next season, on *Monday Night Football*, that former Tampa Bay coach Jon Gruden gushed so much about Williams, going so far as to say Williams was likely the best back in the NFL (his fellow announcers ribbed Gruden, asking if he had ever heard of Adrian Peterson).

Undoubtedly Carolina's best-ever running back tandem, DeAngelo Williams (34) and Jonathan Stewart (28) show off their touchdown dance in 2010 against the Saints.

Williams has not approached his 2008 production since then, but it's not as if he has been unproductive. In 2009, he and Stewart became the first NFL tandem in history to each rush for at least 1,100 yards in a single season.

When the Panthers drafted Cam Newton No. 1 overall in 2011, however, the offensive dynamic changed for the Panthers. Newton was so much bigger than Williams—and to a lesser degree Stewart as well—that the Panthers started calling No. 1's number on an increasing number rushing plays, especially at the goal line. As a result, Williams' touches, yards, and TD numbers all dipped significantly.

Williams has generally been a good soldier about all of that, although he has occasionally expressed his frustrations via interviews or social media. He once said on his Facebook page after one bad statistical game, "Also to all the people that think I'm not the same tailback I was before don't know football....So step away from your fantasy league and watch football." He also has retweeted fans' gripes about his lack of carries on Twitter.

For the most part, though, Williams has done whatever he has been asked of him throughout his career—albeit with a side helping of "I told you so" after some of his best games. After he set a franchise high with 210 yards rushing on only 21 carries in the 2012 season finale against New Orleans, ripping off runs of 54 and 65 yards, he was asked what was different about that day compared to others. Williams said it was the fact that the Panthers "actually called runs."

Because the Panthers have invested more in their backfield than any other team in the NFL—Williams, Stewart, and Mike Tolbert have combined contracts worth north of $100 million—there have been trade rumors swirling around both halves of "Double Trouble" for several years. One day that may happen, or else one of them will inevitably be released when their combined production falters. But it's important to remember that no matter how the story ends, as of this writing Williams is undeniably the best running back in Panthers history.

35 Jonathan Stewart

Jonathan Stewart can play the piano by ear. He instinctively finds the melody in a series of notes in much the same way he determines whether to cut back or find a different hole if the original one a running play calls for is already closed.

Stewart came to the Panthers in 2008, a first-round draft choice (No. 13 overall) of a team that already had invested a first-round pick in DeAngelo Williams in 2006. Their careers and lives have been intertwined ever since, as they christened themselves "Double Trouble" in Stewart's rookie year after bonding while watching pro wrestling together.

Always a fine team player and a little thicker-skinned than Williams when it comes to criticism, Stewart said once he liked the "Double Trouble" moniker because of its equality. "It's more focused on unity than anything," Stewart said. "Whether DeAngelo or me is in, the defense has trouble on its hands."

In that 2008 season, quarterback Jake Delhomme came up with another nickname for them, too—"Penn and Teller." It was a joke, but it had a ring of truth. In case you're not familiar with that duo, Penn and Teller are eccentric, sometimes violent, very successful magicians. Penn does all the talking in their act; Teller is silent.

Williams would be Penn; Stewart is Teller. Stewart can and does go weeks at a time without speaking to the media (although he is now fairly active on Twitter) and so fans don't know a great deal about him.

A powerful, surprisingly fast running back whose specialty is the inside run, Stewart (5'10", 235) grew up in the state of Washington and was raised by a single mother. He stayed on the West Coast for college, going to Oregon. After a very successful

Tolbert Time

The Panthers spent more money on their running backs in 2012 than any other NFL team in the league, and this was a bone of contention among fans since quarterback Cam Newton takes a lot of the carries and in fact led the team in rushing yards that season. Plus, the NFL has become far more of a passing league than it used to be, and so lots of teams try to get by rather cheaply (by NFL terms anyway) at least at the backup running back position.

But all three of the Panthers running backs do bring a little something different to the table. Williams and Stewart are the best known, but former San Diego Chargers fullback Mike Tolbert made his mark in 2012 too and seems primed to contribute more in the future.

In the Panthers' final game of the season, against New Orleans on December 30, 2012, Tolbert scored a career-high three touchdowns. That gave him seven rushing TDs for the season, which ranked second on the team to Newton. Tolbert (5'9", 245) is shorter and squatter than the already fairly short and squat Stewart, and Tolbert's extremely low center of gravity frequently makes people compare tackling him to tackling a bowling ball. Tolbert also was an effective pass-catcher in San Diego and will likely grow into that role more with Carolina. He joined the league the same year as Stewart, in 2008.

career there, he left school a year early and the Panthers grabbed him. It was coach John Fox's belief that every NFL team should have two top-notch running backs because the position is so hard on the body and players can thus be injury-prone.

Stewart made an immediate contribution, rushing for 836 yards in the Panthers' 2008 playoff season and then leading the team with a career-high 1,133 in 2009. That was the season he rushed for 206 yards in a single game against the New York Giants—a franchise record until Williams broke it three years later against New Orleans.

Since Cam Newton's arrival, Stewart's touchdowns have gone way down because Newton (and now Mike Tolbert) have taken the majority of the goal-line carries. But his receptions have gone way up. Fox and his staff had the idea that Stewart wasn't a good third-down back. Offensive coordinator Rob Chudzinski refuted that notion, and Stewart set team records in 2011 for the most catches (47) and receiving yards (413) by a running back.

The Panthers gave Stewart a five-year contract extension just before the 2012 season, trying to assure he was not going to hit the open market anytime soon. The deal included $22.5 million in guaranteed money, which was big-time cash for a player who has technically been a backup running back for almost his entire pro career. In reality, though, Williams (No. 1 on the Panthers' all-time rushing list) and Stewart (No. 2) have split carries almost evenly.

Williams had a two-year head start on Stewart as a Panther, so it's not surprising he ranks first in almost all the team's primary all-time rushing categories and Stewart is second. If he can stay healthy, however, it's not inconceivable that Stewart will eventually lead some of those lists.

One disconcerting note, though, for the piano player: Stewart rushed for a career-low 336 yards in 2012 while missing seven games, mostly due to a high ankle sprain. He hopes to be a far bigger part of the offense for the rest of his Carolina career.

Ryan Kalil

In basketball, centers are often the center of attention.

In football, the opposite is true. Centers are usually anonymous. They line up smack in the middle of the scrum that begins every play—snapping the ball to the quarterback and then disappearing into a pile of humanity.

Ryan Kalil, however, has made a name for himself as both the best center the Panthers have ever had and the author of one of the team's most public (and incorrect) guarantees: his Super Bowl promise of 2012.

First, the good stuff. Kalil was one of the best-value picks the Panthers have ever made in the NFL Draft. He was selected deep in the second round of the 2007 draft, not too long after filming a spoof of an NFL training video with fellow Southern Cal alum and comic Will Ferrell. That one is still available on the Internet. If you've never seen it, you need to Google it. Ferrell, as the overzealous trainer, is hilarious. And Kalil holds his own.

Kalil has good genes. His father, Frank, played center in college, got drafted by the Buffalo Bills, and played three years in the old USFL. His younger brother, Matt, is an offensive tackle and was selected fourth overall by Minnesota in the 2012 NFL Draft.

Kalil played on some fantastic college teams at USC before the Panthers drafted him in 2007. After a brief stint at right guard, he became the team's starting center during the 2008 playoff season, and then played in the Pro Bowl for three straight years from 2009 to 2011. The Panthers signed him to a six-year, $49 million contract extension in 2011, making him the highest-paid NFL center ever. He is in particular noted for his quick feet—his balance is exceptional for a 300-pound man.

Noted in the locker room as a solid and somewhat playful guy, in the summer of 2012 he was inspired to take out a full-page advertisement in the *Charlotte Observer*. He did so without telling anyone in the Carolina Panthers organization. The ad began, "Why the Carolina Panthers will win Super Bowl XLVII" and ended with his signature.

It was a grand, flamboyant gesture. The Panthers players and coaches publicly supported Kalil for stepping so far out on a limb. Coach Ron Rivera even had T-shirts made up that read, I HAVE RYAN KALIL'S BACK.

But it didn't work out that way in 2012 for either Kalil or the team. In the Panthers' fifth game, he sustained a Lisfranc injury, rupturing the ligaments in his left foot. He ended up on injured reserve, missing the rest of the Panthers' 1–6 start that season and the fine finish that got them to 7–9 and kept Rivera from getting fired.

The Super Bowl guarantee? It turned out not to be worth the paper it was printed on, although Kalil said later he had no regrets about setting expectations high for the team. And it wasn't the first time a high-profile Panther had said something like that. Owner Jerry Richardson had guaranteed a Super Bowl win within 10 years when he first got the team. Carolina made it to the Super Bowl in their ninth season, but lost.

Kalil said he didn't plan to take out any full-page newspaper ads for the rest of his career, preferring to let his play do the talking.

37 Jordan Gross

As the seasons marched on, year after year, one thing always seemed certain in the Panthers' starting lineup: Offensive tackle Jordan Gross would be playing.

Gross set the team record in 2012 for most starts when he got to 142 midway through the season, surpassing wide receiver Muhsin Muhammad and safety Mike Minter (who were both tied at 141). In his first 10 years with Carolina, Gross missed a total of only nine games—seven of them in 2009 after suffering a broken leg.

On either side of that injury, Gross made the Pro Bowl—in both 2008 and 2010. Extremely nimble for a 6'4", 305-pounder, Gross is actually smaller than a lot of tackles in the NFL but has survived for so long because of his smarts, toughness, and "good feet," as NFL scouts like to say. For most of his career with the Panthers he has lined up opposite the other team's best pass rusher, and he has generally proven himself quick enough to cope with a speed rush to the outside and strong enough to hold down the fort when faced with a bull rush to the inside.

Gross grew up in Idaho, and he still has a 40-acre alfalfa farm there that he works on during the off-season. He went to Fruitland (Idaho) High, where he also was a basketball standout. The Panthers have had a number of players with small-town backgrounds over the years, but not many of them hailed from Idaho.

As Gross said shortly after the Panthers selected him with the No. 8 overall pick of the 2003 draft, "My high school class had 86 members, and my varsity football team had 21 guys. So it's pretty amazing to me that my dream has come true to get to this position."

In his final two years at the University of Utah (where Gross was a college teammate of Steve Smith), Gross did not allow a single sack. He was a dominant lineman in college, an All-American who almost never lost one-on-one battles.

That changed immediately when he got to the Panthers. Gross faced Julius Peppers every day in practice during his first training camp, and Peppers embarrassed him several times with his own dazzling athleticism.

Said Peppers, who was then entering his second year in the NFL, "I'm going to give him everything. I really want to prepare him. He won't see anything new after I get done with him. Because if you can stop me, you can stop anybody."

Gross was up to the challenge. "This is going to make me a better player in a hurry," he said then. "It's a fight-or-flight thing for me."

And Gross fought. While known as one of the nicest players in the Panthers locker room and an unofficial team spokesman on almost every issue, he also has a seriously competitive streak. The Panthers got him up to speed quickly and he started as a rookie for the only Super Bowl team in franchise history. In his third year, the Panthers made it to the NFC Championship Game.

He doesn't think much of his own skills of prediction. "I never have a clue how our team's going to be," Gross said once. "In '03, I didn't know any better, [and] we went to the Super Bowl. In '04, I thought we were going to be just as good and we started out 1–7."

Since 2005 the path has been more uneven, with only a single postseason appearance, in 2008. But Gross has been there in good times and in bad. He attributes some of his longevity to an old-school workout regimen that includes pull-ups and push-ups. He has protected the blind side for quarterbacks ranging from Jake Delhomme and Cam Newton to Vinny Testaverde and David Carr. He said several times during the 2012 season that he hopes to leave the team only after the pendulum swings back toward winning more frequently again, the way it was when he first joined the Panthers. To continue his long tenure with the team, he took a substantial pay cut prior to the 2013 season to ensure the Panthers had enough money to get under the salary cap and to also ensure that he still had a job.

Kris Jenkins

Grunt work.

That is the job of a defensive tackle, who by definition is in the middle of a pileup on every running play and often is instructed to "use up" one or two blocks from the other team so that the linebackers can make tackles.

No one ever did that job better for Carolina than Kris Jenkins, the flaky but fearsome defensive tackle who played for the Panthers from 2001 to 2007 and made the Pro Bowl three times in that span.

Jenkins was a huge man—6'4" and officially 340 pounds for most of his Panthers career, although his weight fluctuated wildly and sometimes neared 400. He also was remarkably athletic for someone that size and very hard to knock off his feet or backward. He was a key factor in the Panthers' run to the 2003 Super Bowl and when healthy was a difference-maker.

The Panthers chose Jenkins out of Maryland in the second round of the 2001 draft—the team's best draft ever and the one that also netted Pro Bowlers Dan Morgan and Steve Smith. Carolina kept him for the next seven seasons until trading him in early 2008 to the New York Jets in exchange for third- and fifth-round draft choices.

Hindsight shows that it was a pretty good trade for Carolina, because Jenkins turned out to be nearing the end of his career. He had one very good year for the Jets, in 2008, but then tore the anterior cruciate ligament in his left knee in both 2009 and again in 2010. He ultimately retired at age 31, before the 2011 season.

When Jenkins was good, though, he was very, very good. And he was one of the few players in the Panthers locker room who didn't mind publicly ripping his teammates in hopes of getting them to play better. After a game in 2007 in which Carolina lost badly at home to Tampa Bay, Jenkins said, "I think the players owe the fans an apology. I would be as upset as they are if I had to sit in the stands for four hours and look at that garbage. I'm going to be honest with you. That's what it was: garbage."

He also said after that game, "As a team collectively, we have no heart. We have no energy. We have no drive."

Such outbursts and Jenkins' unusual style didn't endear him to some in the locker room, but his talent was respected by all. In

2003, for instance, he saved a sure loss to Tampa Bay by blocking the extra point after a Buccaneers touchdown as regulation ended. Buccaneer kicker Martin "Automatica" Gramatica had been 129-for-129 in his career on extra points until then, but Jenkins got such good penetration he actually blocked the kick with his elbow. The game instead went into overtime, and the Panthers won with a field goal. It was the first time in NFL history that a player blocked an extra point to send a game into overtime.

Jenkins grew up in Ypsilanti, Michigan, raised mostly by his father. His younger brother, Cullen, was of a similar build and, while undrafted, eventually became an NFL starter on the defensive line for Green Bay before going to the New York Giants in 2013.

Kris Jenkins played four years with the Terrapins and was second-team ACC as a senior in 2000 when he had eight sacks. The Panthers made him a starter for most of his rookie season, and by his second season he was pushing the pocket back constantly and playing in the Pro Bowl. By his third year, in 2003, he was a Pro Bowl starter.

That was as good as it got. Jenkins missed most of 2004 with a shoulder injury and most of 2005 with the first of what would be several serious knee injuries. He did start 31 of 32 games in the next two years for Carolina before going to the Jets, where he missed slightly more than half the games over a three-year period due to injury before retiring.

After retirement, Jenkins worked with the *New York Times* on a series of interviews for a first-person story about the pain football inflicts on all who play it. In the story, he said he had had "more than 10" concussions in his college and pro careers. He also expressed no remorse about his career and his actions in the pileups that dominate the life of every defensive tackle.

"Somebody has to be the grunt," Jenkins said in that story. "That's why there's no better position on the field than interior defensive line. Forget quarterbacks or specialists. They've got it easy. If we don't come to play, nobody else on defense can do their job. Piles, oh my God, they're brutal. I've had my ankles twisted. I've been bit... I've tried to break guys' elbows, pinching people, twisting ankles, trying to bend up their arms, pop an elbow out. Why? I had to fight back."

39 Steve Smith's 218-Yard Game

Entering the Panthers' road game against Chicago in the 2005 playoffs, Steve Smith was at the height of his powers. The Panthers' 5'9" ball of blue fire had led or tied for the NFL lead in the three key receiving categories that season: yards, receptions, and touchdowns. He had already burned Chicago earlier that season with 14 catches for 169 yards, so it seemed like the Bears would be primed to do whatever they needed to stop him.

They weren't.

On the second play from scrimmage, Smith scored on a 58-yard touchdown, faking out Bears defensive back Charles Tillman so badly that Tillman ended up facedown on the ground.

Later, Smith caught a 46-yard "jump ball" pass between two defenders and scored on a 39-yarder. He said after the game that he was just doing his job. "If you lined up my mama out there, I've got to catch it over her too," he said.

The result was a 29–21 upset playoff win for Carolina, with Jake Delhomme throwing for 319 yards and three touchdowns and John Kasay adding three field goals. Delhomme had had a poor game in the Panthers' 13–3 loss to Chicago earlier that season, getting sacked eight times and intercepted twice. This time he was close to perfect against a Bears defense that had ranked No. 1 in

The Panthers beat the Bears to advance in the playoffs, and it will always be remembered as the game in which Steve Smith gained 218 yards.

scoring defense in the NFL coming in to the matchup and allowing just an average of 12.9 points per game.

Who was the defensive coordinator for the Bears in that game? Ron Rivera.

Of course, 69 percent of those 319 yards Delhomme threw for went to Smith. Give Delhomme credit for knowing when to feed the hot hand. The Bears knew he was going to get the ball but still couldn't slow him down.

When asked what had happened to Chicago after the game, Bears linebacker Brian Urlacher growled, "Steve Smith. That is what happened to us."

Carolina coach John Fox hardly ever uttered a memorable quote in his nine years at Carolina, but he had one after that game. Referring to Smith's height, Fox said, "It's not how big the wand is, it's how much magic is inside."

In this game, Smith had enough magic to make Harry Potter jealous. He took a fire-pole slide down the goal post after one TD. Another time, when it appeared Tillman was going to make an interception, Smith simply yanked the ball out of his hands.

"He did catch the ball," Smith said, "but I wanted it a little more than him."

Smith always has wanted the ball. And on his incredible day in Chicago, he made an impact every single time he touched it. Urlacher also called Smith the best offensive player in the league after the game.

It was the last playoff game Fox would win at Carolina—the Panthers lost by 20 points at Seattle the next week in the NFC championship and would also lose their first game in the 2008 playoffs—but it was something else.

Mike Minter

For 10 years, Mike Minter was one of the steadiest players the Panthers ever had. He started 141 games, which at the time he retired in 2006 was the most of any Panther ever. He made 953 tackles, which is still a Panthers best.

Time and again, No. 30 was the man who made his position of safety seem appropriate by being the man who saved something. Oftentimes, he turned a possible 25-yard gain into a five-yarder with a sure tackle. Sometimes he did more with one of his 17 career interceptions. He returned four of them for TDs, and those four pick sixes remain a team record).

Minter was one of the most beloved Panthers players of all time, both inside and outside the locker room, renowned for his friendliness, honesty, and hard hits. That's why I asked him to write the foreword for this book in his own words, which, if you haven't read yet, you absolutely should before reading this supplemental text.

Was Minter perfect? Of course not. Minter remembers a few times when he felt totally helpless on the football field, like when he watched the San Francisco 49ers offense of the 1990s run up and down on his defense. Like all defensive backs, he got beaten sometimes. But he was always a stand-up guy no matter what happened, which is one reason he was voted a team captain for the final five years of his Panthers career. NFL players can smell a fake a mile away, and Minter was never one of those.

Minter came to the Panthers as a second-round pick in the 1997 draft. He had played on two national championship teams at Nebraska in college and—given that the Panthers were coming off a playoff appearance—he expected that the winning would continue.

It didn't. The Panthers got old quickly, and Minter didn't play on a winning team for his first six years in the NFL. He won a starting job by the sixth game of his rookie year and basically never left it except for when he suffered a serious staph infection that cost him most of the 1998 season.

The team didn't win regularly until his year seven, in 2003, when he was a starter on the Panthers' Super Bowl team. Having to work that long for it made that year especially sweet for Minter. Then he got to experience one more playoff season as a starter, in

2005. He planned to play in 2007, but his creaky knees had other ideas. He went to training camp that year and then suddenly retired in a tearful ceremony that the *Charlotte Observer's* Pat Yasinskas wrote was "the franchise's most emotionally charged day since the funeral for former linebacker and assistant coach Sam Mills."

Minter said that afternoon, "At the end of the day, there wasn't anything left. But I can walk away knowing I left it on the field—everything."

Team owner Jerry Richardson cried during that news conference and later challenged Julius Peppers to step into Minter's leadership role (which didn't work). Coach John Fox cried too. Fans were saddened as well—many had come to love Minter over the years. World-ranked tennis player John Isner was among them—he owned a Minter jersey and wore it to games.

After Minter's retirement, quarterback Jake Delhomme said, "Football hasn't defined Mike Minter. You've got to put that out there first. He's much more than just a football player."

What he later became was a football coach. Minter first coached a private school in Concord, North Carolina, to two state championships in three years. Then he served as an assistant coach at Charlotte's Johnson C. Smith and Liberty in Lynchburg, Virginia, before getting the head-coaching job at Campbell University in Buies Creek, North Carolina, for the 2013 season.

Mike Rucker

He wasn't the most gifted defensive end, but Mike Rucker was a relentless worker. He once told me he identified with the tortoise, not the hare, in that old fable. And that's the way he played. Slowly, steadily, Rucker would get an advantage on his man, until finally sometime in the second half No. 93 would beat the opposing left tackle and get a sack on the quarterback's blind side.

Rucker played all nine of his NFL seasons for Carolina. A second-round draft pick out of Nebraska in 1999, he only started one game in his first two seasons. But the tortoise just kept on going, and in Rucker's last seven seasons he always started at least 14 games.

An eloquent, classy, and deeply religious man, Rucker nevertheless was a trash talker on the field. But it was relatively mild trash. If an offensive lineman tried the same blocking technique several times in a row, Rucker would growl, "That's the same soup—just reheated." He would get so psyched up before and during games that he occasionally had to come out for a few plays because he was hyperventilating.

His best season dovetailed with the Panthers' best-ever season: 2003. In that Super Bowl year, Rucker had 12 sacks in 14 games and made the Pro Bowl.

Rucker eventually became the Panthers' all-time sacks leader, surpassing Kevin Greene. He did not hold that title too long, however, as he was in turn surpassed by Julius Peppers. The two started together as defensive ends for six straight years. Rucker was the more unsung of the two but also the more consistent worker.

Rucker's Three Favorite Panthers Memories

- The plane ride home from Philadelphia after the Panthers won the NFC Championship Game in 2003.
- Sacking Brett Favre.
- Being assigned the locker right next to Reggie White's as a young player, and soaking in the wisdom from the gravelly voiced Hall of Famer during the 2000 season (White's only season with the team).

When Rucker retired in April 2008, he had a retirement ceremony at Bank of America Stadium during which he thanked everyone from the team's security guards to owner Jerry Richardson. With tears glistening in his eyes, he told coach John Fox, "I just want you to know I gave you everything I've got. The tank is empty."

Rucker kept his tank full longer than most, though, with an NFL career that more than doubled the league average. He credited part of that for deciding to eat a more healthy diet about halfway through his career, thanks in part to something he had seen about it on Oprah Winfrey's show.

Rucker was like that. Even if it didn't sound cool in the testosterone-fueled world of the NFL, he would admit to watching *Oprah* occasionally. Or renting a minivan—which he did once to drive cross-country—and really digging it.

Like his close friend Mike Minter, Rucker was one of those Panthers players who was well liked by everyone he came in contact with because of the way he treated people. He has done the TV color analysis for Panthers preseason games and is as gracious behind the microphone as he was when he was the one being interviewed.

42 Follow the Panthers on Twitter

One of the simplest ways to get uncensored thoughts from the Carolina Panthers players—as well as a raft of useful information about the team from those who cover it—is to use Twitter judiciously.

If you don't know what Twitter is, don't despair. It's free and very easy to use. Go to Twitter.com on the Internet, create your own profile, and then just start "following" people whom you are interested in hearing from. You can easily find them by using the "search" box on Twitter's home page. Then, whenever you are signed into Twitter, you will get dozens of "tweets"—140 characters at a time—that range from the ridiculous to the sublime.

If you do know what Twitter is—and since it's now a social-media giant, I'm guessing many of you do—then you may already follow a lot of the folks listed below. But maybe you can get a couple of ideas to improve your Twitter experience.

Here are some people I follow for Panthers-related news and observations, listed in no particular order. Most of these are current or former Panthers players, with a few media types thrown into the mix:

@randywattson. This is really an alias for defensive end Charles Johnson, who is as prone to post thoughts on life as he is on football. For instance: "If life gives you lemons - make grapejuice. Then sit back and let people wonder how you did it." Johnson also likes to comment on Panthers news not long after it happens.

@JonathanStewar1. Panther running back Jonathan Stewart uses Twitter regularly for all sorts of things—to inform his followers that he's going to a Bon Jovi concert in Charlotte, for instance. His profile reads: "This is jonathan stewart. my passions are football and music... i love Jesus!"

@RyanKalil. The Panthers' deep-thinking and funny center doesn't tweet that often. When he does, though, it's usually more thoughtful than your average tweet. For instance, Kalil once quoted writer F. Scott Fitzgerald, tweeting: "Never confuse a single defeat with a final defeat."

@DeAngeloRB. The Panther running back occasionally retweets fans' comments as well as giving his own opinions.

@Captain_41. Panthers nickelback Captain Munnerlyn is one of the team's most frequent participants on Twitter.

@FrankGarcia65. The former Panther offensive lineman cohosts a popular radio show in Charlotte and is always good for an opinion.

@ItsGHardy. Panthers defensive end Greg Hardy—whose self-proclaimed nickname is the "Kraken"—is an active tweeter and, like defensive line teammate Johnson, doesn't censor himself much.

@GregOlsen82. The Panthers tight end comments on University of Miami sports teams and occasionally gives updates about his own young family.

@JJJansen44. The Panthers' long snapper occasionally hosts Twitter trivia contests many Tuesdays during the NFL season and gives away valuable prizes.

@RosinskiBill. The former Panthers play-by-play announcer is a popular Charlotte radio personality who is never short of an opinion.

@JosephPerson. There is no one more informed about the Panthers' daily doings than Joe Person, the *Charlotte Observer's* Panthers beat writer, who frequently breaks Panthers news via Twitter.

@JJones9. The *Observer's* backup Panthers beat writer, Jonathan Jones, is an inveterate tweeter who often points readers to good stories on other sports subjects—especially around the ACC—as well as Panthers news.

@Scott_Fowler. That's me—I comment most often on Panthers news and direct people to other random stories or blogs I like on the Internet. My blog Scott Says on CharlotteObserver.com is the place where I often expand my tweets past the 140-character limit.

@TD58SDTM. This is Panthers linebacker Thomas Davis, a frequent tweeter and the man who came back from three ACL surgeries on the same knee.

@Blafell1. This is Panther wide receiver Brandon Lafell, one of the Panthers' rising young players and one who does not lack for confidence.

@espn_nfcsouth. This is the account of Pat Yasinskas, who is ESPN's designated blogger for the NFC South and thus is very good at covering both the Panthers and their three divisional opponents.

@TomSorensen. My sports columnist colleague is caustic and funny in his tweets.

@Panthers. The Panthers' official feed gives a rather rosy view of Panthers news, much like the team's official website (Panthers. com). That makes sense given that it is in the team's interest to put the Panthers in the best possible light. But it is also very helpful in terms of the team's schedules, fan giveaways, and more.

@PanthersPR. This is a useful follow. Run by the Panthers media relations department, it often points out interesting and relevant statistics about Carolina players.

@CameronNewton. Panthers quarterback Cam Newton once established a Twitter account, then thought better of it. Newton has close to 100,000 followers despite never sending a single tweet during his first two Panthers seasons. Twitter fans keep hoping he will join the community, and I imagine one day he will.

Here are a number of other Charlotte-area media folks who are also simple to look up on Twitter, tweet often about the Panthers, and are worth a follow: Darin Gantt, Bill Voth, Mike Solarte, Kelli Bartik, Russ Owens, Tim Baier, Marc James, Brett Jensen, Mike Persinger, David Scott, Langston Wertz, Rob Paul, and Taylor Zarzour.

43 Dan Morgan and the Incredible 2001 Draft

With Dan Morgan, the Panthers' No. 1 draft choice in 2001 and for a while one of the best middle linebackers in the NFL, the questions still loom.

All of them relate to injury. How good could Morgan really have been? What if his body hadn't let him down so often? What sort of difference could he have made?

Already, the 2001 draft was the best in Panthers history (see the sidebar that accompanies this chapter for why that was). But what if Morgan had been healthy 90 percent of the time instead of 50 percent?

When he was healthy, Morgan was very good. Sometimes even great. In the 2004 Super Bowl against New England, Morgan sometimes seemed like he was the only one playing defense for Carolina. According to the coaches, he made a team-record 25 tackles in that game. (Generally, a game of 15 tackles is a cause for celebration for any NFL linebacker.)

In 2004, he made the Pro Bowl. He was a fearsome hitter and completely dedicated to his craft. "Football is me," he told me once, shortly after the Panthers drafted him with the 11th overall choice in 2001. And it was. The son of one of Dan Marino's former bodyguards, Morgan had grown up around the game and lived for it.

But oh, those injuries. In seven seasons for Carolina (2001–07), Morgan's ratio of games played to games missed was almost 50–50. He played 59 out of a potential 112 regular-season games and missed 53.

The most problematic injuries for Morgan were his concussions. Linebackers inevitably get hit in the head, and he had at least five (by his count) concussions as a Panther. He tried different sorts of helmets and wearing a mouthpiece, but nothing worked forever.

Despite that, the injury that ultimately ended his NFL career in 2007 was actually a partially torn Achilles' tendon. He only managed to play in four games in his final two NFL seasons. The Panthers released him in early 2008. Although no one likes to be fired, Morgan took the news with grace. "They always treated me

The Three Best and Three Worst Drafts in Panthers History

The Three Best

1. **2001**—Notable players: **Dan Morgan, Kris Jenkins, Steve Smith, Chris Weinke.** Smith is the best and most electric player in team history, Jenkins and Morgan were both Pro Bowlers, and Weinke started as a rookie (albeit for a 1–15 team).

2. **2002**—Notable players: **Julius Peppers, DeShaun Foster, Will Witherspoon, Dante Wesley.** Not only was Peppers a beast and a possible Hall of Famer down the line, but the next three players in the draft also made major contributions for years. That's why this draft is listed but Cam Newton's (2011) isn't—Newton hasn't had much help from the rest of his group.

3. **2007**—Notable players: **Jon Beason, Ryan Kalil, Charles Johnson, Dwayne Jarrett.** Kalil and Beason have both made multiple Pro Bowls. Johnson took a few years, but worked his way up to becoming one of the NFL's best pass rushers. Jarrett (2nd round) was a major bust.

The Three Worst

1. **1997**—Notable players: **Rae Carruth, Mike Minter, Kris Mangum.** Carruth was simply the worst person to ever put on a Panthers uniform and as a first-round pick brings this class down by himself. Minter was a jewel and Mangum a solid tight end, but there wasn't much else.

2. **1998**—Notable players: **Jason Peter, Chuck Wiley, Mitch Marrow, Donald Hayes.** Peter was a first-round bust who had off-field issues. Wiley, a defensive end, once managed to start an entire season without recording a single sack.

3. **2009**—Notable players: **Everette Brown, Sherrod Martin, Corvey Irvin, Captain Munnerlyn.** Brown (2nd round) and Irvin (3rd round) were major busts, while Martin and Munnerlyn have been defensive backfield starters.

with class," he said of the Panthers. "They stuck with me, even when some people thought they stuck with me too long."

Morgan then signed with the New Orleans Saints, but never played a game for them. He tried to come back with the Saints twice—in 2008 and 2009—but both times retired before the season began due to injury, the second time for good.

To remember Morgan only for his injuries, however, is not to give him his due. There were those 59 games he played, after all, and he was at his peak in the 2003 sprint to the Super Bowl.

"We're just so much better with Dan on the field," Panthers coach John Fox said during that Super Bowl run. Morgan had an important interception in the Panthers' 14–3 NFC championship victory at Philadelphia, a game in which the Panthers had five sacks and four pickoffs and allowed only three points.

In 2003, the Panthers were 11–1 in contests that Morgan played in their entirety. "I've had a lot of frustrations," Morgan said then. "A lot of injuries. A lot of negative comments. But I know that when I'm healthy, I'm one of the best linebackers in the NFL."

The late Sam Mills was Morgan's position coach for the Panthers for several years and told me that Morgan could have been Hall of Fame material if No. 55 had stayed healthy. As it was, Morgan still was a key part of the best draft in Panthers history— the 2001 draft in which Morgan (first round), defensive tackle Kris Jenkins (second round), and wide receiver (Steve Smith) all made at least one Pro Bowl.

After retirement, Morgan stayed in Charlotte with his wife and young children. Widely known as one of the nicest Panthers to ever wear the uniform, he got into the restaurant business and is an active member of the community.

44 Michael Bates

It may be difficult to believe in this era where a touchback is the most common result of an NFL kickoff, but there was a time in the late 1990s where no true Carolina fan dared miss a kickoff received by the Panthers.

When Michael Bates was back deep, anything could happen. A former Olympic bronze medalist in the 200 meters in 1992, he was also one heck of a football player. You did not go to the bathroom or get a snack when Bates was about to get the ball.

Bates was easily the best kickoff return man the Panthers ever had, setting a team record that has never really been approached with five career kickoff returns for touchdowns. But he was more than that. He played on the cover teams too, usually as a "gunner" in one of the outside spot on punt returns. He made the Pro Bowl in five straight years for Carolina, from 1996 to 2000, in recognition of his various special-teams accomplishments.

Even if Bates didn't take it all the way back, he often got it close to midfield. In his 11-year NFL career, he had 30 returns of 40 or more yards. He also fumbled 20 times in his NFL career—once on the opening kickoff of a Panthers season, resulting in a New Orleans touchdown only 12 seconds into the game. So it was never completely clear what was going to happen when he got the ball, but he sure did worry opposing coaches.

Said Oakland head coach Joe Bugel once when he prepared to face Bates with the Panthers, "He's what we call scary. He's got crazy speed. He's a legitimate tough guy. He has no respect for his body or anybody else's."

In 1996, Bates' best season, he was the first NFL player in 19 years to average more than 30 yards per kickoff return (he averaged

30.2). That was his first year with the Panthers—Bates was a low-profile free agent acquired by Panthers general manager Bill Polian.

A two-sport standout at Arizona in college, Bates immediately made waves with Carolina for the way he stormed up the field with the ball. He wasn't much for jukes. He would make one move and then run straight ahead, as fast as he could. The other thing he could do that most returners couldn't—he could play as a gunner on the punt coverage team, or he could rush the punter. Bates still leads the all-time Panthers list with three blocked punts.

Bates had a younger brother, Mario, who was awfully good, too, and in some ways better. Mario Bates had a seven-year NFL career as a running back for three teams, once gaining 951 yards in a season in New Orleans. He had 38 career TDs compared to his older brother's five.

For all his speed, Michael Bates was never an effective offensive player like another Olympic medalist–turned–football player—former Dallas Cowboys wide receiver Bob Hayes. Bates was technically a wide receiver, but in 11 years in the NFL he caught only 12 passes.

In the Panthers locker room, Bates was known as an incessant practical joker. He often enlisted close friend and fellow special-teamer Dwight Stone as his accomplice. "It gets boring around here and I'm a playful type of guy," Bates said once.

And he liked to playfully taunt his teammates on the field, once angering the defensive backs so much that they chased him down as a group (hard to imagine, but true) and taped him to a goal post. "Mike worked hard for that taping," said cornerback Eric Davis, who led the successful corralling of Bates. "We figured he'd earned it."

The Panthers employed Bates twice, but the second time didn't work out well. After Bates had a one-year hiatus returning kicks for Washington, he came back to Carolina in 2002. But he missed that year due to an injury sustained in the preseason. And then the next year, Panthers coach John Fox cut Bates and instead kept

Rod "He Hate Me" Smart as his kick returner. Smart had a better nickname, but neither he nor anyone else has ever proved Bates' equal as a returner.

Although Bates was known for his practical jokes and blazing speed, he also had a kind heart. Several times he paid for other Panthers special teamers to accompany him to Hawaii on his annual trip to the Pro Bowl. Bates received one of his biggest honors when voters for the Pro Football Hall of Fame chose him as the kick returner for the NFL's Team of the Decade of the 1990s. He joined linebacker Kevin Greene as the only two former Panthers players to make that squad.

45 Luke Kuechly

A tackling machine.

That is the most frequent description of Panthers linebacker Luke Kuechly, and it certainly fits him. Kuechly was the NFL's 2012 Defensive Rookie of the Year mostly because he led the NFL in tackles—164 by the press box stats, but an astounding 205 by Panthers coaches' stats based on game film.

The latter number set a team record by a mile. By either number, Kuechly became the first rookie to lead the NFL in tackles since San Francisco linebacker Patrick Willis did so in 2007.

But Kuechly—drafted No. 9 overall by the Panthers in 2012—is not a machine. He's a soft-spoken young man from Ohio with Midwestern family values, one who will be counted on to become one of the cornerstones of the Panthers for the next five to 10 years.

At only 21 years old, Kuechly was thrust into the Panthers starting lineup from day one in 2012. He started the first four games

A punishing tackler, Luke Kuechly is one of the stalwarts of the current Panthers defense.

of his career at weakside linebacker, but once Jon Beason got hurt again Kuechly moved to middle linebacker—his natural position—and stayed there for the rest of the season. Not coincidentally, once he took over at the middle, the Panthers moved from 24th in the NFL in total defense to No. 10 in the final 2012 statistics.

"Luke is a wonderful person," said Panthers quarterback Cam Newton, who first realized Kuechly was as good as advertised at training camp in 2012, when the rookie kept messing up the first-team offense's plays. "Secondly, he's an unbelievable football player. Looking at him, you don't think he has that fierce attitude on the field—but looks may be deceiving."

Kuechly can get starstruck. He once ended up at a dinner with Newton and Michael Jordan—he knew he was eating with Newton, but MJ was a surprise guest. Kuechly (pronounced KEEK-lee) was so intimidated that he hardly said a word the whole night.

And, as Newton indicated, when Kuechly comes off the team bus he doesn't look like the first guy the other team would worry about. He's a sturdy 6'3" and 235 pounds, but he wears glasses off the field and has slightly curly hair. His teammates at Boston College sometimes called him "Superman." The glasses made him look like Clark Kent, and on Saturdays he put on his uniform, took off the specs, and transformed.

Kuechly first made his name at Boston College, where he led the ACC in tackles for three straight seasons and averaged an NCAA-record 14 tackles per game in his career. In his junior year, he was the ACC's Defensive Player of the Year and won a number of national defensive awards, including the Bronko Nagurski Award as the nation's best defensive player. He made at least 10 tackles in 33 straight games, another NCAA record.

Originally from Cincinnati, Kuechly was modestly recruited out of high school—mostly by schools known for their academics. Then a 210-pound safety, he visited Northwestern, Duke, Stanford, and Boston College.

BC's football program is known more for the two NFL quarterbacks it has produced—Doug Flutie and Matt Ryan—than anything else. But Kuechly felt comfortable there, signed, and started 37 games in three seasons. When the Panthers drafted him, Kuechly was a rarity. He was going to be a high NFL pick, and because of that he was invited to go to New York for an all-expenses-paid appearance at the draft. Instead, he decided to stay home with his family. Kuechly's draft party included about 50 friends and family. When NFL commissioner Roger Goodell announced his name, Kuechly was on a couch in his basement.

Kuechly's impact on the Panthers was immediate. By the team's third exhibition game, when Carolina played on national TV against the New York Jets, analyst Cris Collinsworth watched Kuechly get into double digits in sacks and said Kuechly was "already one of the best players on this team."

Kuechly isn't perfect. Although he is good both dropping back against the pass and defending the run, he could cause more turnovers and he rarely gets to the quarterback (although he also is rarely called upon to blitz).

But Kuechly's first step is remarkably good. Coach Ron Rivera, a former NFL linebacker himself, has noticed that Kuechly's instincts are so good that his first step is generally forward and toward the ball, rather than laterally as is the case for many linebackers who have to wait a half-second longer to diagnose the play. It's part of the reason why Kuechly mows down so many opposing ball carriers and stands tall as one of the most important pieces of the Panthers' immediate future.

46 The 1–15 Season

Although 2001 turned into the worst season in Carolina history, no one knew that in Week 1.

In fact, the headlines after Carolina's first game were positively glowing for what would turn out to be George Seifert's last Panthers team. Rookie Chris Weinke won his first start at quarterback. Rookie Steve Smith returned the opening kickoff 93 yards for a touchdown—the first TD scored in the entire NFL that season. The Panthers won convincingly, on the road at Minnesota, 24–13. It looked like a very interesting season was about to unfold.

And it was interesting all right. The Panthers went on to lose the next 15 games in a row, setting an NFL record for most consecutive losses in a single season. (Detroit would later break that mark by going 0–16 in 2008.)

In a league in which every team plays under the same salary cap and thus has at least some talent—and indeed, the Panthers would carry over 20 of their players from 2001 to the Super Bowl team of 2003—it takes some seriously bad timing, bad luck, and bad quarterbacking to lose 15 straight. The Panthers managed all of that, ending the season with a 38–6 home loss to New England in front of more than 50,000 empty seats in Charlotte.

After the 12th loss in a row, to a one-win Buffalo team, Seifert said, "The problem here is that we haven't solved the problem. And it's been an ongoing problem."

He got that right. The Panthers lost leads all the time that season. They were up by 18 against Buffalo and lost. They were up 14 against Washington and lost. They lost twice in overtime.

Over and over, they played teams close and blew it. The Panthers ended up 0–9 that season in games decided by eight points or fewer.

Quarterbacking was a big issue. Weinke had a QB rating of only 62.0, throwing 11 touchdowns but also 19 interceptions.

Coaching was an even bigger issue. Seifert had jettisoned highly respected quarterback Steve Beuerlein in the off-season, thinking Jeff Lewis was ready to assume the starting job. Then he changed his mind about Lewis after Lewis had a horrible preseason, which left him with the not-ready-for-prime-time Weinke.

Seifert also had the best player in team history in Smith, a rookie—and buried him on the bench. He instead played a rotation of Muhsin Muhammad, Donald Hayes, and Isaac Byrd at wide receiver. "Moose" was a justified choice, but Hayes and Byrd were average players at best. It was decisions like that which would cost Seifert his job following the season.

The Panthers were a team that was almost void of big plays. They didn't have a reception of 50-plus yards the entire 2001 season, nor a run of 30-plus by a running back. Only Smith—with three return TDs of 70 or more yards and a 39-yard run on a reverse—was capable of dazzling. And No. 89 had just 14 touches on offensive plays from scrimmage all year (an average of less than one per game).

There were a few bright spots. Cornerback Doug Evans had eight interceptions for the season, which remains a team record. Tight end Wesley Walls scored five times. Defensive end Mike Rucker had nine sacks. Weinke showed a knack for getting into the end zone himself, hammering the ball in on six scoring runs.

But it was a season in which the Panthers routinely found a way to lose. They were 1–0 for nearly two full weeks—the NFL postponed games originally scheduled for September 16, 2001, because of the terrorist attacks on 9/11, pushing those games back into early January 2002. So the Panthers—who had originally been scheduled to play New England at home in mid-September—ended up playing that game against a red-hot Patriots team on a very cold day in January.

Would it have mattered? Maybe a little; probably not much. This Panthers team certainly had some talent, but it was badly mismanaged and had lost all its confidence by midway through the season.

So Carolina set a low water mark in 2001, one that even the 2010 team quarterbacked by Jimmy Clausen couldn't equal when it went 2–14. Just as it's hard to go 15–1 in the NFL, it's also hard to go 1–15—but in 2001 the Panthers managed to do so.

47 The Sean Gilbert Trade

It seemed like a good idea at the time.

At least it did to the Panthers when they made Sean Gilbert the highest-paid defensive player in the history of the NFL in 1998.

The money was bad enough. However, the worst part of this horrible deal was the fact the Panthers had to give the Washington Redskins their first-round picks in both 1999 and 2000 as compensation.

In the news conference the proud Panthers held in April 1998 to announce Gilbert's acquisition, Gilbert said, "I don't have a cape on, so I'm not Superman."

Was that ever true. Gilbert played for five seasons for the Panthers and Carolina didn't make the playoffs in any of them.

That wasn't a coincidence. Gilbert wasn't a total bust—he was durable, starting 56 games in those five years. And he did have 15.5 sacks in his Panthers career. But he was never dominating enough to make up for all the Panthers gave up to get him—two No. 1 picks who likely would have become starters, and so much salary-cap space that it made it difficult for Carolina to plunge into the free-agent pool for years.

The man who masterminded the Gilbert mess was head coach Dom Capers, who by 1998 had also assumed the responsibilities of general manager because Bill Polian had left for Indianapolis. Capers was a wonderful defensive coordinator, an okay head coach, and a great guy. He was, however, a terrible general manager—and the Gilbert signing is No. 1 on the list of the reasons why.

Gilbert was signed to put more bite in the Panthers defense. But in his first season, the Panthers ranked dead last in total defense. By the end of it, Capers had been fired.

Gilbert was popular in the locker room and genuine in his Christian convictions. He also could be self-deprecating about the immense value of his contract, once saying he believed it was natural for Panthers fans to think that he should be able to be a great defensive player for $46.5 million, as well as "split the atom" and "find out what's on Mars."

The Panthers released Gilbert after the 2002 season. The *Charlotte Observer* reported that the actual amount of money Gilbert had received from Carolina was $27.43 million (NFL contracts are not fully guaranteed) and that he had restructured his deal four times and taken a pay cut in his final season in Charlotte.

Still, Gilbert was no bargain. It turned out that even at 6'5" and 320 pounds, he wasn't great at holding the point of attack. He got pushed backward too often. He was more effective on pass plays, when he could rush upfield.

Gilbert sat out the 2003 season, played part of the 2004 season with Oakland, and then retired. He stayed in Charlotte after that with his family, staying active in his church, raising his family, and dabbling in several pursuits, including movie actor, record producer, and assistant high school football coach.

48 Fred Lane's Rise and Tragic Fall

The rise and fall of Fred Lane stands as one of the most tragic episodes in Panthers history.

Lane was an undrafted free agent out of tiny Lane College in Tennessee (the fact that his last name matched the college's name were coincidental). The Panthers gave him a tiny $5,000 signing bonus to be training-camp fodder in 1997.

"Basically, I thought I was going to be sent home on the first cut," Lane told me shortly after he signed in 1997. "I thought they just had me in to be a practice body."

Instead, Lane had a breakthrough game in an intrasquad scrimmage in Charlotte and eventually became the Panthers' starting tailback. He scored 13 touchdowns and had six 100-yard games in his three-year career with the Panthers.

Lane had several huge moments, including a 147-yard, three-touchdown performance at home against Oakland in 1997, during which he did a dance he called "the Fred Lane Shuffle" after each TD. Perhaps his best moment came a few weeks after that on *Monday Night Football*, when Lane gored the Dallas Cowboys for 138 yards on 34 carries in a road win at Texas Stadium.

But Lane was shot to death on July 6, 2000, by his wife, Deidra Lane, just after he arrived at their south Charlotte home. He was only 24.

His wife shot him twice with a shotgun. His keys still hung in the door lock.

Deidra Lane would ultimately plead guilty to voluntary manslaughter in 2003 in connection with her husband's death. In 2009, she was released from prison. At the time of the shooting, Deidra and Fred Lane had a newborn daughter who was seven days old. That child is now a teenager.

In Deidra Lane's trial, prosecutors portrayed her as a money-hungry woman who ambushed her husband just inside the front door because she wanted to collect on a $5 million life insurance policy. Her attorneys defended her by saying she was a battered wife who feared for her life when she shot her husband. In her 2003 sentencing hearing, Deidra Lane faced her late husband's parents in court and said, "I am sorry for the loss of Fred. I loved Fred dearly. He was a good man. At times, he scared me, and I didn't understand him then. I'm sorry for the pain I've caused."

Lane's father was the first Fred Lane, and when his son came along they were called "Big Fred" and "Little Fred" to differentiate the two. Big Fred taught and coached for 32 years at the middle-school level in Tennessee. They went to the same high school, with Little Fred breaking all of Big Fred's records, and the school ended up retiring both of their numbers.

When Little Fred went to college—he had academic problems or likely would have gone to a bigger college—his father would enter the stadium each Saturday before the game and let out a high-pitched whistle. That would alert his son, warming up on the field, and the son would smile and wave. They were a close family. Little Fred called his parents frequently and ended every conversation with "I love you."

Panthers fans loved Lane too—especially at the beginning, in 1997. In what was otherwise a down season, they couldn't get enough of the undrafted rookie who suddenly became a starter. They ate up the details: Lane's favorite food was spinach. He said he read his grandmother's well-worn Bible every night.

Lane was not a choirboy in his three years at Carolina, however. He had some immaturity issues. Once, he was held out of a game because he missed the team plane. He was suspended for another

Fred Lane's was a career and life cut tragically short. When he was killed in 2001, he was the Panthers' all-time leading rusher.

game after celebrating a touchdown by grabbing his crotch. He and teammate Tshimanga Biakabutuka were roundly criticized when before one game they did not stand for the national anthem. Long before the shooting, Lane's wife filed a domestic violence complaint against him.

In April 2000, the Panthers traded Lane to Indianapolis for a forgettable linebacker named Spencer Reid. But Lane would never play a down for the Colts, so he is always thought of as a Panther. And for good reason—he was a fine player in Charlotte for three years. When he was killed, he was the Panthers' all-time leading rusher with 2,001 yards, and his total still ranks sixth.

"I try to only remember the good times," Fred Lane Sr. told me on the 10th anniversary of his son's death. "And every day with him was a good time. Fred loved life. He was a joy to be around."

49 Shutting Out the Giants

The Carolina Panthers have won six playoff games in their history. Their 23–0 victory against the New York Giants in the 2005 postseason wasn't the most exciting of them, but it was undeniably the most dominant.

The Panthers so thoroughly throttled the Giants—in the Giants' own stadium, no less—that New York fans were leaving in droves by the time the fourth quarter began. The victory was predicated on Carolina's defense, which forced quarterback Eli Manning into four turnovers and had star running back Tiki Barber stating flatly that Giants coach Tom Coughlin was outsmarted by Panthers coach John Fox.

Said Barber after the game, "I think, in some ways, we were outcoached... They were in our huddle a little bit. They kind of had us dissected and figured out and we couldn't get anything going consistently."

Barber would back off those comments a few days later, but by then the damage was done. The Panthers had pounded the Giants in the stadium where Fox had once served with distinction as New York's defensive coordinator.

Eli Manning would eventually become the Giants' franchise quarterback, winning two Super Bowls later in his career. That day, however, he looked nothing like the clutch QB he would become. To that point, Manning's teams had never been shut out—in the pros or during his college career at Mississippi.

Not only did the Giants not score, they also only had the ball for 17 minutes and 15 seconds and never advanced past Carolina's 35-yard line. Current Panthers general manager Dave Gettleman worked for the Giants at that time and remembers this dismantling vividly, although he prefers to forget it.

On offense, the Panthers constructed their game plan around familiar tenets in the Fox era. With the Giants committed to putting two defenders on Steve Smith, Carolina ran the ball repeatedly. DeShaun Foster ended up with 151 rushing yards and Nick Goings had 63. And still Smith was able to score the only two TDs of the game. The first was on a 22-yard dart from Jake Delhomme, which Smith took into the end zone. No. 89 then sprawled onto his back and made a pretend snow angel.

Later, in the third quarter, Smith got the ball on a reverse and scored from 12 yards out. That made it 17–0 and the Giants were done. Carolina ended up as the first team to register a shutout on the road in the playoffs since the L.A. Rams had managed it in the 1979 postseason. The defense allowed New York only 132 yards, a season low, and sacked Manning four times. Marlon McCree had two of the interceptions for Carolina and Ken Lucas had the other.

"If you can make it in New York, you can make it anywhere, right?" Carolina defensive tackle Brentson Buckner quipped to reporters as he walked into Carolina's locker room.

It was one of those days where everything seemed to go perfectly. Barber had rushed for at least 100 yards in six of his past seven games but was held to only 41. Plaxico Burress, the Giants' best receiver, didn't catch a pass.

Giants defensive end Osi Umenyiora had said a few days before the game that he and Michael Strahan were the best defensive ends in the league. But on this day Julius Peppers and Mike Rucker were the tandem going home with the shutout win.

The Panthers would win one more playoff game that 2005 postseason—the 29–21 victory at Chicago when Smith had the best day of his career—before losing in the NFC championship at Seattle.

50 The Arizona and Seattle Playoff Losses

In the 10 playoff games in the Carolina Panthers' history, two games stand out like sore thumbs for the sheer ineptitude displayed by the men in black and blue.

They were played three years apart, following the 2005 and 2008 seasons. They both resulted in 20-point losses, the sort of beatdowns that make a lot of the previous good feelings dissipate.

Seattle administered the first whipping, 34–14 in the NFC Championship Game in 2006. That one at least was a bit more understandable, since it was on the road and Seattle was favored.

The second one was worse. The Panthers played at home in 2009 after having secured a first-round playoff bye. They were 9½-point favorites, and then they got absolutely blistered by Arizona, 33–13.

While Jake Delhomme had many great moments as Carolina's quarterback, including five playoff wins, those two games constituted his two lowest points as a Panther. He threw three interceptions against Seattle and then five at home against Arizona, losing a sixth turnover in that game on a fumble.

Cruelly, the Arizona game happened on his 34th birthday, and Delhomme was never the same quarterback after that showing.

Delhomme's poor performances were the biggest commonality in the two games, but there were several others. The Panthers trailed 27–7 by early in the third quarter in both games, so by then it was basically over in both matchups. The Panthers weren't able to run the ball well in either game—they gained only 36 yards on the ground against Seattle and 75 vs. Arizona. Whenever John Fox's teams weren't able to run the ball, the Panthers were always in trouble.

The Panthers defense also was unable to stop the biggest threat on the other team. Against Seattle, it was running back Shaun Alexander, who bulled his way to 132 rushing yards and two touchdowns. Against Arizona, it was wide receiver Larry Fitzgerald, who carved up the Panthers for 166 receiving yards (151 in the first half alone) and a touchdown.

And in both games, Steve Smith was effectively double-covered on most every pass play and wasn't able to have a good game receiving—and he was instrumental to the Panthers offense in both years. In 2005, coming off a career-high 218-yard game against Chicago, Smith only caught five passes for 33 yards against Seattle. He did score Carolina's only touchdown, however, on a 59-yard punt return. Against Arizona, he managed only two catches for 43 yards.

In the Seattle game, at least, the Panthers had gone on a fine road playoff run to get that far. They shut out the New York Giants 23–0 and then watched Smith almost single-handedly beat Chicago, 29–21. But the NFC title game was never really close. Seattle slew the Panthers by jumping to a 17–0 lead by the time seven seconds had elapsed in the second quarter. Carolina never made a serious charge.

It didn't help that Nick Goings sustained a concussion early in the Seahawks game, leaving the Panthers' running game to the overmatched Jamal Robertson, a fourth-stringer. Seattle held the ball for nearly 42 minutes.

Against Arizona, the Panthers entered their first home playoff game in five years at 12–4 and fresh off that first-round bye. But Delhomme was totally outplayed by his former Amsterdam Admirals teammate, Kurt Warner of Arizona, who had also beaten him out for the starting QB job on that NFL Europe team back in 1998.

"We got a butt-whooping," Panthers safety Mike Minter said after the Seattle game.

Overall, Carolina is 6–4 in its postseason history. The other two losses are more understandable—the Panthers lost 30–13 at Green Bay in only their second season to a formidable Packers team that went on to win the Super Bowl. And of course, the Panthers lost a thriller in the Super Bowl to New England following the 2003 season.

But neither Arizona nor Seattle would go on to win the Super Bowl after defeating Carolina, and the Panthers were not clearly overmatched in talent in either game. They just were outcoached, outplayed, and overpowered in both cases, setting up the twin playoff losses that are still remembered with a grimace by all Panthers fans.

51 Go to a Road Game Against a Divisional Rival

Of the Panthers' eight road opponents every NFL season, only three are guaranteed. The other five road sites rotate among 28 NFL teams. But Carolina always plays NFC South divisional rivals Atlanta, New Orleans, and Tampa Bay twice each season—once at home and once on the road.

Panthers players set special stock in divisional games, since winning the division guarantees at least one home playoff contest.

And those games are also important for playoff tiebreakers. Intensity is never a problem.

So if you were going to go to one Panthers road game, which would it be? Atlanta, Tampa, or New Orleans? Here's an alphabetical rundown, taking into account both the stadiums and the cities.

ATLANTA—For Panthers fans in the Carolinas, this is the easiest and cheapest game to get to because you can drive there in half a day or less. From Charlotte, Atlanta is about 250 miles on Interstate 85.

The downside of the "I–85 rivalry" from a Carolina fan perspective is that the Panthers have won far less in Atlanta than they have in Tampa or New Orleans—for whatever reason, the Georgia Dome usually has been a personal house of horrors for Carolina. Michael Vick used to terrorize them routinely there. Kerry Collins quit after a 28-point loss there. Haruki Nakamura gave up a 59-yard pass there in 2012 to allow the Falcons a last-minute field goal to win.

The Georgia Dome is located in the heart of Atlanta's downtown, where there are hundreds of lodging options. If you stay a few miles outside downtown, costs can drop by 30 to 50 percent. The Georgia Aquarium is one of the best aquariums in the world and is located very near where the Falcons play. It's well worth the money if you have kids. There's a Six Flags nearby, too.

Atlanta hosted the Olympics in 1996 and the city's infrastructure improved significantly for that event. Atlanta is a very easy place to entertain yourself and has an underground subway called MARTA that many Atlanta fans take to games to avoid parking hassles.

As for the stadium itself, it's a fine and loud building. Yet it is scheduled to be replaced for the 2017 season with a new retractable-roof structure that will cost a billion dollars and be constructed about a half-mile away from the current Georgia Dome. So if you want more bells and whistles, you may want to wait for that one, although the current model is perfectly serviceable. When the team is good, as it has been in recent years, tickets to Falcons games can be hard to find unless you pay an online premium. But Atlanta's fans are fairly fickle, and tickets run cheap when the team is playing poorly.

NEW ORLEANS—The best home-field atmosphere in the NFC South is found at Saints games, where fans love their team so much, win or lose, that every Sunday feels like a party.

To get the full New Orleans experience, you absolutely must stay in or near the French Quarter. The Panthers sometimes stay in Metairie, Louisiana, about 20 minutes away, but that's purely so the players won't be distracted by the revelry.

Don't do that. After all, you want to be distracted, don't you? Why else would you come to New Orleans?

So walk down famous Bourbon and Canal Streets and sample the ample nightlife. Look at the artists' work set up outside Jackson Square. Eat some Cajun food. Go to Café du Monde for coffee and beignets (there's a great Jimmy Buffett song that references the place). Take an early morning run or walk at the park right beside the Mississippi River. Go to the casino.

And do yourself a favor—fly to New Orleans if you can afford to. It is 715 miles from Charlotte and seems to be a long way from practically anywhere. Once you get there, you won't need to rent a car, as New Orleans' downtown is very compact.

For sheer uniqueness, New Orleans has it all over Atlanta, Tampa, and almost every other city in the U.S. The Saints' Superdome seems cavernous and ancient, but it rocks as loudly as any stadium in the NFL when the home team is doing well. The Panthers win there close to half the time, though, so it's not a bad place to hope for a Carolina win. Tickets are fairly difficult to come by, as Saints fans show up no matter how the team is doing. But they can be found online and sometimes outside the stadium before the game.

TAMPA—A Panthers game in Tampa has a few things going for it. First, the weather is almost always nice, which matters because it's the only outdoor stadium among Carolina's three NFC South rivals. Second, tickets are always easier to get than they are for Falcons or Saints games. The Buccaneers rarely sell out their games and the upper deck in particular yawns with emptiness most times when the Panthers come to town. Third, the Panthers often play well in Tampa.

Carolina fans who make the trip to Tampa often combine the game with some of Florida's many other family attractions. Busch Gardens is a great place to spend a day in Tampa. And the many amusement parks of Orlando—including the Disney parks—are only 85 miles away on Interstate 4.

The flip side? Tampa is a long way from Charlotte—580 miles. So it's either a really long drive or a really short flight from most places where Panthers fans live. And the NFL atmosphere leaves a lot to be desired (although the pirate ship in one end zone is cool and is open to fans—be sure to walk through it if you go). Unlike going to a Panthers game in Atlanta or New Orleans, you don't feel like you are at a big-time event at a Buccaneers game. But it's not as expensive a city to visit as New Orleans and—because of the "blah" attitude many Floridians have about the Bucs—is the safest place of the three division rivals to wear a Panthers jersey to the game without fear of reprisal.

52 Panthers in Prime Time

Nighttime has too often *not* been the right time for the Carolina Panthers, whose record in prime-time games under the lights has been spotty.

In their first 18 years, the Panthers played 27 regular-season games at night. They went 11–16 in those contests, so they lost about 59 percent of the time. There were a number of very good wins sprinkled in among the disheartening losses, however.

Here are the best three and worst three games the Panthers have ever played at night (only regular-season games are counted in this total, not preseason or postseason games played at night). All six of these games were played in Charlotte, where for some reason most of the Panthers' most memorable night games have occurred.

Best Three Prime-Time Games

Carolina 38, Tampa Bay 23—December 8, 2008. Carolina piled up 299 rushing yards in an NFC South division battle of two 9–3 teams in Charlotte. The Panthers dismantled the Bucs so convincingly in this home win that Tampa Bay coach Jon Gruden would be fired a month later.

Carolina 31, Green Bay 14—November 27, 2000. Undrafted rookie Brad Hoover was switched from fullback to tailback and had the biggest individual night of his career, rushing for 117 yards. Forevermore in home games, he would be known as "Hoooooov!" Coach George Seifert said after the game of Hoover, "We thought we had somebody that had multiplicity in his abilities."

Carolina 26, Minnesota 7—December 20, 2009. Matt Moore outplayed Brett Favre in an unlikely upset of a very good Vikings team that entered the game 11–2 (Carolina entered 5–8). Moore had three touchdown passes and Steve Smith and Julius Peppers both had monstrous games in the upset.

Worst Three Prime-Time Games

Green Bay 24, Carolina 14—September 13, 2004. The year after the Super Bowl, the Panthers got to open on Monday night at home and got whipped. Not only that, but wide receiver Steve

Julius Peppers creams Brett Favre in a prime-time matchup against Minnesota.

Smith was lost for the year due to injury. This dud began a 1–7 start for Carolina.

Washington 24, Carolina 10—August 31, 1997. Another terrible home opener following a great season. Coming off an appearance in the NFC Championship Game, the Panthers proved fame was fleeting, losing by two touchdowns to the Redskins on their way to a 7–9 season.

NY Giants 36, Carolina 7—September 20, 2012. In a game that helped push Panthers general manager Marty Hurney out the door, Carolina was stomped by the New York Giants. Cam Newton was benched late in the game after his third interception and then sat alone on the sideline, causing Smith to verbally light into him for not standing up and supporting his teammates with what Smith would memorably label "unchoice words."

Mark Carrier

One of the most gracious players in the Carolina locker room during the team's first four years was wide receiver Mark Carrier. Already Tampa Bay's all-time leading receiver by the time he got to Carolina at age 29, Carrier was productive enough from 1995 to 1998 that he still ranks fourth all-time in receptions for Carolina, with 176.

The classy Carrier was one of the most popular players on the early Carolina teams. Even though his speed wasn't tremendous, Carrier was a big-play threat from day one because of his precise routes and fine hands. While often mistakenly characterized as a "possession" receiver, Carrier finished his Panthers career averaging 14.5 yards per catch while with Carolina and 15.4 over his entire NFL career. That's comparable to Steve Smith's career average of about 15 yards per catch.

"I run as fast as I need to," Carrier often said.

Carrier had a number of fine games in the team's first two seasons, during which he posted all five of his 100-yard receiving games. He led the team in reception yards in both 1995 and '96 and scored the first-ever touchdown in the Panthers' home stadium. The Panthers nevertheless tried to phase him out in each of the next two seasons. In 1997, general manager Bill Polian did not bring Carrier to training camp and planned to part ways with him permanently.

Before Week 4 of the 1997 season, however, the Panthers realized they had miscalculated. Although no one else had picked him up, they missed Carrier when he was gone. So they re-signed him, and he was starting by Week 7. Polian would later admit that not bringing Carrier back sooner was one of his biggest regrets of the 1997 season, when the Panthers thudded from 13–5 in 1996 to 7–9.

By 1998, though, the Panthers were effectively phasing Carrier out again. They started Rocket Ismail and Muhsin Muhammad all that season, with Carrier often playing less than a dozen snaps a game as the No. 3 receiver in a conservative offense that hardly ever used three wideouts. Nevertheless, that season he found a way to win a game ball—without catching a single pass.

It was late in the fourth quarter in a lost season. The Panthers, 1–9 at the time, were clinging to a 24–20 lead. Carrier was in the game, but he hadn't seen a pass all day.

Then Steve Beuerlein threw an awful one to someone else, and Rams linebacker Roman Phifer intercepted it and started chugging toward the end zone. Carrier, way out of the play, started motoring toward Phifer, trying to chase him down.

It was one of those rare 40-yard dashes that actually meant something. That's how far Phifer had run when Carrier caught him at the 2, neatly stripping the ball just before Phifer crossed the goal line. Panthers offensive guard Frank Garcia fell on it and the Panthers had ultimately preserved their second win of the season. Carrier, normally very calm on the field, went into boxer mode, throwing lefts and rights and uppercuts at the sky. Beuerlein gave Carrier a hug and the game ball in the locker room as his teammates whooped and hollered.

"It's probably, of all the plays I've ever seen in my life, the most awesome hustle play I've ever seen," Beuerlein said. To long-time football fans, it was similar to the play Buffalo wide receiver Don Beebe made in the Super Bowl when he chased down Dallas defensive lineman Leon Lett and knocked the ball away and out of the end zone for a touchback even though the Cowboys had already put the game away.

It was Carrier's last great moment as a Panther. The team cut him in April 1999 and he didn't play in the NFL again. But he would return to the Panthers as the team's player engagement director in 2011, a fitting choice to serve as a liaison for players in all of their off-the-field activities.

54 Chad Cota's Interception

He was a seventh-round draft choice in 1995, a safety who had only started two games in his first two seasons. But Chad Cota made one of the most famous plays in Panthers history on December 22, 1996, intercepting a Kordell Stewart pass in the end zone to preserve Carolina's 18–14 win in Charlotte and clinch a first-round playoff bye.

Cota's play was not only clutch, it was mysterious. It was difficult to see the ball from any vantage point, as Cota and Pittsburgh's best receiver at the time, Andre Hastings, wrestled for the ball in a scrum of players. Cota came up holding the ball aloft, though, and the home crowd exploded. It was one of those moments that everyone who was there remembers. As Panthers play-by-play man Bill Rosinski said on the radio, "Stewart back to throw, fires in the end zone. What is it? What is it? INTERCEPTED! The Panthers have it! The Panthers have it!"

Cota was a small-town Oregon kid with movie-star looks and a quiet personality. He was a skier, a snowboarder, and a fine safety who played more and more during the 1996 season as safety Brett

Maxie kept getting bothered by nagging injuries. He was the sort of guy who was admittedly intimidated by shadowing Jerry Rice for the first time on the field but then played Rice relatively well. He had stayed in-state for college, going to Oregon and playing on the Ducks' "Gang Green" defense. In the Panthers locker room, cornerback Eric Davis sometimes called him "Cota-chrome."

Cota would tie for the Panthers' lead in 1996 with five interceptions. His most spectacular pick came with Pittsburgh trying to beat the Panthers behind the scrambling Stewart, a dual threat who had run for an 80-yard touchdown earlier in the game—still the longest TD run by an NFL quarterback.

Of the final two minutes of that game, 90 seconds were spent with Pittsburgh inside the Carolina 10, trying to erase a four-point Panthers lead. The Steelers actually got to a first-and-goal at the Carolina 1 on a defensive holding call on Kevin Greene, only to move back to the 6 on a false-start penalty. Then, on third-and-goal from the 8, the Panthers misfired on their substitutions. Linebacker Sam Mills was supposed to come out of the game for a defensive back because Pittsburgh had five wide receivers on the field. He didn't.

Cota gambled that the pass would go to Mills' area, and it did. The Steelers ran the same play that they had scored on earlier on a throw to Hastings. This time Cota and Hastings got to the ball at the same time, but Cota had a stronger grip on it.

"I had it," Cota said after the game. "He was trying to get it from me. I knew I had it. I didn't even know they were debating it."

"He had a little more leverage than I did," Hastings said.

Panthers defensive coordinator Vic Fangio would later say he thought Cota's play was the one that forever changed the team. "I just think some kind of love affair—I mean true love affair—started then," Fangio said. "The town was in love with the Panthers before that, but from that fourth quarter on it was much bigger."

In the locker room, Cota was still holding onto the ball he intercepted an hour after the game.

"You can let go of that ball now. We won," Eric Davis teased him.

Cota kept a firm hold on the ball, however. "Ain't nobody getting this ball, bro," he said.

Cota was not with the Panthers much longer. In 1997, he became a full-time starter in his third year and led the team in tackles (Mills would finish second).

The New Orleans Saints then signed him away from Carolina as a restricted free agent in 1998, offering more than the Panthers wanted to pay him. In one notable game against his former teammates, Cota intercepted an ill-advised halfback pass from Carolina's William Floyd to help key a Saints victory.

"There's nothing fancy about Chad," Mike Ditka, who coached Cota in New Orleans, once said. "He just plays old-fashioned football and gives you everything he's got. He's a good kid. He's been wonderful."

Cota would end up also playing for Indianapolis (Panthers general manager Bill Polian had originally drafted him before leaving for the Colts) and St. Louis before retiring before the 2003 season following an eight-year NFL career.

Cota would then move back to Oregon, where he and his wife are raising two sons. He had 15 career NFL interceptions, but none of them were as big as the one against Pittsburgh.

Rae Carruth

The darkest episode in Carolina Panthers history was caused by team's No. 1 draft pick in 1997—a wide receiver out of Colorado named Rae Carruth.

Carruth was an egocentric brooder who also happened to be very fast. That speed was the main reason the Panthers drafted him so high. His best NFL season was his first, when he had 44 catches for 545 yards and four touchdowns as a rookie in 1997. Those who knew him thought of him as a little weird—but not as someone who would conspire to murder his pregnant girlfriend.

That, however, is exactly what a jury convicted Carruth of doing. He was convicted in January 2001 of conspiring to murder Cherica Adams, who was pregnant with Carruth's unborn son. Adams survived the shooting initially, long enough to make a haunting 911 call in which she described the circumstances: She and Carruth had gone to see a movie together and were driving away from the theater in separate cars. She was following him.

Then Carruth slowed down. Another car pulled up beside Cherica Adams and someone inside it shot her four times. Carruth then drove away, as Adams said on the call.

The baby survived and remains alive today. Chancellor Lee Adams is a teenager now being raised by Saundra Adams in Charlotte—she was Cherica's mother and is his grandmother. Called "Lee," the boy was delivered 10 weeks prematurely via an emergency Caesarean section. The bullets missed the boy, but loss of blood and oxygen left him severely handicapped. He has cerebral palsy.

Cherica Adams died a month after the November 1999 shooting. Carruth was arrested just hours after that. When FBI agents found him, he was hiding in a car trunk at a Best Western motel in Tennessee.

His trial was nationally covered, with much of it being broadcast live on Court TV. Prosecutors claimed that Carruth had organized the attack to get rid of the child because he didn't want to pay child support. Carruth did not take the stand in his own defense.

Eventually, Carruth and three other men went to jail for the heinous crime. Van Brett Watkins, the man who pulled the trigger, pleaded guilty to second-degree murder and is serving a 40-year sentence. Two other men inside the car served time as well but have since been released.

Carruth was sentenced to approximately 19 years in prison—although he was found not guilty of first-degree murder—and has a scheduled release date of 2018. While in jail in eastern North Carolina, he has worked a variety of jobs, including janitor, groundskeeper, and barber. The player who once signed a four-year, $3.7 million rookie contract with the Panthers has been paid around one dollar per day for his jailhouse work. He has routinely declined interview requests, although shortly after the trial he did do an interview with CNN/SI and said: "I feel guilty about none of it. I didn't have anything to do with it." He explained that he was hiding in the car trunk before being arrested simply to "clear his head."

No one believed that, of course. But it was also hard for the Panthers and their fans to believe how far their first-round draft pick had fallen. Adams was murdered during coach George Seifert's first season, in 1999. He and the players were very careful not to overstep their legal bounds as Carruth's case slowly worked its way through the court system and mostly ignored it publicly. Quarterback Steve Beuerlein was the only one who addressed the topic to any real extent with the media.

Although I was around Carruth for a couple of years before he conspired to do such a horrific thing, I won't claim to know him well. He didn't like to talk to the media and generally avoided reporters. I only knew small things about him: he remains the only Panther ever to carry a skateboard to training camp, for instance. He worried a whole lot about his appearance. He was slim, but told me once that he looked fat in any jersey that didn't contain the number "1." He tried out about five different jersey numbers in his brief time with the Panthers, always trying to find the perfect number that apparently didn't exist for him. He seemed to be an introvert and also fairly smart.

It was the death of Cherica Adams—and only seven months later, in 2000, the death of Fred Lane at the hands of his estranged wife—that really shook up the city of Charlotte and gave Panthers fans a lesson about the dark side of what it means to have an NFL team.

It's not all wins and losses, fun and games, Super Bowls and near-misses. Sometimes, it's far worse. Sometimes real life—and gruesome death—intrudes in the most horrible of ways.

If the Panthers could only have a "do-over"—if they could take back one draft pick in their entire history—there's no doubt who it would be. It wouldn't be some player who merely failed to fulfill their potential on the field.

It would be Rae Carruth.

56 Catman: The Trick and the Truck

It was one of the weirdest stories I've ever covered. And ultimately, one of the most gratifying.

In August 2006, at the end of a meaningless exhibition game in Charlotte, Panthers superfan Greg "Catman" Good was made to look like a fool on national television. It was a poorly executed, badly planned trick that some people at Fox Sports had thought up to juice up the final quarter of the preseason game.

Simply put, they told "Catman"—who has come to Panthers games forever in his electric-blue wig and black-and-blue cape—that they were going to give him a car. Then Fox sideline announcer Tony Siragusa gave him a toy car instead. Good, believing the toy car to be a symbol for the real thing, acted excited for the cameras. Then Siragusa simply walked away.

I wrote a column about the incident for the *Charlotte Observer*, ripping what Fox did and saying the only way to make it right was to fulfill the promise and give Good a real vehicle. The reader response was among the largest I've ever received for any column—I was bombarded by close to 1,000 e-mails and phone calls in eight hours.

At first, Fox Sports offered only an apology. But after a blizzard of e-mails by *Observer* readers and the intervention of Fox Sports chairman and CEO David Hill, that decision was reversed.

Hill was a stand-up guy about it. He called me on the phone to say that he was going to personally fly from Los Angeles to Charlotte to give Good the keys to a new F-150 pickup. He also criticized the Fox TV crew that pulled the practical joke for "an appalling piece of misjudgment."

"I'm coming to Charlotte to apologize to Mr. Good for a joke that went terribly, terribly wrong," Hill said. Hill also said there would be internal discipline at Fox Sports due to the incident but that no one would be left "hanging from the gallows."

Hill indeed met Good in Charlotte, apologized, and presented him with the truck, which became Good's vehicle of choice for many years.

But let's back up for a second. This is a story that people always seem to want to hear at cocktail parties, even many years later, so I will tell it more fully. I first had met Good in 1996 after Panthers wide receiver Mark Carrier had handed him the football after scoring a touchdown. Carrier appreciated that Good always came early and the two had talked sometimes during warm-ups. I had exchanged occasional e-mails with Good since then.

Good, who is from Winston-Salem and a college graduate, had bought permanent-seat licenses on the first day they were available.

He has sat in the first row of the end zone since the Panthers moved into Bank of America Stadium in 1996.

Through the years, "Catman" has become the Panthers' most well-known fan because of his striking outfits, his enthusiasm, and his front-row seat in Section 104. He was part of an exhibit on super fans at the Pro Football Hall of Fame. He created his own bobblehead, financing it himself and having 1,000 of them made.

So he was a natural choice to put on camera for the nationally telecast game against the Miami Dolphins from Charlotte in 2006. Here's how it worked.

First, with 2:37 left in the third quarter, Fox Sports analyst Daryl Johnston made the first mention of the car giveaway. Said Johnston, "Now all you fans out there, you might be thinking, *Well, the starting units are out, we might change the channel.* We're going to do something special to try and keep you here tonight. We're giving a car away tonight."

Then, with 1:56 left in the fourth quarter, the announcers brought up the giveaway again. Said play-by-play man Dick Stockton, "Someone's going to get a car tonight, Daryl."

Said Johnston, speaking of on-field reporter Siragusa, "Hopefully, Tony has assembled all the criteria, and he's got a worthy selection down there."

Said Siragusa, "I'm looking. I'm looking."

After a Miami kickoff return, the camera flashed back to Siragusa on the sideline. He was standing close to Good, who was still in the stands in his front-row seat.

Siragusa introduced Good, asked him to scream for the Panthers and then said, "The car is coming in right now. Here it comes. Beautiful. It's white. It's a Porsche."

On air, Siragusa asked, "Do you have a car?"

"I need a car so bad," Good said. Siragusa also said that Good, who is 6'4" and weighed 340 pounds at the time, would need "oil" or "butter" to fit into the car.

Then Siragusa handed a tiny toy car to Good.

Good thought the real car was too big to roll into the end zone, which was why he looked so happy. "Thank you! Thank you very, very, very much! It's a blessing and a prayer answered!" he said.

A few seconds later, Stockton returned to the game action and said: "So our lucky fan is going to drive off with a new car. First-and-10 at the 28."

Good still believed he was getting a free car from Fox Sports that night and most of the next day, when he first contacted me in an exultant e-mail. When I didn't hear back from him after responding, a few days later I asked what had happened. Some fans online had been wondering, too. Good told me the story and, eventually, all ended well.

"I'm grinning from ear to ear," Good said shortly after hearing of the new truck, "because this time it's for real."

Good, who had been driving a 1991 Chevrolet Astro with 130,000 miles on it, harbored no hard feelings toward Fox Sports. He has continued to come to games, changing his outfit slightly every year. He is relatively well known by the players—not by his given name, but by his "Catman" moniker. His notoriety also helped him land a gig for a while with the Charlotte Bobcats, where he substituted in an orange wig to match the Bobcats' colors.

At Muhsin Muhammad's 2010 retirement news conference, one of the people "Moose" thanked during his time at the microphone was Good. The fan had always loved the way Muhammad played and had routinely incorporated Muhammad's No. 87 jersey into his outfits.

57 The Original 10

On December 14, 1994, the Carolina Panthers had a helmet, a color scheme, and a few employees—and not much else.

Most notably, they had no players. But that changed the next day, when with great hoopla the Panthers announced their "Original 10" players at a press conference in Charlotte.

"The Panthers are alive and breathing," team president Mike McCormack said as the players, dressed in suits and ties, signed their contracts for the cameras. "We can now give you some physical evidence we are a football team."

The "Original 10" were not high-profile players. They were, in NFL parlance, "street free agents." The 1994 NFL season was still going on, with all 28 teams playing. But these 10—who, by coincidence, all played offense—didn't have a job anywhere. They were on the street, clinging to wisps of a pro football dream.

"We'll be pleased if two of these guys make our team," Panthers general manager Bill Polian would say that day, throwing a splash of cold water on the hoopla. "Personnel selection in this league is always a crap shoot."

"Oh, yeah, we all loved hearing that!" offensive lineman Kevin Farkas would joke later. "Nothing like a 2-in-10 chance."

But Polian was about right. Two of the original 10 made meaningful contributions to the Panthers in the next couple of seasons. Wide receiver Willie Green—who had given himself the nickname "Touchdown Machine"—was a starting receiver for most of the 1995 and '96 seasons and caught a 44-yard TD pass in Carolina's very first game. Matt Campbell hung around for one season as an overweight and somewhat slow tight end. Then he was converted to an underweight and fast offensive lineman, where he thrived.

The Original 10—and No. 11

The Panthers' "Original 10" were wide receivers **Willie Green** and **Eric Weir**; tight end (and future offensive tackle) **Matt Campbell** and TE **Lawyer Tillman**; running backs **Randy Cuthbert** and **Tony Smith**; and offensive linemen **Kevin Farkas, Mike Finn, Carlson Leomiti**, and **Darryl Moore**.

Green and Campbell both made a lasting impact—the other eight never really could get on the field for Carolina. But there was also an "11ᵗʰ Panther" who started for a while. That was offensive lineman **Matt Elliott**—who was supposed to be included in the first 10, but whose contract details didn't get worked out until a month later. Elliott was called the "Lego Lineman" because he was smart enough to learn every position on the line and thus could fit anywhere.

But, like every person in the world, these 10 had a story to tell. Offensive lineman Darryl Moore, for instance, came from a small town in Louisiana. His mother had lost four children in a horrific house fire. She prayed for a "replacement child" for each one of those she had lost, and Moore was one of those replacement children. I went down to Louisiana to write the Moore family's story and came away deeply moved by it.

Carlson Leomiti was a huge Samoan offensive lineman and also a talented musician. After that first news conference, Leomiti played the piano and sang the song "Easy" by the Commodores. Unfortunately, it wasn't easy for Leomiti to keep his weight down—it sometimes neared 400 pounds—and he never played a down in a real game for the Panthers. There were other stories like that among the other players. But the ones that people most remembered were those associated with Green and Campbell, since they played the longest and the best of that charter class.

One of their best combined moments came in 1996, when Carolina beat the San Francisco 49ers on the road, 30–24, to clinch a playoff berth. Green caught seven passes for 157 yards and a touchdown. Campbell, playing left tackle by then, held the 49ers' standout pass rusher Chris Doleman without a sack.

Campbell had beaten the odds to make the team after first being seen in a open tryout along with more than 200 hopefuls at Winthrop College in 1994. He made it to the "Original 10" press conference only after getting the day off from his part-time job delivering prescriptions for a Columbia, South Carolina, pharmacy.

Campbell was a tight end throughout 1995, playing in 10 games and actually catching three passes. He ended up playing 69 games for the Panthers altogether and cashed in bigger than any of the other Original 10. After becoming a sought-after offensive lineman in free agency, he signed a contract with Carolina that included a $3.2 million signing bonus.

Green played only two years for Carolina and then left for more money in Denver—the flamboyant receiver got a $900,000 signing bonus to go there—and caught passes from John Elway for a while. Green would later return to North Carolina after retiring and was an entrepreneur involved in numerous businesses.

Because Green had already been an NFL starter, being a member of the "Original 10" didn't mean as much to him as it did to the other nine players that day in Charlotte. But for everyone, having the Panthers brought them back into the NFL fold.

"The day didn't really seem like it was real," remembered Farkas—a mountain of a man who went to Appalachian State and stuck around on Carolina's practice squad for a while. "The Panther logo didn't look real. No one was used to it yet. It didn't look or feel much like a real NFL team. We didn't even have a coach yet. But it sure was fun."

58 Rod "He Hate Me" Smart

If not for his nickname, Rod Smart would just be another nondescript Panthers player. He scored just one career touchdown. He was a reliable special-teams player for four years, but not an exceptional one like Michael Bates.

Yet Smart made one move early in his career that had "marketing genius" stamped all over it, and it followed him ever since. That's why Panthers fans still smile when they talk about Rod "He Hate Me" Smart, and that's why you still see an occasional No. 32 jersey in Bank of America Stadium with Smart's nickname embossed on the back.

Before he got to the NFL, Smart played running back in the XFL—a forgettable version of minor-league football that lasted only for one season in 2001. The XFL was always trying to be edgy, and one of the things it allowed was for players to put a nickname on the backs of their jerseys instead of their real name. Smart's was "He Hate Me," and he was the XFL's No. 2 rusher that year. The moniker was so memorable that it stuck with him the rest of his career.

Smart came up with the nickname himself as an updated version of the old Rodney Dangerfield "I don't get no respect" refrain. The "He" in question was any coach who wouldn't play Smart, or any personnel man who wouldn't draft him or who would later fire him (Smart was cut by Philadelphia and San Diego, as well as the CFL's Edmonton Eskimos, before sticking with Carolina).

As Smart explained once, "Football is very political at the pro level. And because I came in [to every training camp he went to] as the last back, if I didn't get a carry, I'd talk to the other running

From the XFL to the Super Bowl: Rod "He Hate Me" Smart revels in Super Bowl media day festivities in 2004.

backs and say, 'He hate me, man. This coach hate me.' I was always saying that."

Smart played collegiate football as a running back at Western Kentucky and wasn't drafted. He struggled to find a spot in the NFL. So when he got there, he didn't mind sticking out. His lone Panthers touchdown—a 100-yard TD on a kickoff return in 2003—was punctuated by Smart beating his chest six times. He also blocked a punt in 2003 that forced a safety and ended up being crucial to the Panthers' opening-day win against Jacksonville.

Other than that, Smart wasn't really hated or loved much as a Panther—he made a lot of special-teams tackles and came close to scoring on a few other kickoff returns. He did break another one for a TD once, but it was called back due to penalty.

But the best thing about it, as far as Smart was concerned, was that he had an NFL job for four seasons. And the best thing about it, as far as Panthers fans were concerned, was that he provided the team with the best player nickname it has ever had.

59 Go to the Panthers' Free Days

You certainly can debate whether a Panthers game is worth the money. I think everyone should experience a home game in Bank of America Stadium at least once, but those who shell out several hundred dollars to take their family to a game only to watch the Panthers get shelled themselves usually don't feel real good about that expenditure walking out of the stadium. That's understandable.

There are two days every year, however, when the Panthers open their stadium to the public and you absolutely can't beat the price: it's free. It's worth checking out either or both.

One is in late April for the Panthers' draft party, a fairly recent tradition. The other comes in early August and used to be reserved for permanent seat license holders but is now open to all: a team practice that is generally held the Saturday before the Panthers' first exhibition game.

The Panthers announce the dates for both several weeks or months in advance, and you can always check the team's official website (www.Panthers.com) for details about when to come and what is provided on each day.

Other Bank of America Stadium Events

The Panthers control access to their stadium and are very particular about renting it out, so it isn't used as a venue for other big-ticket events very often. Here are a few that have been in the stadium, however, since it opened in 1996:

- Billy Graham crusade (1996)
- Rolling Stones concert (1997)
- Kenny Chesney / Tim McGraw concert (2012)
- Belk Bowl (college football bowl game held annually in late December)
- ACC football championship (several times in early December)
- International soccer matches (several times—one game featuring Mexico drew 63,227 fans)

The draft party is a one-night event during the three-day NFL Draft weekend. Sometimes the Panthers host their party on the first day of the draft—which is on a Thursday—and sometimes they wait until the third and final day because that's Saturday and more people are off from work and school. The Panthers not only open the stadium and broadcast national NFL Draft coverage on big screens, but they also give free behind-the-scenes tours of the team's locker room and weight room. This serves as the only chance most fans will have to see either one of those places (check out the excerpts of Sam Mills' "Keep Pounding" speech on the weight-room wall if you go).

Fans also can go on the playing field on that night to participate in a kid-oriented NFL "combine," where kids can kick field goals and throw and catch passes. A few former Panthers players, team mascot Sir Purr, and the team cheerleaders are usually around to interact with fans. Food and drinks are available for purchase. Panthers-themed vehicles are often on display. It's a good time.

The August event is a little more serious—there are no locker room tours during that one and no field access for fans, either. And it's always hotter, since it's in the afternoon. By then, the team is in training camp in Spartanburg (where practices can also be watched for free from late July to mid-August). The Panthers traditionally make a one-day trip to Charlotte to allow fans to take a look at the newest version of the Panthers.

While in the early years the Panthers would design the event almost like an intrasquad scrimmage—memorably, one year Fred Lane had a great afternoon and it helped him make the team—in recent years it has become not much more than a glorified practice, with very little tackling in order to prevent injury.

Still, the stadium is open, the event is free, and thousands of fans always attend. For many supporters near Charlotte, it's easier to go to the free August practice than to drive down to Spartanburg to see basically the same thing.

Also, at the end of the practice, the players all walk to the edge of the field and sign autographs for at least 10 minutes or so. You can't get everybody you want—there are too many fans clamoring for signatures and too little time—but you can always get a few if you stick around for the entire practice (which usually lasts around 90 minutes).

Charles Johnson

It took Charles Johnson a while to figure out the NFL game. In his first three seasons, he had combined totals of only five starts and 10 sacks.

But beginning in 2010, Johnson became one of the best pass rushers in Panthers history. The defensive end out of Georgia parlayed an 11.5-sack season in 2010 into a whopping six-year, $76 million contract extension, which led media outlets to tag him with the nickname "Big Money." Johnson earned his cash big-time in 2012, posting a career-best 12.5 sacks and also ranking second in the entire NFL with seven forced fumbles.

Johnson's teammates just call him "Chuck." In contrast to boisterous defensive end Greg Hardy, Johnson is a quiet guy from rural Georgia who prefers not to draw attention to himself. He leads more by example than words—you would never, ever see Johnson do a Ray Lewis sort of pregame dance. But he does lead well enough that the Panthers gave him a *C* for captain on his jersey midway through the 2012 season once Jon Beason got hurt, asking Johnson to step up even more on a team where he is clearly one of the best players.

"I felt like I always was a leader on the field, but that *C* made it official," Johnson said at the time. "I'm trying to be a more vocal leader. That takes time. But we're growing as a defense, and we have to keep growing."

Johnson now ranks third on the Panthers' all-time sacks list, trailing only Julius Peppers and Mike Rucker. He passed Kevin Greene in 2012, a season for which some thought Johnson should have received Pro Bowl consideration (Johnson has yet to make the all-star game).

The Panthers took Johnson in the third round of the 2007 draft, and he didn't become a full-time starter until 2010. In a dark 2–14 season that year, he was probably the team's MVP, once posting sacks in six consecutive games. Johnson's best individual game came in 2012 in the first game against Atlanta—Johnson recorded a franchise-record 3.5 sacks of Falcons quarterback Matt Ryan.

Johnson has been helped considerably by the emergence of Hardy, who endangers quarterbacks from the other side. In 2012, the two became the first Panthers duo since 2002 to each register double-digit sacks (Hardy had 11). Given the Panthers' long-term commitment to Johnson, it seems quite possible that his best years in a Carolina uniform are still ahead of him.

Greg Hardy

The Panthers have had their share of characters over the years, but probably the biggest one on the current team is defensive end Greg Hardy.

Hardy calls himself the "Kraken" on game days, referring to the mythological sea monster, and he takes his alter ego quite seriously. He paints his face. He sticks in either black- or white-colored contacts. He writes "Kraken" on a strip of tape and covers the name on the back of his jersey (he peels the tape off before the pregame warm-ups—it's against NFL rules to doctor up a uniform in such a fashion during a game).

"The Kraken is a giant monster that just demolishes everything that moves," Hardy told me once. "On Wednesday or Thursday,

---

Top Panther Sack Tandems

The sack-happy season of 2012 for Charles Johnson and Greg Hardy was the second-best in Panthers history. A look at the best duos over team history:

1996—Kevin Greene (14.5) and Lamar Lathon (13.5) combine for 28 sacks, still the team record. Greene nicknames the duo "Salt and Pepper."

2012—Charles Johnson (12.5) and Greg Hardy (11) post 23.5 sacks, with each having at least three in a single game.

2002—Julius Peppers (12) and Mike Rucker (10) post 22 sacks, even though Peppers is sidelined during this, his rookie year, with a four-game NFL suspension for taking a banned supplement.

1998—Greene (15) and Sean Gilbert (6) combine for 21 sacks, with Greene doing most of the heavy lifting as a pass-rushing linebacker in Dom Capers' 3-4 defense.

2008—Peppers (14.5) and Johnson (6) combine for 20.5 sacks in a season that was the Panthers' most recent playoff season.

Greg Hardy releases the Kraken in a game against Green Bay in 2011.

I go down in my subconscious. I find him, and I unlock the cage. About Saturday he usually comes out. Then he's always out on Sunday. I don't control him then. What he does when I'm not there, I don't know."

This is all viewed as harmless fun by his teammates, particularly since Hardy has emerged as such a force. Keep calling yourself the Kraken, they say, as long as you're finding the quarterback.

In high school, Hardy was a teammate of offensive tackle Michael Oher, whose life inspired the book and movie *The Blind Side*. The two practiced against each other not only in high school but also in college at Mississippi and remain good friends.

A sixth-round draft pick out of Ole Miss in 2010, Hardy was once viewed as a first-round talent until injuries and attitude issues caused him to plummet down draft boards. But he was such an athlete—Hardy also caught three passes for Mississippi in his career, all for TDs—that the Panthers took a chance on him and it has paid off.

After a modest seven sacks in his first two seasons, Hardy had 11 sacks in 2012. He teamed with Charles Johnson (12.5 sacks) to post the second-best combined sacks total ever for a Panther pair—their 23.5 sacks trails only Lamar Lathon and Kevin Greene's combined 28 in 1996.

Hardy's happy-go-lucky ride through life has had its problems. In 2011, he had a motorcycle wreck that left him with severe abrasions and a foot injury and sidelined him throughout most of the preseason. "I thought I was going to be dead," Hardy said of the wreck.

In 2012, he posted a picture on Twitter that appeared to show him driving in excess of 100 miles an hour. Coach Ron Rivera has given him the "you gotta be more careful" talk more than once.

But man, can Hardy run. He has even occasionally played outside gunner for the Panthers' punt coverage unit, a position usually reserved for defensive backs who might weigh 80 to 100 pounds less than the 6'4", 290-pound Hardy. His athleticism is so outlandish—in Julius Peppers fashion, Hardy played a while for the Mississippi basketball team—that Johnson swears that Hardy could be the best defensive end in the NFL one day. Johnson has no problem saying Hardy has "more ability than me."

"He's in his own world sometimes," Johnson said. "But he's a freakish athlete."

62 Trying to Trade for Peyton Manning

Before Cam Newton, the Panthers tried for years to find a franchise quarterback. The closest they ultimately came was the rip-roaring Jake Delhomme—although Delhomme himself would tell you he didn't fit the classic description of what a franchise quarterback should be.

But the Panthers did make the effort. For instance, they tried to trade for Peyton Manning.

More specifically, they tried to trade for the pick that *became* Manning. This was in 1998. Bill Polian, the former Panthers general manager, had left Charlotte after the 1997 season for more money and more power with the Indianapolis Colts.

Polian was a major Kerry Collins guy. Polian had drafted Collins No. 5 overall—the Panthers' first-ever pick—out of Penn State in 1995. He had been a Collins defender in front-office meetings, even when the quarterback would get in off-the-field trouble.

The Panthers, however, weren't as sold on Collins. They wanted Manning, who at that time was coming out of the

University of Tennessee. Some NFL teams liked Manning. Some liked Ryan Leaf. The Panthers liked Manning.

So negotiations began. Polian said publicly he would want a "king's ransom" if the Colts were to give up the No. 1 pick, which they had gotten by virtue of having the worst record in the NFL in 1997. The Panthers tried to make him an offer he couldn't refuse: Collins, wide receiver Muhsin Muhammad (who had just finished his rookie year and had also been drafted by Polian), and a slew of draft picks.

"I thought Bill would do it because he wanted Kerry," Panthers owner Jerry Richardson would tell the *Charlotte Observer* many years later.

But Polian ultimately declined that offer and all the others that the Colts received. He held onto the No. 1 pick and drafted Manning, who will become a surefire Hall of Famer and is one of the best quarterbacks in NFL history.

Collins, meanwhile, would quarterback only four more games for Carolina before his controversial "my heart's not in it" conversation with coach Dom Capers that would lead to Capers waiving him later in 1998. Collins did recover from his various problems, of course, and wound up playing 17 years in the NFL. Polian would rehire him years later in trying to replace an injured Manning in Indianapolis. That experiment was unsuccessful, as Collins quickly got hurt himself.

But what if that trade had been made in 1998 and the Panthers had had Manning as their quarterback for the next decade or so? How many playoff appearances would they have made? How many championships would they have won?

Instead, Polian said no, and what would have been one of the biggest days in Panthers history vanished into smoke.

63 Marty Hurney

The longest-serving general manager in Panthers history, Marty Hurney was a former sportswriter who worked for the team for 15 years before being abruptly fired midway through the 2012 season.

Although the end of his tenure was stark, Hurney had an excellent run at times with Carolina, putting together three playoff teams, one of which advanced to the Super Bowl. While most NFL GMs only get to hire one head coach—and last as long in their own job as that coach does—Hurney got to hire two. He tabbed New York Giants defensive coordinator John Fox for the head job in 2002, and for nearly a decade after that the two seemed to be joined at the hip.

After Fox and the Panthers parted ways following the 2010 season, Hurney was retained as GM and hired coach Ron Rivera. But when Rivera's second team began the 2012 season with a 1–5 record, Panthers owner Jerry Richardson put aside his longtime friendship with Hurney and fired him.

That ended Hurney's 15-year run with the team. Hired in early 1998 from San Diego after Bill Polian left for Indianapolis, Hurney worked with all four Panthers head coaches, starting as a salary-cap expert and contract negotiator for Dom Capers and George Seifert and then assuming more responsibility until he was promoted to GM in 2002.

Hurney's biggest regret was that the Panthers never had consecutive winning seasons during his tenure—indeed, they have never been able to do that in franchise history. He was gracious following his dismissal, saying he understood it was time because Richardson had to "make changes to change an atmosphere that really has become a losing environment."

Hurney's Hits and Misses

Five of Hurney's best and worst moves as Panthers general manager:

Best Moves

- Drafted three NFL Offensive or Defensive Rookies of the Year with high first-round choices: Cam Newton, Luke Kuechly, and Julius Peppers.
- Signed Jake Delhomme and Stephen Davis to relatively inexpensive free-agent contracts in 2003. Both were essential to the Panthers' Super Bowl run.
- Drafted Jon Beason, Ryan Kalil, and Charles Johnson in his best draft (2007); all three became cornerstones of the franchise.
- Hired John Fox in 2002, the head coach who took the Panthers to three of their four playoff appearances.
- Traded third-round pick to Chicago in 2011 for tight end Greg Olsen, who immediately became one of Newton's favorite targets.

Worst Moves

- Traded three picks to Philadelphia, including a first- and second-rounder, to be able to pick tackle Jeff Otah at No. 19 overall in 2008. Otah was an injury-prone disappointment.
- Traded up with New England to acquire Appalachian State quarterback Armanti Edwards in the third round in 2010, and then converted him to a wide receiver. The second-round pick the Panthers gave up wound up being the 33rd overall choice in 2011. Edwards has struggled with the position change and never has become the electrifying player Hurney envisioned.
- Drafted second-round busts Dwayne Jarrett, Everette Brown, and Eric Shelton.
- Fired kicker John Kasay in favor of hiring Olindo Mare, who didn't last long and showed little of Kasay's ability to come through in the clutch.
- Overloaded the team with high-paid running backs (DeAngelo Williams, Jonathan Stewart, and Mike Tolbert) in a league that was becoming more passing-oriented, lessening the Panthers' ability to spend that money in other ways.

That was indeed the case. While the Panthers compiled the seventh-best record in the NFL from 2002 to 2009—the first eight years of Hurney's span as GM—they fell off a cliff after that. From the beginning of the 2010 season to October 2012, when Hurney was fired, the team went 9–29—the worst mark in the NFL in that span.

Hurney said in a conference call with several reporters shortly after being fired that the Panthers lacked a take-charge leader like Ray Lewis, the Baltimore linebacker who fueled the Ravens for so many years. "It just seems like when you get in a situation where you lose close games, the teams tend to lose close games throughout the season," Hurney said. "And the teams that win close games do it. So somebody has got to step up and say enough is enough."

Like all personnel men, Hurney had some hits and misses. His most notable hits occurred in the first round of the NFL drafts, when he picked players like Cam Newton, Luke Kuechly, Jon Beason, Jordan Gross, and Julius Peppers. The Panthers had a history of misfiring on first picks before Hurney started making the final call—Jason Peter, Rashard Anderson, and Rae Carruth, to name three—but he was very good with them.

Hurney's most notable misses often came in later rounds, and he occasionally made decisions seemingly out of misguided loyalty. Hurney signed a number of the players he drafted to huge contract extensions, which often kept the Panthers on the brink of salary-cap "jail" for much of his tenure and certainly consigned them there for some time once he left.

Overall, the Panthers went 80–86 in the regular season and 5–3 in the playoffs during his time at GM.

64 Tailgate Before a Panthers Game

If you are running late to a Panthers game, you can certainly arrive 30 minutes before kickoff and rush to your seats. But this approach—while it might work just fine for a movie theater—leaves out part of the joy of the NFL experience.

The anticipation of a Panthers game is sometimes about as much fun as the game itself. So many fans tailgate before Carolina games, much like pro and college football fans around America do.

Because Bank of America Stadium is located in uptown Charlotte, there is no enormous centralized parking lot that can hold tens of thousands of fans. Instead, fans are spread over a multi-block area. It gives the tailgating a more community feel. Fans frequently buy a parking pass that entitles them to park in the same spot each Sunday, and they get to know their neighbors through games of cornhole or throwing a football around with the kids.

Food? Oh, yeah. It's a communal experience—better and cheaper outside, as a rule, than inside the stadium itself. Carnivores are happy at most Panthers tailgates, since barbeque, hot dogs, hamburgers, and grilled chicken or steaks are an essential part of many Panthers tailgate experiences.

As for drinks, since it's the South, the tea is just about always served sweet. And of course a few alcoholic beverages are consumed as well.

If you're coming to a single Panthers game and don't have a reserved spot, don't fret. There are plenty of places that sell parking on a single-game basis, usually from $10 to $40 per spot, depending on how close you want to be to the stadium. If you arrive a couple of hours before the game, you have time to eat, socialize, and leisurely walk to your seat in the stadium (leaving time for the inevitable security check at the gate).

Some fans never make it inside the stadium at all. Instead, they go to tailgate with their friends, and then go back home to watch the game itself back on the comfort of their own couch in front of their big HDTVs. Since the Panthers games always sell out and thus are never blacked out, that works, too.

65 Really Weird Losses

Stick around long enough in the NFL and you're going to lose a lot of games. The Panthers have lost more than 150 times in franchise history, and most of them have been of the garden variety. The other team simply played better.

Turnovers often were an issue. In 1998, for instance, the Panthers managed to turn over the ball at or inside the other team's 1-yard line a staggering 10 times over the course of the season, giving up 70 possible points in the process. That's a sure way to go 4–12.

But a few losses stick out over the years. In this section, I'm not talking about significant losses, such as the Super Bowl defeat to New England or the Panthers' other playoff losses. Those are covered elsewhere in this book. The following three losses were relatively insignificant in comparison, but they were so darn weird that they are still remembered by Panthers fans (especially the masochistic ones) all these years later. In chronological order:

1997: Johnson to Johnson

The Panthers were tied 7–7 with Minnesota in the fourth quarter, trying to make a goal-line stand. It was third-and-goal for the Vikings from the Carolina 3.

Minnesota quarterback Brad Johnson faded back, fired—and had the ball swatted into the air by Panthers nose tackle Greg Kragen. Incomplete pass, right?

Wrong. Johnson alertly caught the ball in the air and carried it into the end zone for a TD, ostensibly "throwing" the pass to himself. It was believed to be the first time in NFL history that a quarterback threw a TD pass to himself.

The official box score read: "Johnson 3 pass from Johnson." Minnesota won, 21–14. Said Johnson, "It was a play that I think will go into the memory banks of Vikings fans for years to come."

2002: Grant's Tomb

In John Fox's first season as Carolina head coach, the Panthers were 3–2 and absolutely dominating Dallas on the road. Carolina led 13–0 with less than five minutes left in the game. The Cowboys were stuck at their own 20 and had the inconsistent Quincy Carter at quarterback.

But then Panthers safety Deon Grant made a bad mistake. He thought he had an interception and cut in front of Dallas receiver Joey Galloway on a mid-range pass. Grant instead only succeeded in deflecting the ball—directly to Galloway. The Cowboy caught it and gratefully sprinted 80 yards for a touchdown.

After that freak play, the Panthers collectively collapsed. The offense couldn't hold the ball, the defense allowed Dallas to convert two fourth-and-long plays on another TD drive, and the Cowboys ended up winning 14–13. The last Dallas TD came on yet another tipped ball. An uncharacteristically emotional Fox said afterward he was more "ashamed" of that defeat than any he had ever suffered.

Dallas running back Emmitt Smith summed it up from the other sideline, saying, "It showed God has a sense of humor."

2012: Nakamura's No-No

The game that changed the 2012 season for the worse came in Atlanta on September 30, 2012, when the Panthers outplayed the Falcons for most of the afternoon. Then came the last two minutes.

First, Cam Newton fumbled on third-and-short on a running play that would have picked up a game-sealing first down. The Panthers recovered, but coach Ron Rivera then made the conservative decision to punt on fourth-and-1 from the Falcons 45. The punt pinned the Falcons back at their own 1, down 28–27 with no timeouts and 59 seconds left.

But Matt Ryan reared back and threw the ball as far as he could, in the direction of Roddy White. Panthers safety Haruki Nakamura had one primary responsibility on the play—don't allow a deep ball—and he blew it. White got behind Nakamura and basically picked the ball off the safety's helmet for a stunning 59-yard gain to the Panthers 40. A couple of short completions later, and Atlanta won 30–28 on a Matt Bryant field goal. A fired-up Ryan started shouting from the sideline for the Panthers to get off the Falcons' field and go home (but he didn't say it quite that nicely, and the Panthers remembered it well when they beat the Falcons in Charlotte two months later).

Nakamura's no-no was only part of one of the worst Carolina defensive back performances. Although he made an interception early in the game, he also had earlier allowed two TD passes to White and whiffed on a tackle that turned a dump-off pass into a 60-yard TD for Atlanta's Michael Turner.

"Basically I cost us the game," Nakamura said afterward. No doubt. It was a preposterous, scarring loss, and it influenced the rest of the 2012 season.

The Richardson Brothers and Danny Morrison

One of the strangest days in Panther history came on September 1, 2009, when Carolina owner and founder Jerry Richardson publicly split with his sons.

Mark and Jon Richardson had both been heavily involved with the Panthers for more than 15 years and had been expected to succeed Richardson as the team owners. Instead, they suddenly resigned their posts as team presidents in a statement released by the Panthers just before the 2009 season began.

Mark had run the team's business operations, while Jon had been in charge of Bank of America stadium. It was widely reported, via unnamed sources in the *Charlotte Observer* and in other places, that the two brothers did not get along well and that the elder Richardson, who was 73 at the time this happened, decided it was time for both of them to step down.

What exactly led to the events of that day has never been fully explained. It only added to the oddity that Jon Richardson was already involved at that time in what turned into a decade-long fight with cancer. He would die in July 2013, at age 53.

The Richardson sons did remain a part of the franchise's ownership group after their resignations, and Mark is in that group to this day.

Only one day after the brothers' stunning resignations, Jerry Richardson hired Danny Morrison as the team's new president. Morrison was the athletic director at Texas Christian University in Fort Worth at the time. But he had previously been the AD at Wofford College in Spartanburg, where the Panthers train each summer. He and Richardson each graduated from Wofford, although decades apart, and Richardson had been impressed with the way Morrison ran the school's athletic program and got Wofford ready for the Panthers' arrival every July. Morrison also had helped TCU enjoy a great deal of success in numerous sports.

Morrison would eventually become the front man in successfully negotiating with the city of Charlotte about major renovations for Bank of America Stadium in 2012–13. He quickly assumed the roles Mark Richardson had played.

Extroverted and smart, Morrison is certainly an able front-office man. But there remains a fascination among Panther fans as to what exactly happened to the brothers and their father and why the "family business" was no longer really in the family after September 1, 2009. It is now unclear what will happen to the team when Richardson dies—although it seems most likely it will be sold to a new owner.

Mark Richardson, who was born a year after Jon, had been one of the successful pitchmen for the Panthers' expansion effort way back in the late 1980s and was officially considered the team's first employee. He played college football at Clemson. A dapper dresser who favored expensive suits, Mark went through a well-publicized divorce in Charlotte but otherwise had stayed fairly under the radar. He worked mostly on marketing.

Jon Richardson was the oldest of Jerry and Rosalind Richardson's three children. He was the brother who managed the stadium, wore jeans and liked to eat lunch at down-home Charlotte diners that served a meat and two vegetables. He had a ready smile, never seemed to be in a huge hurry and was a devout Christian. He was a good athlete, too – a two-year starter at wide receiver for North Carolina in college. Panther players liked him as well.

"Jon Richardson was the most humble person I've ever met," said Dwight Stone, a special-teams standout on the first four Panther teams. "He was such an outstanding guy—working behind the scenes, not ever caring who got the credit. He made a great difference in my life, and in the life of the Panthers just as they were getting started."

It is not unfathomable that Mark Richardson will resurface into the public eye at some point, although it appears unlikely. He also has a sister, Ashley Allen, who is part of the Panthers ownership group as well. She remains on good terms with her father.

Cam Newton's 72-yard TD Run

It was one of those "location" plays—a brief fragment of time that Carolina Panthers fans not only will always remember but will also likely recall where they were when they first saw it.

Cam Newton's 72-yard touchdown run in a 30–20 home win over Atlanta on December 9, 2012 was notable for several reasons—it was the longest run of his career, the longest run by a quarterback in Carolina history, and assured the quarterback's first 100+ rushing yard game in the NFL.

But two other things make the play really stand out as one of the most dazzling in Carolina history. First, wide receiver Steve Smith hustled downfield while Newton was sprinting down the left sideline and was able to take out two Atlanta defenders with a single, devastating open-field block that would later earn him a game ball. Second, Newton had enough left in his tank at the end of the run to do a front flip into the end zone.

Yes, a somersault. Newton wasn't totally happy with it—a Falcons player got a piece of him as he started the flip, so he wasn't able to stick the dismount as effectively as Mary Lou Retton. But it was still a 6'5", 245-pound man doing something so athletic that most quarterbacks could only dream of it.

Said tight end Greg Olsen after the game: "We had a great call there. It was the right time for that look, just like you drew it up

Cam Newton ends his 72-yard run with an exclamation point: a front flip into the end zone for a touchdown.

on paper. But you need a 6'5" quarterback to run 80 yards. That's the problem. Fortunately, we have that."

Well, it wasn't quite 80 yards—just 72. The longest quarterback TD run in the Super Bowl era still belongs to Kordell Stewart, who scampered 80 yards against the Panthers in the same stadium in 1996.

"It was just a zone read play," Newton said of the run in which he first faked a handoff to DeAngelo Williams and then took off down the left sideline. "When I was running I saw No. 23, Dunta Robinson, look back as if the running back had it... The only thing I kept thinking was, *I just can't get caught.*"

The game marked the first time any Carolina quarterback has surpassed 100 yards rushing (Newton ended up with 116). More significantly, it was also the first time any quarterback in NFL history had thrown for more than 250 yards (Newton had 287), run for more than 100 yards, and gotten at least one touchdown passing and running. And it gave Newton his first victory in four attempts against the Falcons, the team he used to cheer for as a kid growing up in Georgia, when he idolized Michael Vick.

Said Newton, "I get hounded so much when I get in Atlanta... I think this game allows me to have a little chip on my shoulder going back home."

Offensive tackle Jordan Gross said after the game that Newton's sideline demeanor had improved late in his second season.

"I tell Cam all the time that the positive energy he brings is as valuable as his athleticism and his physical features," Gross said. "He has a way of getting everybody around him excited about the game and believing we can make good things happen. And that run was part of it. And to see Steve down there in his 12th year, providing a critical block for him—the crowd was excited. That's what our offense needs to be about."

It was one of those magical Sundays—a decisive victory over a fine Atlanta team that would advance to the NFL's final four that season. Too bad it happened for a 3–9 Panthers team that was already out of the playoffs.

Newton's 53-yard screen pass for a touchdown to Williams clinched the win. After that TD, Newton came jogging into the end zone and tried to wrest the ball from Williams to give to a fan. There was a brief, playful struggle between No. 1 and No. 34, and then Newton let the ball go. Williams instead kept the ball and took it to the sideline.

"It has come to a competition of who is going to get the football, " Newton said. "As we call it, the Sunday giveaway. Whoever gets it, I couldn't really care less. Because if we are having those types of arguments, those are good arguments."

There was no argument that Sunday, though. Newton's 72-yard run would be one that Panthers fans would never forget.

Coin Flips

It's rare that a coin flip makes much of a dent in a team's psyche one way or the other.

For the Carolina Panthers, though, coin flips have made the news more often than they have for most NFL teams. Three examples come to mind: one that worked out beautifully for Carolina, one that worked out badly, and one that was so-so. In other words, kind of a coin-flip result—all things ending up even.

The one that worked out beautifully came in 2012, in a coin flip the Panthers actually lost. Carolina and Miami were the contestants, with the winner getting the No. 8 pick in the 2012 NFL draft and the loser getting pick No. 9. Both teams had exactly the same 6–10 records in 2011 and the exact same strength of schedule, forcing the flip at an NFL meeting.

The Dolphins won. With the No. 8 pick in the draft, they selected Texas A&M quarterback Ryan Tannehill and quickly started him. Picking Tannehill wouldn't have done Carolina any good, however—the Panthers already had Cam Newton at quarterback. And with the ninth pick, the Panthers grabbed Boston College linebacker Luke Kuechly, who had a sensational rookie season and was the AP's Defensive Rookie of the Year.

It's been proven true time and again in sports that winning a coin flip doesn't always guarantee the best outcome. For instance, in 1984, the NBA conducted a coin flip between Houston and Portland to decide which team got the No. 1 overall pick. Houston won and picked Hakeem Olajuwon. Portland lost and picked Sam Bowie. But Chicago, which wasn't involved in the flip at all, really won by picking Michael Jordan at No. 3.

The most highly publicized flip the Panthers were ever involved in came in 1994, and they won it. But the outcome was mixed.

At the 1994 NFL Draft, 16 months before the Panthers' first real game, Carolina owner Jerry Richardson and Jacksonville owner Wayne Weaver were the team representatives in a coin flip by NFL commissioner Paul Tagliabue. The winner would get quite a prize— the No. 1 overall pick in the 1995 NFL Draft. The two expansion teams would both participate in that draft for the first time.

The Panthers won that one, and so speculation centered for months on who they would pick. Ultimately, though, general manager Bill Polian traded away the pick to Cincinnati, getting the No. 5 and No. 36 overall picks in return. The Bengals used No. 1 to pick Ki-Jana Carter, a running back who became one of the biggest first-pick busts of all time due to injury problems.

The Panthers fared better than that, but didn't hit the home run you want to hit when originally holding the No. 1 overall pick. With the fifth overall pick, Carolina chose Kerry Collins, who played 3¼ tumultuous seasons as the team's starter. He directed the team to the 1996 NFC title game but was basically allowed to quit the team in midseason in 1998 by head coach Dom Capers. The Panthers picked defensive end Shawn King with the No. 36 overall pick, but his career was short-lived as a Panther, and notable more for his off-field issues than the number of games he started for Carolina (which was two).

The last coin flip that was notable for Carolina was actually a series of coin flips—13 in a row, to be exact, to begin the 2012 season. The Panthers lost every single one of them. The odds of doing that if you tried—losing a coin flip 13 times in a row, or winning 13 times in a row for that matter—is 1 in 8,192. Was there any way to explain this, really, other than the fact that the Panthers have a black cat as their mascot?

One of those 13 lost flips was particularly important, as it came before the overtime period in a game against Tampa Bay. The Buccaneers scored a touchdown on the OT's first possession, so Carolina never got the ball.

The other 12 were during the pregame flip. By rule, the visitor always calls the toss for NFL games. The Panthers were so desperate during the streak that they actually let fans vote on their Facebook page whether to call heads or tails for one game at Kansas City. But the fans missed, too.

Finally, Atlanta broke the coin-flip loss streak on the 14th try of 2012 when the Falcons called the flip incorrectly at a Carolina home game. Panthers fans, well aware of the streak, roared their approval. Panthers captain Jordan Gross was one of the Carolina players at midfield when the streak finally ended.

"I've never heard a crowd cheer so loud for winning a coin toss," Gross said. "It was hilarious. I was pumping my fist. It was awesome."

Newton responded by quickly engineering a TD drive that gave the Panthers a 7–0 lead they would never relinquish in their best victory of the 2012 season, as they beat an Atlanta team that had entered the game with an 11–1 record.

69 The First Win at San Francisco

One of the most unlikely victories for the Panthers came in their 1995 expansion season, when they visited San Francisco for the first time and whipped the 49ers, who were the defending Super Bowl champions.

The Panthers were 15-point underdogs. So their 13–7 win was a stunner—a victory over the most famous team in football at the time. The 49ers had future Hall of Famers Jerry Rice and Steve Young on the roster and a coach—George Seifert—who was three years away from taking over in Charlotte as the Panthers' second head coach.

On this day, though, Young didn't play because of a shoulder injury. That undoubtedly helped, but his backup, Elvis Grbac, threw for 327 yards—the first time the Panthers had ever seen an opposing quarterback go over the 300-yard mark. What undid the 49ers were the five turnovers forced by the Panthers defense, which also scored Carolina's lone touchdown. Seifert later said it was his "team's lowest point" in 13 years, when the 49ers had finished 3–6 in the strike-shortened NFL season of 1982.

Carolina's touchdown came on cornerback Tim McKyer's 96-yard interception return that gave the Panthers a 10–0 lead in the first quarter, just when it looked like the 49ers were about to go ahead, 7–3. On the play, Grbac looked for tight end Brent Jones, but he was well covered, so the QB tried to throw the ball out of bounds. Instead, he threw it to the verbose McKyer, who made the biggest play of his Panthers career.

"My eyes got so large when I saw it coming to me," McKyer said. "The ball kept getting bigger and bigger. When I caught it I said, 'Man, I'm going to take one to the house.'"

The other starting cornerback, rookie Tyrone Poole, forced two fumbles inside the Carolina 5 to save two other potential 49ers touchdowns. Rice, who entered the game with more touchdowns than any player in NFL history, was on his way to another after beating Poole on a play when the Panther punched out the ball at the 1. The ball skipped through the end zone, a touchback, and Carolina took over at the 20.

"I'm human," said Rice, who still had eight catches for 111 yards. "I'll take some of the blame but not all of it."

Poole also tackled San Francisco receiver John Taylor at around the 5 on another series, stripping the ball and causing a fumble that Sam Mills fell on just short of the end zone.

It was that kind of day for the Panthers—one in which every ball seemed to bounce the right way. The Panthers were outgained by 200 yards—404 to 204—and still won.

"This is a very special day for us," coach Dom Capers said.

"Huge," Mills called it.

Rookie quarterback Kerry Collins threw for a modest 150 yards, but the Panthers controlled the ball a little more than half the game by converting on one third down after another. "It seems like one of the more improbable things to come in as a rookie and beat the world champions on their home turf," Collins said.

The win was one of only two the Panthers would have on the road in their first season, as they went 2–6 away from home and 5–3 at their temporary home quarters in Clemson, South Carolina. The 49ers would get revenge a month later in Clemson, creaming Carolina 31–10 when Young returned with 336 passing yards.

That same week, the Charlotte Hornets had made a controversial trade, shipping off their best big man, Alonzo Mourning. "All anyone talked about in Charlotte this week was the Alonzo Mourning trade," Panthers tight end Pete Metzelaars said. "Maybe it's time to change the subject to us."

70 Ricky Proehl

Ricky Proehl made a lot of plays in 17 years as a pro receiver, including 669 receptions and 54 touchdowns while playing for six NFL teams.

For the Carolina Panthers, though, Proehl's first touchdown was more important than any of the rest. In his very first game for the Panthers, in 2003, he reeled in a 12-yard TD catch on fourth down with 16 seconds left in the game. That allowed the Panthers to overcome a 17–0 deficit and beat Jacksonville 24–23, cemented Jake Delhomme as the team's starter, and began the run toward the Super Bowl.

Proehl is now the Panthers' wide receivers coach, earning that job after assisting Fred Graves in the role for two years. Coach Ron Rivera let Graves go following the 2012 season and promoted Proehl.

By the time he got to Carolina in 2003, Proehl was already almost a coach on the field. He had been in the league since 1990, after all, after a standout college career at Wake Forest.

The Panthers installed him as their No. 3 wide receiver on what was the most effective trio of wideouts they ever had— Steve Smith, Muhsin Muhammad, and Proehl. All three of them caught a touchdown pass in the Super Bowl that season, and with Delhomme at the controls they helped propel the Panthers to one late-game comeback after another.

Proehl was never a speedster like Smith, but he was crafty, tough, and could sneak behind a defense. He scored eight regular-season TDs for the Panthers in his three seasons. But the team did not re-sign him prior to the 2006, instead signing Keyshawn Johnson.

Proehl seemed to have a knack for getting on—and often improving—good teams throughout his career. He actually caught game-tying Super Bowl passes in the final two minutes of games *twice*—once for Carolina and once for St. Louis. In both cases, coincidentally, field goals by New England's Adam Vinatieri beat his teams.

During his three seasons with Carolina, the Panthers reached the Super Bowl once and the NFC championship twice. Proehl also won a Super Bowl with St. Louis, helping the team get to get there with a spectacular TD catch in the Rams' 11–6 NFC championship victory over Tampa Bay.

And after his time with the Panthers ended, he had one final hurrah. Indianapolis signed him out of semi-retirement late in the season as veteran insurance, so he got a second Super Bowl ring with the Colts in the 2006 postseason. (It may have helped that Vinatieri was on his side that time.)

Proehl then opened a family sports complex and fitness center in Greensboro, N.C., called "Proehlific." But he wanted to become a coach, and Panthers head man Ron Rivera was impressed once when Proehl jumped into a workout for then-college quarterback Blaine Gabbert at Missouri and ran some routes. Ron Rivera hired Proehl in early 2011, a couple of months after getting the head job.

"I really got a big kick out of how much he reminded me of myself—wanting to start, saying, 'Hey, look, I'll do whatever. I'll start at the bottom,'" Rivera said of Proehl. "I used to want that opportunity because I really thought I could help. We were really intrigued by that."

For the Panthers, Proehl has the unique opportunity to coach a player in Smith that he used to team with on the field. But given that Smith knows about all the wide receiving tricks in the book by now, Proehl's knowledge is probably even more valuable as he passes it along to the Panthers' corps of young receivers.

71 Mike McCormack

You could argue that Mike McCormack had the most successful front-office tenure in Carolina Panthers history, even though it was a very brief one.

Panthers owner Jerry Richardson hired McCormack as a consultant in 1989, and his main job was to help Richardson and his partners win an NFL franchise for Charlotte.

"Just his presence gave our ownership instant credibility," Richardson said once.

That's because McCormack by then had already been in the NFL for nearly 40 years. He was a Hall of Fame offensive tackle, earning that honor in 1984 after creating holes for Jim Brown in Cleveland. His old coach, Paul Brown, once said McCormack was "the finest offensive lineman I ever coached."

McCormack then turned to coaching. He was the head coach of three different NFL teams in his career—the Philadelphia Eagles, Baltimore Colts, and Seattle Seahawks. He also served as the Seahawks' president.

So when Richardson hired McCormack in 1989, he got a man known for being "the ultimate gentleman," as Panthers linebacker Sam Mills once described him—as well as somebody that everyone in the NFL offices knew and respected.

The Panthers were awarded an NFL franchise on October 26, 1993. McCormack was the team's first general manager, but later was elevated to president when he and Richardson hired Bill Polian as the GM.

Then McCormack stayed on through the heady first two years of the Panthers—the better-than-expected 7–9 season of 1995 and the NFC Championship Game appearance in 1996. Right after that, McCormack retired, so he got to skip the next six years of playoff misses.

Richardson thought so much of McCormack that he made McCormack the first inductee into the Carolina Panthers Hall of Honor. A statue of McCormack was unveiled outside the stadium in 1997.

McCormack would wonder later if he had retired too soon. He had a year left on his contract, and his moderating influence was obviously missed in the front office. He was 65 by the time the Panthers began play in 1995. He thought he was leaving the team in the hands of a strong front-office man in Polian—his handpicked successor—but Polian left for the Indianapolis Colts only a year later.

"When I left, I felt it was in good hands and everything would be fine," he said once. Instead, the team slowly unraveled, although McCormack hastens to say that he might not have been able to stop the decline himself. But McCormack, who moved back to the West Coast after his retirement, remained a fan of the team and was cheered by its three playoff appearances in the 2000s. He is still one of the men remembered most fondly from the Panthers' early days.

As Richardson said when announcing McCormack would be the first man in the Panthers Hall of Honor: "Mike is a person who typifies everything the Panthers stand for. We think he's the best benchmark for all of us in the organization. There is no more appropriate person than Mike to start our Hall of Honor. It sets a high standard for all who follow."

72 Visit the Mills and McCormack Statues

Unlike some of the older NFL franchises, the Panthers don't have their own hall of fame that fans can go inside and visit. Maybe that will happen sometime down the road.

In the meantime, though, the Panthers do have a "Hall of Honor"—which is not a hall at all, but is most noticeably represented by two life-sized bronze statues at the northeast corner outside the stadium.

The statues are of former Panther president Mike McCormack and former Panther linebacker and assistant coach Sam Mills. McCormack, the first inductee, was instrumental in securing the Carolina franchise in the first place, and then helped the team get off to a great start in its first two seasons.

Mills played for the Panthers for the first three years of the franchise, making the Pro Bowl in 1996, and then was a steadying influence for the team as an assistant coach before dying of cancer at age 45 in 2005. Both men were respected for their many accomplishments and beloved due to their gentlemanly ways.

There actually is a third inductee in the Hall of Honor, but this one doesn't have its own statue. In 2004, the permanent seat license holders who helped make the stadium and franchise possible were honored. The Panthers sold more than 60,000 PSLs to help fund the construction of Bank of America Stadium.

The names of the three inductees can also all be found inside the stadium on the ring that encircles the stadium between the upper and lower decks.

The McCormack and Mills statues are a ready-made photo opportunity, although they are sometimes overlooked because of the sheer immensity of the six Panther statues that ring the stadium entrances (and which were made by the same sculptor, Todd Andrews).

Panther fans like to play a parlor game of "Who will get their own statue?" There is a committee of one who makes those decisions—team owner Jerry Richardson—and his statue standard is extremely high. McCormack was inducted in 1997 and Mills in 1998, and as of this writing there hasn't been an individual inducted since then. Kicker John Kasay, wide receiver Steve Smith, safety Mike Minter, and several others have all been mentioned as possibilities by fans, and at some point the Hall of Honor is going to need some new statues. The ones of McCormack and Mills have looked lonely, with no new company for more than a decade. Richardson has remained silent on the issue, but he is expected to eventually add a few more names to help fill in this very small hall (and will likely be inducted himself at some future date, although that honor may occur posthumously).

73 Thomas Davis

Some would look at Thomas Davis' right knee and see only a series of scars. Others would see a jagged miracle.

Davis, a Panthers linebacker, returned to play in 2012 after the third anterior cruciate ligament reconstruction on that right knee. He was believed to be the first athlete in any professional sport—and certainly the NFL—to come back from three ACL tears on the same knee.

And he came back at a high level. Originally, the Panthers eased Davis in as a situational backup linebacker. But after a series of injuries, Davis started the final 12 games of 2012 and made 118 tackles, second-best on the team. Offensive tackle Jordan Gross proclaimed that someone "should make a movie" about Davis' return.

It was "tremendous," to borrow coach Ron Rivera's favorite word for Davis' comeback. Davis had missed 39 of a possible 48 games from 2009 to 2011 for the Panthers, with each year cut short due to injury. There was great trepidation surrounding his comeback in 2012 given that, but he made it through the season, missing only one game and providing inspiration in the locker room as a team captain.

How long will that knee ultimately last? Who knows? But the fact that Davis got through a whole season was amazing.

Davis joined the Panthers in 2005, as a first-round pick out of Georgia. The team wasn't sure at first whether it would use him as a strong safety or a linebacker. I still remember what Davis said before he had ever played a game for Carolina when he was asked about his tackling philosophy: "Get to the ball with bad intentions."

Davis turned out to be very fast for an NFL linebacker but a little too slow to be a safety. So the Panthers turned him into a linebacker, and a good one. It's difficult to remember now because of all the knee injuries, but Davis was once considered one of the team's most durable bedrocks. From 2005 to 2008, he played in 62 of a possible 64 games for Carolina.

Then the injuries began—three ACL tears in less than a two-year period. After the third one, Davis admitted, "I thought I was done." But after considering it carefully, he decided that if the Panthers would give him a chance to earn a spot on the 2012 team, he would go through the rehab once more. Once he got the team's blessing, he started working again.

Each time he tore his ACL, his wife, Kelly, would help him through the rehabilitation. Before the 2012 season, linebacker Jon

Beason was often rehabbing alongside Davis, since he had sustained a ruptured Achilles' in 2011.

Beason had been the player most expected to make it through the 2012 season unscathed, but instead he got hurt again and Davis kept on going. One of the most emotional moments for Rivera came after Carolina's 30–20 win over Atlanta in December.

Davis made seven tackles and a key interception against the Falcons, and Rivera presented the Georgia native with a game ball. "I know he really wanted to make it through both Atlanta games," Rivera said. "As a head coach, when you have a guy that looks you in the eye coming off three knee surgeries, he makes you believe in him. And that's what it's really about."

Rivera then got choked up and had to abruptly leave his own press conference, apologizing on the way out.

Davis' comeback had that sort of effect on the people who saw him go through a grueling rehab—day after day, year after year. He became the rare player who got three strikes and still was not out.

74 Greg Olsen

For the first 16 years of the Carolina Panthers, the team had a total of exactly one exciting tight end. His name was Wesley Walls, and he was a lot like a good wide receiver in that 1) he always thought he was open and 2) he could catch just about anything. He was also fortunate not to play under John Fox, who thought a tight end was basically a sixth offensive lineman in disguise.

Then, in 2011, Greg Olsen came along via trade—and the Panthers had their new Walls. Olsen shared many of the routes and playing time during that first season with Jeremy Shockey, but then became an every-down tight end in 2012 and had a superb season in which he broke several of Walls' single-season records.

Olsen's journey to the Panthers was an unusual one. Trades in the NFL are generally uncommon. The Panthers have almost always built their team through the draft and occasional, mostly low-profile forays into free agency. But they got Olsen from Chicago for a future third-round pick—the Bears were de-emphasizing the position at the time under then–offensive coordinator Mike Martz—and it turned out to be one of the best bargains the Panthers have ever gotten.

Olsen is a smart, old-school, detail-oriented tight end whose father was his high school football coach in New Jersey. Olsen also could catch a Lifesaver shot out of a bazooka. To watch Olsen snagging passes from a JUGS machine is to be amazed. Like Steve Smith, Olsen's hand-eye coordination is extraordinary.

So Olsen understandably became a favorite target of Cam Newton. They joined the Panthers the same year and learned the playbook together. In 2012, Newton found Olsen so often that Olsen set Panthers tight end records for catches (69) and yards (843)—although Walls still holds the single-season TD record (he had 12 in 1999; Olsen had five TDs in 2012).

While Olsen was with the Panthers in 2012, he went public with a very difficult personal issue. The Olsens already had one young child, and his wife, Kara, was expecting twins—a boy and girl. But an ultrasound turned up a possible abnormality in the boy's heart. Further testing confirmed that the boy would be born with a congenital heart defect known as hypoplastic left heart syndrome (HLHS), which is marked by an underdeveloped left ventricle and aorta.

The Olsens heard about an experimental in-utero surgery that was being performed at a Boston hospital on some babies with HLHS. They booked a flight to Boston for the next day, where they would be accompanied by both sets of their parents as well.

Before they left, though, Panthers team owner Jerry Richardson called Olsen. "Don't get on that flight," Richardson said, "because I've chartered a plane for all of us. And if you don't mind, I'd like to go with you."

That's exactly what Richardson did, accompanying the Olsens for two days' worth of doctors, hospitals, and tests. It was a remarkable thing to do, the Olsen family thought. And although it turned out their son was not deemed to be a good candidate for the surgery, they never forgot the gesture.

In fact, they made one of their own. When their son was born, they named him T.J.—with the initial *J* standing for "Jerry" in honor of the Panthers' owner.

T.J. and Talbot, his healthy sister, were born in October 2012. T.J. underwent the first of three scheduled open-heart surgeries before he was a week old and spent most of his first month of life in a Charlotte hospital, but he was healthy enough to be released from the hospital before Thanksgiving that year.

Olsen grew up in New Jersey and played collegiately at the University of Miami, where he was one of a string of fine Hurricane tight ends (Shockey was another). He was Chicago's first-round draft pick in 2007 and spent four seasons with the Bears before the Panthers acquired him in 2011 via trade and signed him to a long-term contract afterward. Although Olsen was considered a poor blocker early in his career, he has worked on that to the point where he is an every-down tight end now, able to hold his own at the point of attack when called on to do so.

Still, Olsen's forte is receiving. Smith, who in 2007 wished the Panthers would draft Olsen, has said that he believes if Olsen (6'5", 255) dropped some weight that he could play wide receiver in the NFL.

For now, though, Olsen is happy where he is. A fan of country music and the TV comedy *Modern Family*, he likes playing football by day and being a father by night. Olsen is considered one of the

Greg Olsen shows the love to Carolina fans in September 2011.

Panthers' essential building blocks as the team tries to reach the playoffs for the first time since 2008.

Olsen is also known in both Charlotte and Chicago for his charity work. When Olsen was 16, his mother, Susan, was diagnosed with breast cancer in late 2001 and underwent all sorts of treatments. When her hair fell out, she would simply put on a blond wig every Friday night, put a cap on top of it, and go to the football stadium to watch her son play and her husband coach the team. She would later return to her job as a physical-education teacher.

Greg and the rest of his family established a foundation called "Receptions for Research" in Susan Olsen's honor in 2009. It has raised and given away about $250,000 since then, mostly to fund breast cancer research and cancer treatments.

75 Brad Hoover

They're not saying, "B-o-o-o." They're saying "Ho-o-o-o-o-v."

That explanation was given over and over again—both in the Bank of America stands and on television—when Brad Hoover carried the ball and a chorus of yells reverberated throughout the stadium.

Hoover was never a flashy player for the Panthers—except for on one magical Monday night as a rookie—but he was the lunch-pail type who became popular through sheer dint of his effort. He played his entire 10-year career, from 2000 to 2009, for the Panthers after making the team as an undrafted rookie free agent.

Mostly, Hoover was a fullback. He played tailback during his rookie season only, when he subbed in for the injured Tshimanga Biakabutuka and caught everyone's attention by gaining 117 yards rushing in a 31–14 Monday night win over Green Bay. That was when the "Hooooooov" chant first began.

Hoover would never approach 100 yards in a single game again. There were entire *seasons* when he didn't gain 100 yards rushing. He was a battering ram for other running backs for most of his career, opening holes for DeAngelo Williams and Jonathan Stewart in his final season of 2009, the year the two became the first NFL tandem to each run for more than 1,100 yards. Both of the "Double Trouble" backs said publicly they thought Hoover should have made the Pro Bowl that year, but instead he got a pink slip a few months later.

Fullback Fever

The Panthers fullback with the most longevity is Hoover, but several others have played the position with distinction. Here are three of the best:

Mike Tolbert. The Panthers' current short-yardage back made a fine impact in his first year for Carolina, scoring seven touchdowns in 2012. Built like a bowling ball, Tolbert is very hard to stop from a yard away and a surprisingly good receiver.

Howard Griffith. The fullback for the first two Panthers teams was a lethal blocker who compared the act to running your head straight into a garage door over and over every Sunday.

Nick Goings. Like Hoover, Goings was a versatile player who played both tailback and fullback. He had five 100-yard rushing games while playing tailback—four of them consecutive in 2004 after a slew of injuries to the Carolina running corps.

In his entire career, Hoover carried the ball 284 times. Only once did he have a rush of more than 20 yards—a 35-yarder as a rookie. Late in his career, he had an 18-yard run in a game, and punter Jason Baker joked to him, "You can go that far?"

"That's about my limit," Hoover answered.

Hoover was the rare player who played high school, college, and pro football in the same state. He grew up only about 80 miles from Charlotte in Thomasville, North Carolina, where his father was a bus mechanic and his mother an office assistant at a church. He was a tailback in high school—leading the state in rushing as a senior—and then again in college at Western Carolina, a smaller school that he attended after the big ACC schools didn't recruit him. As a Catamount, Hoover had two 1,000-yard seasons.

It wasn't enough to get him drafted in the NFL. "I've always been underestimated my entire career," he said once. "That's pretty much my life story."

He made the Panthers under coach George Seifert, who was impressed because, as Seifert said, Hoover had "multiplicity in his abilities." That was helpful when the Panthers switched him to full-back, which was the key to Hoover's decade-long stay in the league. He was smart and a good locker-room guy, and he didn't mind doing the dirty work. He once had to crawl in pain toward the side-line. It wasn't uncommon for Hoover to peel off his uniform and find imprints of shoulder pads on his skin. He still kept playing.

The end came earlier than Hoover wanted it to. The Panthers replaced him with the younger, cheaper (although not as good) fullback Tony Fiammetta in 2010. The plus side was that Hoover did get to avoid Carolina's horrific 2–14 season—but he would have liked to stay longer.

"Reality has set in and it's here," Hoover said then. "They decided to go with a youth movement and I'm not part of it, and I'm very disappointed that I'm not."

Adding a little insult to injury was the fact that then-teammate Chris Harris sent out the news of Hoover's firing via Twitter before the team or Hoover announced it. Harris was sympathetic to Hoover's plight, but it still wasn't the way Hoover wanted the story to get out.

Hoover and the Panthers always had a good relationship. Coach John Fox in particular liked him. "Brad has been here since the day I arrived in Carolina," Fox said after Hoover was released. "When things were difficult, he was a leader and someone both the players and coaches knew would always be accountable. On the field, he was the ultimate competitor and set a physical tone in both his style of play and attitude."

Hoover has since represented the Panthers on several "goodwill ambassador" types of missions. The stadium replay boards some-times played a message with him and his family urging fans to be good sports. He once announced the Panthers' third-round draft pick from the NFL podium in New York.

He now lives in the Charlotte area. In 2013, he took the head-coaching job at a small charter high school in Monroe, North

Carolina, called Union Academy, where he hopes to teach the values and skills he learned over his own career.

76 Stephen Davis

For Carolina, Stephen Davis was a one-year wonder.

What a year it was, though. In 2003, Davis joined the Panthers, was installed as the team's feature running back, and ripped off 1,444 yards—the largest season total of his career. The Panthers made it to the Super Bowl partly due to a steady diet of No. 48, whose punishing runs made the play-action passes from Jake Delhomme to Steve Smith and Muhsin Muhammad far more effective.

Davis actually had four seasons of 1,300 or more rushing yards in his stellar career, but only his final of those was with Carolina. The other three came for Washington from 1999 to 2001, where he played his first seven NFL seasons after going to college at Auburn.

The Panthers got him in 2003, signing him to a five-year free-agent contract for $15.5 million. Davis had grown up in Spartanburg, South Carolina, so it was a homecoming of sorts for him. At training camp, he was only a 10-minute walk away from the housing project where he grew up, a place where he had been carefully shepherded away from trouble by his mother, whose real name was Queen Elizabeth Davis.

Davis was beastly that first season for Carolina, breaking off one big run after another. One of the biggest came against his old teammates, when he scored on a three-yard, third-down run with 1:09 left to beat the Redskins 20–17 in Charlotte. Davis had the ball knocked from his grasp just after crossing the goal line, but the TD counted.

Davis rushed for more than 100 yards in each of his first four games as a Panther. He said before the season he wanted the ball 300 times as a rusher—he ended up getting it 318 times. And to call him only an inside runner with no burst was incorrect—Davis was a three-time high school champion in South Carolina in the 100-meter dash. Even a dozen years later, Davis still had enough speed to break off one 64-yard run in the playoffs for Carolina (although he got hurt on the play). After that first season in 2003, he was suddenly responsible for posting five of the top eight rushing games in Carolina history at the time.

But by the time the 2004 season started, Davis was 30, and most workhorse NFL running backs have a hard time playing at that age. He ended up having microfracture knee surgery in 2004 and missing almost the entire season, and when he came back in 2005, he wasn't the same player. He still had a nose for the goal line, scoring 12 times, but he gained a modest 549 yards and lost his starting job in the middle of the 2005 season to DeShaun Foster.

The Panthers released Davis before the 2006 season in a salary-cap move. He played ineffectively for one more season, with St. Louis, before retiring with 8,052 rushing yards and 65 rushing TDs. In 2012, he would join one of the lawsuits against the NFL for concealing the long-term effects of concussions. Davis, who lives with his family in Columbia, South Carolina, told a reporter from the *Washington Times* then that due to repeated concussions his short-term memory was iffy, that he suffered from headaches and blurred vision and that he no longer liked to be in sunlight.

In 2003, though, Davis was a bright light for the Panthers, literally carrying them to victory in several games while earning a visit to the Pro Bowl. When the Super Bowl season comes up, his is always one of the first names mentioned.

77 DeShaun Foster

In the category of "What Might Have Been Except For Injury" for the Carolina Panthers, save a locker for DeShaun Foster alongside players like Dan Morgan, Patrick Jeffers, and Tshimanga Biakabutuka.

Foster, a second-round pick in the 2002 draft, was long thought by the Panthers brass to be a potential 1,000-yard rusher and game-changer at running back. Occasionally, he would look like one—especially in the playoffs. Foster had several huge playoff moments—a 33-yard touchdown run in the Super Bowl against New England, a 151-yard rushing day against the New York Giants, and the most dazzling one-yard TD run in Panthers history, at Philadelphia.

But on a week-to-week and year-to-year basis, Foster disappointed. He never gained 900 yards in a single season. Nearly always, injuries played a role. For instance, the week after that 151-yard day against the Giants in the 2005 postseason, Foster broke his ankle against Chicago.

Foster suffered major injuries in three of his first four NFL seasons. Why? Who knows? As Foster said once, "I do have 11 people chasing me. They're all bigger than me."

The Panthers kept Foster around for six years, always as a part-time back. He originally backed up Stephen Davis. Then he became the starter and had DeAngelo Williams as his backup. In early 2008, the Panthers released him and made Williams the starter. Foster would play one more season—a below-average year with San Francisco—before leaving the NFL.

It wouldn't be fair to characterize all of Foster's time as a failure with the Panthers, though—far from it. When the Panthers fired him, he was the team's all-time leading rusher. He still ranks third on that list, behind Williams and Jonathan Stewart. And although he didn't like to be interviewed much and was thus not particularly well known by the Panthers fan base, his coaching staff and the front office thought a lot of him.

Offensive coordinator Dan Henning once characterized Foster this way: "Sometimes he'll surprise us. He's the Jake Delhomme of the running backs. Sometimes, he'll make a play where you say, 'How in the [heck] did he ever make that?' And then he'll miss one."

Said Marty Hurney, the general manager who drafted Foster, nurtured him, signed him to a contract extension, and ultimately released him in early 2008, "He is everything you draw up as a person and a player that we want as a Panther. He's loyal. He's been an excellent player for us. He's done everything we've asked. We certainly wish him the best because he's always going to be at the top of the list when we think about the players who were here."

78 The Reggie White Experiment

"The Minister of Defense" only spent one year with the Panthers—the last of his 15 NFL seasons, in 2000. Having moved to Charlotte and sat out the 1999 NFL season in retirement, he decided to play one more time. The most well-known Christian in the NFL for many years, White said God had led him to play for the Panthers, who signed him to a free-agent contract as a situational pass rusher.

Ultimately, it was a tease of a season—a worthy risk for Carolina that never quite paid off. White had 5.5 sacks, easily the worst season total of his Pro Football Hall of Fame career. Meanwhile, the Panthers went 7–9. White was 38 years old when he signed and he had finally slowed down from the 6'5", 300-pound defensive end who at his peak could run a 4.6-second 40.

Then White retired again—this time for good. And in 2004, on the day after Christmas at his home on Lake Norman just north of Charlotte, he died suddenly at age 43. The cause of death was later determined to be respiratory failure, caused by the sleep apnea White had battled for a number of years.

White's time in Charlotte is remembered in a bittersweet way. The Panthers enjoyed having him for a year. His gravelly, baritone voice was an important one in the locker room during that single season. He was surprisingly playful, doing outlandishly good impressions of Muhammad Ali and Howard Cosell. He was a good mentor to young players like Mike Rucker.

But he wasn't what he had once been on the field. Who could be at age 38?

Still, the Panthers had hoped for more. White had a remarkable career and for a long time had seemed ageless. At age 36, for Green Bay, he had 16 sacks and was the NFL's Defensive Player of the Year. But time had finally caught up with him by the time he got to Carolina, and any Panthers fan would be hard-pressed to come up with any significant highlights for White in that 2000 season.

And then he died far too early. His funeral was in Charlotte and his family—a wife, a son, and a daughter—stayed in the area for many years afterward. So much of what is remembered about White, the Panthers and Charlotte has to do with what might have been rather than what actually was.

White's impact on the NFL is undeniable. He made a record 13 consecutive Pro Bowls (and was inducted after his death into the Hall of Fame, in 2006). He was also a plaintiff in a suit against the NFL that established up the league's current form of free agency. He won a Super Bowl in Green Bay—beating the Panthers in the 1996 postseason on the way there. In the Packers' Super Bowl win over New England, he had three sacks.

An ordained Baptist minister by the time he was 17 and a man who didn't smoke, drink, or swear, Sunday always seemed like a holy day for White no matter how he spent it. He occasionally whispered to offensive linemen he had just run over, "Jesus loves you."

After he retired from the Panthers, White took up an intensive study of ancient Hebrew. He was trying to glean a deeper meaning of the Bible's Old Testament by studying it in its original language, sometimes for hours a day. He told former teammates including Mike Minter that something was being lost in the translation.

On the day White died, Panthers owner Jerry Richardson spoke for many associated with the team when he said, "Like everyone who knew Reggie White, we are saddened and shocked by his passing. We were fortunate to get to know him during the season he played with the Panthers and he remained a good friend of the team after his playing career. We'll miss him."

79 Tshimanga Biakabutuka

Once upon a time, the story of Tshimanga Biakabutuka sounded almost like a fairy tale. With his parents, he moved from Zaire to Montreal at age six, in search of a better life. English was his third language.

His high school in Canada started a football team as a way to ease racial tension and Biakabutuka surprised himself by being extremely good at it. He was the rare Canadian high schooler who went onto the University of Michigan, where in 1995 he rushed for a startling 313 yards to key an upset against Ohio State. His name (pronounced TEE-mong-ah Bee-ahk-ah-buh-TOO-ka) rolled off the tongue during the 1,818-yard season he had for the Wolverines as a junior.

Panthers general manager Bill Polian coveted Biakabutuka—especially after that 313-yard game—and was ecstatic when the running back was still available for the Panthers' No. 8 overall slot in the 1996 draft. Polian's right-hand man, Dom Anile, then the team's personnel director, described Biakabutuka like this as a pro prospect: "He's got excellent acceleration out of the hole. He can break tackles. He's got good long speed. There's certainly no question about durability or toughness."

Almost immediately, though, the questions about his durability began.

Biakabutuka got through four games as a rookie and played relatively well before tearing the anterior cruciate ligament in his knee, which finished him for the season. In 1997, he played in only half the Panthers' games due to lingering effects from that ACL tear, as well as a new rib injury and the emergence of Panthers rookie running back Fred Lane.

That became the pattern for Biakabutuka's six-year career as a Panther. A few flashes of brilliance. An injury—sometimes devastating, sometimes nagging. An unrealized potential.

Occasionally, he could be spectacular—the player the Panthers had thought they were getting when they used such a high draft pick on him. He rushed for more than 100 yards in a game seven times. In 1999, he scored three touchdowns in five carries and ran for 123 yards against Washington—*in the first quarter.*

More often, though, his career could be labeled in one word—a word Biakabutuka used himself to describe it once in our interview: "Frustrating."

Due primarily to injury, he never had a 1,000-yard season. Not even close, really—his best was 718 rushing yards.

Biakabutuka—whose friends sometimes shorten his first name to "Tim"—finished his career in 2001 as Carolina's all-time leading rusher, with 2,530 yards rushing, but that meant he gained only an average of about 422 per season. He has since been surpassed in that category by DeAngelo Williams, Jonathan Stewart, and DeShaun Foster.

Personally, Biakabutuka was always a delight to talk to—spiritual, humble, and boasting a wide range of interests. He would later go into the business field with Charlotte as his home base, attempting several ventures—including owning Bojangles' restaurants and running two high-end, Christian-themed jewelry stores.

It's a shame that the Panthers never really saw the back that Michigan saw in Biakabutuka's junior year of 1995, when his knees were whole and the world was at his feet. But as we all know, fairy tales don't always have a happy ending—at least the ones that haven't been sanitized by Walt Disney. And, at least from a football perspective, Biakabutuka's fairy tale was among them.

80 Hang Out with Sir Purr

Depending on your age, you probably think of Panthers mascot Sir Purr...

...not at all.

...only during the annual mascot football games that remain the most popular halftime show each year at Bank of America Stadium.

...as the best part of any Panthers game or event.

Sir Purr has been a Panthers fixture since the team's inaugural season in 1995. With an oversized, cartoonish black head, a

Sir Purr gets the crowd going with a patriotic display in 2011.

blue Panthers jersey, and an otherwise black outfit that must get devilishly hot in the summer, Sir Purr also has mastered the skill of signing an autograph more legibly than any actual Carolina Panther, despite those big black paws. Seriously. His signature is something to behold. Get it sometime for your kids. And he doesn't charge for photos, either.

While the six-foot-tall furry Panther scares some very small children, who must be reassured that he's "not real," Sir Purr has become one of the most popular features of the team for kids of a certain age.

You would be surprised—or maybe you wouldn't, depending on whether you are mascot-phobic or not—by how many children run straight at him for a hug. He makes numerous appearances at hospitals, schools, charity, and corporate events. (If you want to contact him for some reason, his phone number is 704–358-PURR. Again, I'm not kidding.) Sir Purr has actually performed well outside of the Carolinas, too—in Hawaii, Hong Kong, and New York.

Only once, though, has Sir Purr had a tangible effect on the action in a Panthers game. That happened way back in 1996, when the Panthers' Rohn Stark punted the ball into the end zone in a home game against Pittsburgh.

At the time, Sir Purr was played by a young man named Tommy Donovan. Previously, he had been Cocky, the South Carolina Gamecocks mascot, for three years while in school at USC. Donovan was one of the best Sir Purrs ever—athletic, funny, and always trying to get a rise out of the crowd. He had received national recognition for his work as Cocky. (Yes, there are competitions for mascots, I'm serious—okay, you know that by now.)

Stark's punt reached the end zone. It was still technically a live ball as it bounced around, with no Steeler or Panther within 15 yards. Sir Purr didn't realize it was live, though—and he hopped on it.

When some stern-faced officials approached him, Donovan realized he had overstepped his bounds. He tried to hide behind a goalpost. Then he tried to hide behind a groundskeeper. The head official saw that huge head, though, tracked him down and said to him, "If you want to be out here, you can't come on the field like that."

Donovan was afraid the officials would call a penalty on him for delay of game or something similar. After some consultation, however, they didn't.

Meanwhile, Pittsburgh coach Bill Cowher was almost doubled over in laughter watching the replay of Sir Purr "downing" the punt. Panthers coach Dom Capers, too worried about field position, never cracked a smile.

Later, ESPN would run an on-screen graphic that read, SIR PURR. PUNT RETURNS: ONE. YARDS: ZERO.

81 Mark Fields

Linebacker Mark Fields served as one of the inspirations for the Carolina Panthers in their Super Bowl appearance in 2003.

Like Sam Mills, who by that time was the Panthers linebacker coach, Fields was diagnosed with cancer. His type was less serious than what Mills had. Fields had Hodgkin's disease, which wreaked havoc with his football career but was not life-threatening, as Mills' cancer was.

Fields had an on-again, off-again career with the Panthers because of the cancer. He played well in 2002 for the Panthers, setting a team record with seven forced fumbles. He sat out the 2003 Super Bowl season. He made a stirring comeback in 2004, being voted as a first alternate to the Pro Bowl and then playing in the game itself after one of the other linebackers pulled out due to injury. And then in 2005, he had a recurrence of Hodgkin's disease, sat out another season with the Panthers, and never played in the NFL again. He would ultimately move to Arizona, get into a bit of legal trouble, and decline numerous interview requests.

When Fields was an active Panther, however, he was very popular. While Mills is the one with the statue outside the stadium and the "Keep Pounding" slogan, Fields was the active player in 2003 when Hodgkin's sidelined him. Panthers players wore white T-shirts with both No. 51 (for Mills) and No. 58 (for Fields) under their jerseys during games. Fields did a press conference alongside Mills at the Super Bowl, and then he returned in 2004 with Mills as his position coach.

Fields, a former No. 13 overall pick for New Orleans in 1995, came to Carolina relatively late in his career, at the age of 29. The 2004 season, Fields' last with Carolina, started slowly for him. He became a situational player for the first half of the season and had trouble getting back into football shape. But in the second half of the year he was far better.

In a memorable 37–27 win over San Francisco, he ran a fumble back for an apparent touchdown on one play, only to have the 49ers challenge the call and the fumble get overruled. Undeterred, on the next play, Fields intercepted a pass and returned it to the San Francisco 1 to set up a Panthers TD. Fields would later win an ESPY Award for his comeback in 2004.

An enthusiastic man with a large personality, Fields sometimes kept a talking doll of the singer James Brown in his locker. When you pressed the doll, it sang, "I feel good," echoing one of Brown's greatest hits.

Fields didn't always feel good when he was with the Panthers. But he had some nice moments with the team. And he also is part of its heritage in terms of his No. 58. When Thomas Davis was switching numbers early in his career to denote his change from strong safety to linebacker, he had 47 but wanted 58. Fields wasn't an active player for the Panthers by this time, but as a gesture of respect, Davis asked Fields first if it would be okay.

Fields said sure. So many years after Fields had to leave the NFL due to cancer, No. 58 still roamed sideline to sideline for the Panthers.

Curtis Whitley

Curtis Whitley was a cowboy at heart, favoring a hat, boots, and jeans when he was off the field. When he was on it and unencumbered by the twin demons of alcohol and drugs that haunted part of his adult life, he was a natural at center.

A free spirit who started all 16 games for the Carolina Panthers in their inaugural 1995 season, Whitley played enough that year that the team rewarded him with a new three-year contract entering the 1996 season.

But the NFL suspended Whitley for four games during that 1996 season, and both his life and his Panthers career were ultimately cut short. In a 1997 interview for a book I cowrote with Charles Chandler about the first two Panthers teams, *Year of the Cat*, Whitley told me, "Maybe I'm the example. Maybe I'm the guy *not* to be. Maybe that's my value to this team… Don't be that guy. That may be my place in history for the Carolina Panthers. Who knows?"

In 2008, while living in a small town in west Texas and working in construction, driving heavy machinery, Whitley died inside the mobile home he was renting from his boss. There was no evidence of foul play, but the cause of death was not determined beyond a shadow of a doubt. He was 39.

In 2012, Whitley's two children filed a wrongful-death lawsuit against the NFL, alleging that their father suffered from traumatic brain injuries and multiple concussions which helped explain his behavior and could be linked directly to the six years he spent in the league.

Whitley had some of the deepest Carolina roots of any Panther. Born and raised in Smithfield, North Carolina, on a 200-acre farm, he would sometimes jog along besides his father's tractor as his dad harvested tobacco and beans. He loved horses—riding them, breeding them, and raising them. He had an RV suitable for family camping trips. It boasted a bumper sticker that read, Have you hugged your horse today? He was naturally funny, with a down-home drawl and a quick smile.

Most of his collegiate career was spent at Clemson. He was always one of the strongest players on any team he played despite the fact that he mostly avoided the weight room. "For me, playing football has been easy," he once said. "I've never had to train hard for it." Whitley was an expert at recognizing an opponents' rushing package and calling it out to his fellow offensive linemen. It was his decision-making off the field that got him into trouble.

Whitley's behavior problems began at Clemson. Head coach Danny Ford kicked him off the team in the aftermath of a bar fight, forcing his transfer to a smaller school called Chowan in North Carolina. He begged for another chance when new Clemson coach Ken Hatfield took over and got one. Whitley played well enough then to catch the NFL's attention, although he got sent home early from a bowl game for violating team rules.

The San Diego Chargers drafted him in the fifth round in 1992. He spent three years there, but in 1994 he had a car wreck in which he had run a stoplight while driving drunk and injured another motorist. The Chargers sent him to an alcohol rehab facility. After the 1994 season they made him available in the expansion draft and the Panthers selected him in early 1995.

Whitley became an immediate starter for the Panthers and would sometimes pop an unlit "victory cigar" into his mouth after Panthers wins. As he told me once, "I've always been good with fresh starts for about a year and a half. Then the wheels start coming off."

Whitley started the first 24 games in Panthers history. But a four-game NFL suspension for violating the league's substance abuse policy spelled the end of his time with the Panthers, who never started him in another game and ultimately released him in 1997. He was then signed by the Oakland Raiders and played one solid year for them, but later tested positive once more in violation of NFL policy and was suspended for at least a year by the league. He never played in the NFL again.

Teammates who played with him in the mid-1990s at Carolina still remember "Whit" fondly, as a fun-loving man whom they wish had been able to live a long and happy life. Said quarterback Kerry Collins shortly after Whitley's death, "For those of us who knew Curtis, we are greatly saddened. I considered Curtis a friend who had a huge heart and, like many of us, he battled a number of things during his life."

83 Obscure Panther Quarterbacks

The four most famous quarterbacks in Panthers history are also the four men who hold almost all of the Panthers passing records: Jake Delhomme, Steve Beuerlein, Kerry Collins, and current QB Cam Newton.

Each member of that quartet has his own chapter in this book, in which his career and personality are explored in some detail. The late Jeff Lewis also has his own section, not because he was great, but because the Panthers and specifically coach George Seifert invested so much in him.

But there have been 10 other Panthers quarterbacks who have also made a substantive mark—either good or bad—during the franchise's span. Longtime Carolina fans will remember at least some of these names. Here's a thumbnail look at each of them, ranked in order of the number of regular-season passing attempts for the team. That number is in parentheses.

Chris Weinke (687 attempts): The former Heisman Trophy winner at Florida State had a tremendous beginning to his NFL career, quarterbacking a win in the 2001 season opener as a rookie. It was downhill after that. The Panthers lost 15 straight games and Weinke was basically a backup from then on. At one point, he had lost 17 consecutive starts—then won one in 2006, throwing only seven times in a 10–3 win over Atlanta.

But Weinke did have a few moments. Owner of one of the three 400-yard passing games in Panthers history, Weinke is the only quarterback not named Cam Newton to have one. And, at IMG Academy (a private training facility for athletes), Weinke helped tutor Newton before his rookie season and by all accounts did a fine job.

Rodney Peete (392): At age 36, Peete ended up as John Fox's surprise opening-day starter in 2002 when Fox decided he didn't trust Weinke. Peete was old and slow but threw a pretty accurate ball and seemed to know everybody. He was also funny. Peete would laughingly say his wife, actress Holly Robinson Peete, was more famous than he was. The Reverend Jesse Jackson had officiated their wedding.

Matt Moore (392): An affable Californian, Moore had several good games subbing for Delhomme in the late 2000s, enough so

Panthers TD Passes

Here's a list, current prior to the 2013 season, of all the men who have ever thrown a touchdown pass for Carolina (statistics include only TD passes for the Panthers, not those thrown for other teams):

Player	TD passes
Jake Delhomme	120
Steve Beuerlein	86
Kerry Collins	47
Cam Newton	40
Matt Moore	16
Rodney Peete	15
Chris Weinke	14
Vinny Testaverde	5
David Carr	3
Jimmy Clausen	3
Frank Reich	2
Brian St. Pierre	1
Matt Lytle	1

that the Panthers decided he would be their starter in 2010 and released Delhomme. Then Moore started the 2010 season but got an early hook from Fox, who despite his conservative reputation could be quite mercurial about quarterbacks. Fox inserted Jimmy Clausen in only the third week of the season after Moore proved ineffective early—and that turned out to be a very bad move.

Moore returned later that season but then hurt his shoulder. He would sign with the Dolphins in 2011 when Carolina made no effort to re-sign him and has had some modest success in Miami.

Jimmy Clausen (299): The Panthers' second-round draft choice in 2010, Clausen ended up being the player most identified with the team's 2–14 season. That wasn't totally fair to him—he was a rookie in a tough situation, after all.

But Clausen was also very overmatched all year and was incapable of getting the ball to Steve Smith. The Panthers offense was never so routinely awful as it was under Clausen, who went 1–9 as a starter in 2010 and finished with the NFL's worst quarterback rating.

Vinny Testaverde (172): His best moment came in a one-week period in 2007 when the Panthers signed him off the couch on Wednesday, started him Sunday—and he won against Arizona. In the process, Testaverde (43 years and 335 days old at the time) became the oldest quarterback in NFL history to win a game that he started. He only played that one season for the Panthers before retiring, but Testaverde is still remembered fondly and had a 2–4 record as a Panther starter. While at Carolina, he helped inspire DeAngelo Williams and several other young players with an exemplary work ethic.

Even though he was the Panthers' third quarterback by the end of the season, as a goodwill gesture the Panthers sent Testaverde onto the field to take the final snap of his 21-season career in the last game of the 2007 season.

David Carr (136): He is remembered far less fondly than Testaverde. Carr, a former No. 1 pick for Houston, was supposed to be Jake Delhomme's well-paid backup, ready to take over at a moment's notice. When he did take over for an injured Delhomme in 2007, however, it was mostly disastrous.

All the sacks in Houston had apparently rattled Carr—he seemed skittish and overwhelmed in the pocket. Carr also wore gloves on both hands when playing, which wouldn't have been something people made fun of except that his play was so poor. Carr's gloves made him look a little like Michael Jackson, and he played quarterback in Carolina about as well as Michael Jackson would have.

Frank Reich (84): The author of the greatest comeback in NFL history—Buffalo was down 35–3 to Houston and came back to win a playoff game, 41–38, with Reich at the controls—thought he was going to quarterback the Panthers for much of their inaugural season. Instead, he lasted only the first three games (all losses) before Dom Capers inserted Kerry Collins.

Still, the deeply religious Reich threw the very first TD pass in Panthers history.

Randy Fasani (44): Fasani's brief tenure in 2002—necessary after a slew of injuries at the position—was notable for its futility. He actually had a 0.0 quarterback rating in his lone start, a 12–9 loss to Tampa Bay. He ended his time with Carolina with an 8.8 QB rating. That's only possible if you go 15-for-44 with four interceptions, no TDs, and 171 total yards, which is precisely what Fasani did.

Matt Lytle (30): Weinke can't be held solely responsible for the 1–15 record of 2001. Lytle started one of those games—a 48–14 loss at St. Louis vs. the "Greatest Show on Turf." Needless to say, it didn't go very well.

Brian St. Pierre (28): In another one of those desperation moves, career backup St. Pierre was signed off diaper duty with his young child and made his first NFL start at age 30 for Carolina in 2010.

St. Pierre threw an 88-yard touchdown pass to David Gettis in a 37–13 loss to Baltimore. The game had been close—until St. Pierre threw two interceptions returned for touchdowns in an 11-second span of the fourth quarter. Yes, 11 seconds. He got hurt in his one start for Carolina and never threw another pass for the team.

Others worth mentioning: Jack Trudeau, Brett Basanez, Tony Pike, Dameyune Craig, Josh McCown, Steve Bono, and Derek Anderson, all of whom threw between three and 17 passes for Carolina over the years.

Of this group, the best was Anderson, but because of Newton's durability in 2011–12, the former Pro Bowler at Cleveland has yet to be able to showcase what he could do in a Panthers uniform. The Panthers like him, though, and signed him again as a backup to Newton for the 2013 season.

84 Jeff Lewis

What happened to the late Jeff Lewis while playing for Carolina wasn't totally his fault. He wasn't the guy who pulled the trigger on a trade in which the Panthers shipped a third- and a fourth-round pick to Denver to get him; that was George Seifert. He didn't give himself the "quarterback of the future" nickname at Carolina; that was simply what Seifert wanted him to be. He didn't pay himself millions before he ever took a snap at Carolina; the overzealous Panthers did that too.

But it is undeniable that when given the chance to replace the popular and accurate Steve Beuerlein as the Panthers' starting quarterback in 2001, Lewis blew it. Seifert had fired Beuerlein earlier that year with the idea that it was time to watch Lewis blossom in a starting role, but then reversed field after Lewis had an unimpressive training camp and then two terrible preseason games in a row. Instead, he demoted Lewis to fourth string and then cut him only a few days later, installing Chris Weinke as his starting quarterback instead. Lewis was indeed a mobile quarterback, which was what had made Seifert fall in love with him, but he also turned out to be a quarterback who couldn't make the right decision in the pocket under pressure.

Lewis was classy when asked to exit the premises. "I'm not going to make any excuses, " he said after Seifert released him in 2001. "Obviously, I'm disappointed it didn't work out. I tried as hard as I could. I probably tried too hard."

When asked if anything could have been different about his time at Carolina he said then, "I want to take the high road on this whole thing. I played as hard as I could every time I was out there."

Most Panthers fans lost track of Lewis after that. He never resurfaced in another NFL regular-season game and instead began a career as a football coach. He was an assistant at the University of Louisville for three years. In 2012, he got hired by Northern Arizona to coach wide receivers. It was a good fit—Northern Arizona was Lewis' alma mater, where he had been a four-year starter and a member of the school's hall of fame.

But in January 2013, Lewis died in Phoenix, with the cause of death not fully explained in public. He was only 39. Police did say foul play was not suspected as a cause and that Lewis had a preexisting health condition—but didn't say what it was.

The autopsy report filed by the local medical examiner in Arizona later said Lewis died of an accidental drug overdose. Listed at 6'2" and 211 pounds when he played for the Panthers—he was actually two inches shorter than that—Lewis weighed 265 pounds when he died. The report actually cited obesity as a contributing factor to his death as well as a preexisting heart condition.

His death hit former teammates hard. "Jeff was just a great, lighthearted, clean-cut guy," said Mike Rucker, who played alongside Lewis.

"He was kind of a tough guy, and very competitive," former Panthers safety Mike Minter said. "It didn't work out the way he wanted it to in Carolina, but he was always a guy with high character."

Lewis' death inspired a tweet from John Elway, whom Lewis backed up in Denver during the Broncos' two Super Bowl-winning seasons. Elway called Lewis "a great teammate."

Because the Panthers are a relatively young team, they fortunately have not seen too many of their former players die. Among the deaths the team has suffered besides Lewis are: center Bryan Stoltenberg (who, coincidentally, died one day before Lewis in 2013), linebacker Sam Mills, defensive end Reggie White, defensive tackle Al Lucas, running back Fred Lane, and center Curtis Whitley.

85 Brentson Buckner

The middle of the defensive line is often an anonymous position. The defensive tackle's primary responsibility is generally to use up blocks so that the linebackers can roam freely and make plays. An occasional sack or fumble recovery livens up this grunt work.

Brentson Buckner, however, was far from anonymous in his five seasons with the Panthers. "Buck," as everyone called him, was a quotable football philosopher—a 310-pound man with a full beard who liked to sit in the locker room and pontificate about NFL topics past and present.

Buckner also sported a collection of more than 300 throwback jerseys, and Panthers teammates drew entertainment from watching what Buckner walked into the locker room wearing each day. He once named the five men he most would have wanted to play with in the NFL: "Mean" Joe Greene, Walter Payton, Jack Tatum, Johnny Unitas, and Jim Brown. He got a manicure every two weeks during the season and wasn't afraid to admit it.

"Our hands get so messed up in the season," Buckner said. "I've got to pamper myself a little bit."

No one watched the rest of the league more intently than Buckner, who spent the final five of his 12 years in the NFL with the Panthers. A self-proclaimed football junkie who made frequent guest appearances on NFL Network even during his playing career, he could rhapsodize about the personnel on other teams and just about any other subject. That talent should serve him well as he transitions into the NFL as an assistant coach. Arizona coach Bruce Arians hired Buckner as his defensive line coach for the 2013 season, even though Buckner's only real full-time coaching experience had been at a private high school in Charlotte.

Buckner also was a good player—not as good as Kris Jenkins, who was the best defensive tackle the Panthers ever had, but plenty good. Buckner was part of the best Panthers defensive line in history—along with Julius Peppers, Jenkins, Mike Rucker— when the team went to the Super Bowl in 2003. He remained a starter on the squad that advanced to the NFC championship in 2005.

Buckner hemmed and hawed about retirement in his final few years, once expressing it this way: "As long as you've got a big bowl of ice cream and you're eating it, it's good. When you get to the end, it starts tasting better because you know it might be your last spoonful."

It turned out the decision was made for him—his last spoonful came in the Panthers' lopsided loss to Seattle in the 2005 postseason. The Panthers released him before the 2006 season, and he ultimately retired.

Buckner stayed in Charlotte, coaching youth football and cohosting a local radio show with former Panthers offensive lineman Frank Garcia for a while. He interned as a "training-camp-only" assistant coach for the Pittsburgh Steelers for three seasons, which led to his big break when Arians (who was a full-time member of that Pittsburgh staff) got the Arizona head-coaching job.

Buckner grew up in Columbus, Georgia, the only boy of eight children. With seven sisters, he was "pretty spoiled," as he once recalled. "They did make me do some of the manly chores—taking out the trash and washing the car," he said. "But I knew I was going to eat good every day."

In high school, he was a good enough athlete that he returned kicks and occasionally kicked field goals. He went to Clemson, playing nose guard, and had 22 sacks—third-best in school history when he left.

Pittsburgh drafted him in the second round and he stayed there for three years, playing on a Super Bowl team (they lost, just as the Panthers did, so Buckner does not have a Super Bowl ring). He also played for Cincinnati and San Francisco before joining the Panthers for the 1–15 season of 2001 and then enjoying the team's rise to prominence in his final four seasons.

86 Chris Gamble

Chris Gamble had the perfect surname for a cornerback, because by definition the position he played for nine years for the Panthers was one of the riskiest on the field. A bad gamble by Gamble—a mistimed jump, a miscalculated pass route—and the other team had six points.

Gamble played that position well enough from 2004 to 2012 to end up as the Panthers' all-time interception leader, with 27. The Panthers released him in March 2013, but not before he had surpassed Eric Davis, Mike Minter, and every other Panthers defensive back in terms of picks. After the release, Gamble said through his agent that he planned to retire—a surprising move, and one that might not stick, given that he was only 30 at the time.

Gamble was never as well-liked by fans as some of his contemporaries. Part of that was his quiet, reserved nature. Gamble treated interviews like trips to the dentist, always antsy to get away from the microphones.

Part of it was also that even though he had those 27 interceptions, it was hard sometimes to pick out the ones that really mattered. Quick, do you remember any of them? The most memorable play Gamble was involved in with the Panthers was actually a bad one. He fielded a punt against Minnesota in 2006 and, on a called trick play, tried to throw it across the field to Richard Marshall. The pass was terrible, a late Panthers lead evaporated after the ensuing fumble, and Carolina lost in overtime.

Gamble never had that one huge game, like, for instance, Ricky Manning Jr., who had three interceptions in the NFC Championship Game at Philadelphia. But Gamble did consistently hold down his starting position, year after year. His 117 career regular-season starts are the most by a cornerback in franchise history.

His best years were his first two in terms of ball-hawking. Gamble had come out of Ohio State as a Panthers first-round draft pick and was highly renowned for his athletic ability—he played both ways as a Buckeye, starting 19 games at cornerback and 14 at wide receiver. In 2004, as an NFL rookie, he became the first rookie to solely lead the team in interceptions when he had six. The next year he led the team again, with seven on a good Panthers playoff squad.

After that, however, Gamble's totals went down. And to be fair, some of that was attributable to the fact that he was more established and teams threw to the other side more often. The Panthers certainly still liked him in late 2008, when they gave him a staggering $53 million contract extension (one of general manager Marty Hurney's most questionable decisions) to be a "shutdown" cornerback.

But after that gamble by his own team, Gamble tailed off. His tackle numbers went down. Coach John Fox once angrily benched him. Gamble had zero interceptions in 2010—the first year he had been shut out—and then played in only four games in 2012 due to a shoulder injury. Due to his salary-cap figure it was no surprise when the Panthers released him in 2013, thereby saving $7.9 million on their cap.

87 Enemies of the State

Given that the Panthers have lost roughly half of their games over their history, they have seen a lot of great performances on the other side of the ball. Here is a quick alphabetical look at a dozen players who have really given the Panthers fits—either during one game or, in some cases, several of them.

Tom Brady, New England: In the Panthers' most important game ever, Brady played just about like you'd expect a future first-ballot Pro Football Hall of Famer to play. In Super Bowl XXXVIII, Brady was 32-of-48 for 354 yards, three touchdowns, and only one interception as New England edged Carolina 32–29. With the game tied at 29 late in the fourth quarter, Brady led the Patriots to the game's winning field goal on the final drive, helping to cement his reputation as one of the NFL's all-time clutch players.

Drew Brees, New Orleans: Brees is so accurate and smart he's hard for anyone to defend. He has three of the top 10 passing performances ever (in terms of yardage) against Carolina in franchise history. On the last day of the 2011 season, Brees threw five touchdown passes and had 389 yards passing as the Saints admittedly tried to set several NFL records while blowing out the Panthers 45–17. That one really rankled a lot of people in black and blue.

Chris Doleman, San Francisco and Atlanta: Only twice have the Panthers given up more than three sacks to one player in a single game. Both times it was 3.5 sacks to Doleman—once when he was with San Francisco in 1998 and once in 1995 when he was with Atlanta.

Reuben Droughns, Denver: This guy really owes the Panthers a thank-you note. He was a backup fullback for most of his first four years in the NFL, viewed as too slow to play running back. Then the Broncos, decimated by injuries, switched him to tailback for a game on October 10, 2004, against Carolina. Droughns torched the Panthers for 193 yards on 30 carries. He would end up rushing for 1,200 yards in that season and the next and getting a four-year, $13.5 million contract—and it all started against Carolina.

Marshall Faulk, St. Louis: In 2001, in the midst of the Panthers' 1–15 season, Faulk was nearly unstoppable. The two teams were in the same division back then, and Faulk ran for 202 yards in one matchup and 183 in the other.

Brett Favre, Green Bay: The Panthers have beaten Favre a few times—Matt Moore actually outplayed him once when Favre was at Minnesota—but Favre got them a lot of times, too. He threw five TD passes in one 1998 game and also beat Carolina in the 1996 NFC title game.

Matt Forte, Chicago: The Bears' multipurpose running back may be the current player who gets the biggest gleam in his eye when the Panthers appear on the schedule. Forte has not one but two of the best 10 all-time opponent rushing performances in Carolina's history. He blitzed the Panthers for 205 rushing yards in 2011 and also ran for 166 yards in 2010, scoring two touchdowns in each game and leading the Bears to wins.

Rod Gardner, Washington: You'd probably win a trivia bet if you know Gardner is the answer to the question: "Who had the most receiving yards in a single game against Carolina?" The former Clemson receiver beat them up for 208 receiving yards in a 17–14 overtime win by the Redskins in 2001. Gardner was a double whammy for Carolina: The Panthers would later trade for him, and he could barely get on the field for them.

Trent Green, St. Louis: The Rams quarterback threw for 431 yards—still the most ever against the Panthers—on November 5, 2000. Despite that, Carolina still won this one, 27–24.

Dorsey Levens, Green Bay: In the Panthers' first-ever playoff loss, Levens caught for 117 yards and ran for 88 more in the Packers' 30–13 win over Carolina in the 1996 NFC Championship Game.

Michael Turner, Atlanta: The powerful running back was a thorn in the Panthers' side for years. In 2008, against a Panthers team that would go 12–4, Turner scored four touchdowns and rushed for 117 yards in a 45–28 Atlanta win. The Panthers have given up three TDs on at least 10 different occasions to a single player, but Turner is the only one who ever scored four.

Derrick Ward, New York Giants: In general, Ward has been a forgettable NFL back. But he was unforgettable against Carolina in the game to decide the NFC's No. 1 playoff seed in 2008, rushing for 215 yards on only 15 carries in the Giants' 34–28 overtime victory. It's still the most rushing yards the Panthers have ever given up in a game to an individual.

88 The 2001 New England Game

There are a few games for Carolina fans that weren't much fun to go to at the time but over time became stories that they like to tell of how *they were there when....*The "home" games at Clemson in 1995 were like that to a degree—no matter how well the Panthers played, everyone still faced the prospect of several hours on the road in traffic following the game.

But the game that is most often mentioned in the "so bad it was good" category came on January 6, 2002, when New England blistered the Panthers 38–6 on the final week of the 2001 season. Losing to the Patriots in itself wasn't so bad, but the game was played in front of more than 52,000 empty seats and only 21,070 actual fans.

It was terrible. A few Panthers fans wore paper bags over their heads. The crowd was less than half the size of any other crowd for any Carolina game before or since. And that record will never be broken given the fact the Panthers now announce tickets distributed (always well over 60,000) rather than the actual turnstile count, although the latter is a far more honest depiction of what the stands looked like.

The attendance was so low because the Panthers were 1–14 going in, George Seifert was going to be fired in less than 24 hours, and the weather was awful. Much of the game was played in a drizzle. It was a cold and clammy 36 degrees—matching Seifert's personality, some would say. Fog shrouded the stadium starting in the second quarter. At halftime, the *Charlotte Observer* reported on its website that Seifert would indeed be fired the next day.

"It was like the sun was shining only on their side of the field," Carolina defensive tackle Brentson Buckner said. "I would never wish what happened to us that day on anyone in the NFL. It was awful."

The two teams would have a rematch two years later with far bigger stakes, meeting in the Super Bowl. Twenty Panther players on the roster for the Panthers' 2004 Super Bowl played in the 2001 game, too, so Carolina was not without talent.

But the Panthers were without energy in the second half. Some Panthers players would say later that they believed that some of their teammates quit on them that day. "Some guys—the ones who weren't quite as mentally tough and who ended up not being back the next year—they were ready to call it a season," defensive end Mike Rucker said a couple of years later. "That showed."

New England had only a 10–3 lead early in the third quarter, but then started rolling. And once the Patriots began to roll, the Panthers seemed to put up only token resistance. On one play, the

Patriots rushed only two men against five blockers and still banged into Carolina quarterback Chris Weinke to force an incompletion.

By the end of regulation, only about 1,000 fans remained, and many of them managed to walk down into the expensive seats and ring the field. Of those 1,000, probably 900 were Patriots fans, ecstatic at the prospect of the playoffs and a possible first-ever Super Bowl win for the franchise (which New England would indeed capture two months later, upsetting 14-point favorite St. Louis).

The Panthers lost their 15th straight game, an NFL single-season record at the time. Weinke was responsible for four turnovers in the game, with three interceptions and a fumble. The Panthers added a couple of other miscues, which ultimately meant that their turnover and point totals were a matched set: six apiece.

New England scored in about every which way you can. The Patriots ran two of Weinke's interceptions back for touchdowns (76 and 46 yards), and also scored on a punt return (68 yards), a run (32 yards), and a lone Tom Brady TD pass (5 yards). The Panthers managed only two field goals from John Kasay.

Oddly, the Panthers ran the ball extremely well. Richard Huntley, who otherwise barely made a dent as a Panther, set what was then a team record with 168 rushing yards.

At the end of the game, Seifert went to midfield and shook the hand of one man—New England coach Bill Belichick. Then he quickly jogged off the field, followed by a battalion of cameras correctly anticipating that they were chronicling Seifert's last run in that stadium.

The Panthers players were slower to leave, trudging off on a gloomy day. But the game is remembered somewhat fondly by many these days, as evidence of how quickly a team can resurface from rock bottom.

89 The 32-Point Win That Felt Like a Loss

It was a crushing Panthers victory. A complete domination. And yet the Carolina Panthers filed mournfully into their locker room on January 2, 2000, following a 45–13 dismantling of the New Orleans Saints in Charlotte.

It was a game that was odd on several levels—and remains memorable to every Panthers fan among the nearly 57,000 who showed up because of its oddities.

First of all, New Orleans' starting quarterback was a young unknown who went by the name of Jake Delhomme. Three years later, Panthers fans would begin to get to know him very well.

Secondly, the Panthers had to score and score and score in the game to have a chance at their goal—a long-shot playoff berth.

The Panthers entered the final Sunday of what was officially the 1999 season with an 18-point deficit to Green Bay in a critical tiebreaker scenario. If both teams won, the Panthers had to win by 18 points more than the Packers did in their own game in order to have a chance at capturing the final wild-card slot in the NFC in George Seifert's first year. (As it happened, both Carolina and Green Bay missed out on that last spot when Dallas won a game against the New York Giants that started three hours later, trumping them both to qualify for that final playoff spot. But neither team could know that at the time).

So Seifert kept getting minute-by-minute updates of the Packers game as this one was going on. And because Green Bay was scoring in bunches just like Carolina was, he was prompted to keep throwing the ball with a huge lead in the fourth quarter.

At one point—with a 45–7 lead and 1:41 remaining—the Panthers went for it on fourth-and-10 from their own 39. As

Carolina quarterback Steve Beuerlein said afterward, "It was almost like the old sandlot days where you're just out there drawing them up in the dirt, trying to stick a dagger in them every single time you get the ball."

"It was like we were playing a team from 2,000 miles away," wide receiver Patrick Jeffers said.

The Saints were a woeful group that year—coached by Mike Ditka in what would be his final game as New Orleans' head man. New Orleans would finish 3–13. Running back Ricky Williams, the player on whom Ditka had bet so much of the Saints' future upon that he traded an entire draft to get him, had only seven yards in 14 carries.

The Panthers had started the season slowly but finished well—a theme that has resonated throughout many of their non-playoff seasons. They were on fire offensively in this game. Beuerlein threw five touchdown passes—two to Jeffers, two to Wesley Walls, and one to Muhsin Muhammad. Michael Bates took a kickoff back for another score.

But Green Bay was blasting Arizona, so the Panthers kept trying to pour it on. The Packers would ultimately win by 25 points, meaning Carolina would have needed to win by 43 points to have a chance at the final wild-card spot.

Delhomme had a rocky game for New Orleans, throwing four interceptions on the same field where he ultimately would have so much success later in the decade. But he did scramble for a nine-yard touchdown against Carolina with 18 seconds left, ensuring the Panthers couldn't catch Green Bay in the points scenario. Then Ditka, angry at the Panthers' "pile it on" mentality, went for two points but didn't make it.

Said Delhomme afterward of the Panthers' approach, "Personally, I didn't like it. But if that's their playoff chance, you understand."

Although no one knew it at the time, the game also served as the high-water mark for Seifert. The Panthers finished 8–8 with the win—the only season in his three-year tenure when they didn't have a losing record.

90 The Wrestler and the Bachelor

Like all NFL teams, the Carolina Panthers have had a lot of players pass through the team's revolving door without making much of an impact on the field. In Major League Baseball terms, those players had a cup of coffee in the big leagues and then were asked to leave.

Generally, such players fade into anonymity. But there have been a couple of notable exceptions—a wrestler and a Bachelor. They are both pretty useful names to know if you want to win a Panthers trivia contest, because lots of random people vaguely remember them, but very few know they each once suited up (briefly) for the Panthers.

Bill Goldberg—aka "Goldberg"—was the wrestler. Ryan Sutter was the bachelor.

Let's talk about Sutter first, since he was the only one of the two to appear in an actual game for Carolina. He had one of the shortest careers in NFL history—10 seconds. As a rookie safety out of Colorado in 1998, the Panthers first had Sutter on the practice squad. Then they had a spate of injuries and, late in the season, activated him and put him in to cover the opening kickoff. Sutter tried to make a tackle on his first play but instead dislocated his shoulder and never played again for Carolina.

But Sutter would resurface with a flourish. In the first season of TV's then wildly popular *The Bachelorette*, he turned out to be the final pick of bachelorette Trista Rehn. While most of those reality-show pairings don't last and in fact break up before the altar, these two are still together. The two got married in a TV wedding in 2003 and their linked names "Ryan and Trista" became breathless tabloid fodder for several years. The births of their son and their daughter were covered by celebrity magazines. Sutter now works as a firefighter in Colorado and also does endurance racing and triathlons. He has also done some modeling.

Goldberg didn't even get 10 real seconds as a Panther, but his notoriety afterward was much greater than Sutter's. In 1995, the Panthers took the former all-SEC defensive lineman out of Georgia with the 66th pick of the expansion draft (when the team filled its roster with castoffs from other teams—Goldberg had been playing for Atlanta). The Panthers then decided very quickly they didn't need him, making him the team's very first cut.

Former Panthers defensive line teammate Gerald Williams told me once about Goldberg, "I sat in some meetings with Bill. We'd tease each other a little about the Southeastern Conference, since I'm from Auburn and he went to Georgia. For the most part he was a quiet guy, trying to feel his way like most of the younger players. He was a talker, though, whenever he did something good on the field."

That didn't happen often, though. Goldberg was cut before the Panthers even got to their first training camp—he was around less than two months altogether.

But Goldberg resurrected himself as a professional wrestler in the WWE—a tattooed, bald, very rich, very muscular wrestler with a goatee. He dropped his first name and simply went by "Goldberg," and from about 1997 to 2004 he was such a popular pro wrestler that he seemed to "win" everything there was to win in the "sport." He was truly athletic and had a way with working a wrestling crowd into a frenzy.

Like a few other crossover wrestling stars, Goldberg made some appearances in movies as well, including a forgettable slasher flick called *Santa's Slay*, in which he plays a homicidal Santa Claus. And even after his retirement from wrestling he has continued to occasionally show up on TV—he was a contestant during one season of *Celebrity Apprentice* and also has hosted the show *Garage Mahal* on DIY Network.

91 Todd Sauerbrun and the Punters

"A punt is not a bad play."

It was one of John Fox's favorite football sayings—I heard him say it for the first time when we had our first extended interview shortly after he was hired. And although it's not a statement the "Go for it on every fourth down" football fan likes to hear, it is true in some cases.

The Panthers have punted the ball more than 1,000 times in their team history. The man who did it for longer than anyone else was Jason Baker, who kicked 570 punts from 2005 to 2011. Baker also has the highest single-season net punt average for Carolina and the most punts inside the 20. He was a smart punter, going for a repeatable action every time instead of trying to bang a 70-yarder and instead shanking it for 25. Baker was also a well-mannered citizen who never caused a bit of trouble. General manager Marty Hurney called Baker "a model Panther" when he released him before the 2012 season.

Baker, in other words, was the opposite of Todd Sauerbrun. Sauerbrun was brash and occasionally caused trouble. He had public disputes with coaches, got arrested and later pleaded guilty for driving under the influence. According to the arrest affidavit, Sauerbrun told the police officer he drank eight beers with dinner. He was also fingered in a steroid scandal in a *60 Minutes* report in 2005 (as were Carolina offensive linemen Todd Steussie and Jeff Mitchell). And those troubles were just with the Panthers—he would later get in trouble in Denver too.

But Sauerbrun had such a fantastic leg—the best one in Panthers history—that the trouble was sometimes overlooked or downplayed. At least it was until the Panthers finally got fed up and traded him to Denver in 2005 for Baker in a rare punter-for-punter swap.

Sauerbrun made the Pro Bowl in 2001, '02, and '03 for Carolina, booming punts and kickoffs and occasionally making a tackle too (he once drew a 15-yard unsportsmanlike conduct penalty for taunting an opposing punt returner after tackling him). He had 73- and 72-yard punts for Carolina—still the two longest in team history. He encapsulated his punting philosophy in five words: "Just whack the ball, brother."

Once, on the spur of the moment during the off-season, he agreed to go out on an empty high school field and kick about 35 punts to me.

I still remember the look of the ball when Sauerbrun hit it well as it spiraled in an arc toward me. One of them went 85 yards on the fly. It turned out catching one of those nice spirals—they actually whistled through the air—was a lot easier than catching a 40-yard wobbler when he mishit one.

Sauerbrun entered the NFL as a second-round draft pick out of West Virginia. The Chicago Bears drafted him and he showed up with personalized license plates that read HANGTIME—which of course made him an immediate target for hazing by the veterans.

But Sauerbrun kicked in the NFL for 13 seasons because of that tremendous leg—four of them with the Panthers. The Panthers have also employed Ken Walter, Rohn Stark, Tommy Barnhardt, and, in 2012, rookie Brad Nortman as their punters. They have had a number of long snappers who got the ball to those punters over the years, too. Mark Rodenhauser was a computer whiz. J.J. Jansen used Twitter to ask Panthers fans trivia questions and award prizes.

But the two names most remembered among Panthers punters will be Baker, who quietly did his job, and Sauerbrun, who did his loudly. Sauerbrun liked to quote from the movie *Old School,* and you got the feeling he was trying to star in a real-life version of it too.

One last Sauerbrun story: He had a hard time keeping his weight down, and he kept getting fined for it. At one point in the 2004 season, the Panthers had such a desperate situation at place kicker due to injury that there was a possibility Sauerbrun (who once kicked a 62-yard field goal in high school) was going to be asked to do it on a semipermanent basis. Fine, Sauerbrun said—but only if he was refunded the money he was fined for being overweight.

The Panthers passed on that offer, and a few months later they traded Sauerbrun away for good.

92 Try to Get a Touchdown Ball from Cam

Admittedly, this is a long shot. Most of the ideas for Panther-related things to do in this book are sure bets. For instance, no one is going to turn you away from training camp. The team wants you there, and at draft rallies too. And you can always take pictures of the six giant Panthers sculptures or go to the team draft party or visit the Sam Mills statue.

This one, though, is a little like winning the lottery. Panthers quarterback Cam Newton began a tradition as a rookie and carried it over into his second year, giving the football away at home games after a Carolina offensive touchdown. He always does it after his own rushing scores. He sometimes does it—if he can persuade the relevant teammate to hand him the ball—after another Panther player scores.

"The Sunday giveaway," Newton calls it, and those touchdown balls are as prized as Willy Wonka's golden tickets. Newton doesn't throw them into the crowd—which is a good thing, as that would undoubtedly get someone hurt in the resulting battle for the ball. He instead carefully selects the first fan who catches his eye— usually a young one wearing a Panthers jersey—and hands him or her the ball.

So how do you get to be that fan?

First of all, you have to have the proper seat. The only people who have a chance are in the first row at either end zone at Bank of America Stadium. Those seats are not cheap and are all held by season ticket holders. However, you can sometimes buy them on the secondary market at websites like StubHub.com.

Then what? You pretty much have to have a kid with you, and one who is wearing a Panthers jersey. Wearing Newton's No. 1 doesn't hurt. Last, you have to get extremely lucky. The touchdown has to come somewhat near you—if it's Newton's, he will first do his "Clark Kent becomes Superman" routine—and then he has to recognize you in the crowd.

It does happen, though. It happened, for instance, to a 10-year-old kid from Raleigh named Law Waddill in one of the first times Newton gave away a ball, in a 2011 win over Washington. The moment almost overwhelmed the boy with joy.

If you're lucky, this could be you (or, more likely, your kid). Cam Newton gives away a touchdown ball to a young fan during a preseason matchup with the Miami Dolphins in 2012.

SCOTT FOWLER

"He was shaking," father Edmund Waddill said of his son's reaction. "He had tears in his eyes. He said to me, 'Did that really just happen?'"

The idea for this tradition actually came not from Newton but from Mike Shula, who was Newton's quarterbacks coach in 2011 and 2012 before being promoted to Carolina's offensive coordinator in 2013.

Recounted Newton once of what Shula told him, "He says when you celebrate, it's not a celebration unless you give back. He says, 'You do all that riffraff, whatever you do, but at the end you give that football to a little kid. You find a little kid.'"

"So after I did whatever I did," Newton continued, "I heard somebody (Shula) in my headset saying, 'Give it to a little kid! Give it to a little kid!' I looked and there was this kid just gleaming [sic] from ear to ear, so I gave it to him."

It worked out so well that Newton has done it more than 20 times since. Still, the odds are against you, even if you somehow wangle your way into a front-row end zone seat.

But you never know…

93 Keyshawn and Shockey

Keyshawn Johnson and Jeremy Shockey were never teammates for the Carolina Panthers, but their careers ran on parallel tracks.

Both of them were high-profile offensive players who had experienced tremendous success and owned at least one Super Bowl ring when they came to the Panthers very late in their career. Both then played—and played pretty well—for Carolina for a single season. And then, quickly, both were gone.

Johnson played in 2006 for Carolina; Shockey came five years later, in 2011. Shortly after the Panthers released him in 2007—mistakenly believing that second-round draft pick Dwayne Jarrett would be anywhere near as good—Keyshawn officially retired for a TV job with ESPN.

Shockey did not leave the game on his own terms. Carolina signed him to a one-year deal in 2011, and he split time at tight end with Greg Olsen. Believing correctly that Olsen could be an every-down tight end, the Panthers chose not to bring Shockey back in 2012. Shockey didn't play anywhere else in the league that year, either, although he did not officially retire.

Both men provided some interesting moments for the Panthers, along with a dose of star power. Johnson had the better numbers of the two—he had a decent year as the Panthers' No. 2 receiver in 2006, with 70 catches for 815 yards and four touchdowns. He was strictly a 34-year-old possession receiver by then and he was a pretty high-maintenance guy in the locker room. But he was also tough and made a number of third-down catches in traffic.

The play that Johnson may be most remembered for, though, was not a catch but an interception. In Carolina's 27–24 loss at Philadelphia in 2006—a critical defeat for a team that would finish 8–8—Johnson was supposed to get into the corner of the end zone on a fade route in the game's final minute. Instead, Philadelphia's Lito Sheppard beat him to the spot and outmaneuvered him to pick off Jake Delhomme's pass on first-and-goal from the 7.

Some in the Panthers locker room thought Johnson should have taken more of the blame after the game for not making the play. Sheppard, however, later said that the Eagles knew Delhomme's signal for the fade route—a tap on his backside toward the receiver it was coming to—and that's how he knew to stay outside and pick it off.

Shockey had 37 catches for 455 yards and four touchdowns for the Panthers in his lone season of 2011. With his many tattoos

Replacing Keyshawn

The Panthers really didn't miss a beat when they let go of Jeremy Shockey before the 2012 season. Greg Olsen simply got more playing time and posted one of the top two seasons for a tight end in Carolina history.

On the other hand, the Panthers really misfired in trying to replace Keyshawn Johnson. In the 2007 draft, they picked Dwayne Jarrett in the second round. Jarrett had scored 41 touchdowns in only three seasons in college. He seemed like a Keyshawn clone except a decade younger—big and not particularly fast, but with a Southern Cal pedigree and an ability to outfight smaller cornerbacks for the ball.

Although not yet officially retired, Johnson was already dabbling in TV by then. He was part of ESPN's draft coverage when the Panthers selected Jarrett in the second round and said he loved the selection, bubbling: "It's a great pick. And the reason it's a great pick is because we need another wide receiver; we need that third guy… This guy is much like me… He plays exactly like me!"

That's what the Panthers thought too. Only days after the draft, they decided Johnson was now expendable and released him.

But Jarrett turned out to be one of the worst draft picks in Panthers history. By the time he was finally released, in 2010, he had accumulated a number of terrible statistics, the worst of which were these:

1—Number of career NFL TDs
2—Number of DWI arrests

Jarrett turned out to be overwhelmed by the NFL game and lifestyle. And he wasn't exactly a workaholic. Once, talking to reporters as a rookie, Steve Smith walked by his locker and suggested, "Instead of talking to the media, why don't you go watch some film?"

Jarrett smiled a little and kept talking.

"Seriously," Smith said, and walked away.

It turned out that the Panthers really should have kept Johnson around for at least one more year, in 2007. It was one of the seasons in which Smith had to shoulder almost all of the receiving load once again. In 2008, the Panthers got Muhsin Muhammad back, and that finally freed Smith up again. But trying to replace Johnson with Jarrett turned out to be a serious mistake.

and his stories of world travels, he was a unique and opinionated personality. He once ripped officials following a game, saying he should have been offered an explanation for an "offensive pass interference" penalty called on him that negated what would have been a 22-yard TD against Chicago.

"We pay their salary and can't get an explanation," Shockey said. "I'd like to see the explanation when they do get graded. They should be held accountable as well. They get paid a lot of money. They go around and hang out and do whatever they do before the game. Fly for free and do all kinds of [stuff] for free."

While that criticism seemed somewhat petty, on the other extreme Shockey helped save tight end Ben Hartsock's life while with the Panthers. Hartsock was choking on a piece of pork during lunch at the Panthers' 2011 training camp in Spartanburg. Shockey quickly performed the Heimlich maneuver on his teammate to dislodge the offending piece of food. Then Shockey immediately sat back down to finish his own lunch and acted like the whole thing was no big deal.

Said Cam Newton of Shockey once, "My stereotypical thoughts when we signed Shock…[were] extremely different from what it is now. So many people, not just Shock but myself [sic], can fit in that picture sometimes. People hear so much about how he is and this and that. He's been an unbelievable person and an unbelievable teammate."

The bottom line, though, was that neither Johnson nor Shockey made a lot of difference in the Panthers' bottom line. Johnson played for a Panthers team that was 8–8. Shockey played for one that went 7–9. Both squads missed the playoffs. But the two players were certainly entertaining while they were here.

94 Richie Brockel and the Best Trick Play Ever

In general, the Panthers haven't had much success with trick plays.

Once, John Fox went counter to his conservative tendencies—with disastrous results. In 2006, with the Panthers up by a touchdown on Minnesota in the fourth quarter, he allowed Chris Gamble to have the option of throwing a cross-field lateral after catching a punt. Gamble threw an awful pass, the Vikings pounced on it, and Minnesota ultimately won in overtime.

Other misfires: Keyshawn Johnson and William Floyd both threw nasty passes on their lone pass attempts as Panthers; both were intercepted. Punter Todd Sauerbrun threw a Garo Yepremian–style incompletion on a fake punt once.

Even the "successful" trick plays for Carolina usually didn't work. On their final offensive snap of a 25–16 loss to Philadelphia in 2003, the Panthers needed something impossible: a nine-point touchdown.

They still gave it their all, getting off eight laterals in a play that lasted 45 seconds in real time—about 10 times longer than the average NFL play. Three offensive linemen handled the ball. Jake Delhomme touched it three different times. Eventually, Nick Goings scored on a 69-yard TD—but the play was ultimately nullified because one of the laterals was obviously a forward pass.

With that as background, you can see why some Panthers viewed the best trick play in the team's history with some trepidation. In 2011, shortly before a game against Houston and the NFL's No. 1 defense, inventive offensive coordinator (and future Cleveland Brown head coach) Rob Chudzinski decided to install a play nicknamed "the Annexation of Puerto Rico" after a similar play in the 1994 Pop Warner football comedy *Little Giants*.

The Panthers wide receivers—who weren't involved—weren't too sure about it. "When we put it in, I never thought in a million years that that play was going to work, let alone get a touchdown," wideout Brandon LaFell would say later.

Chudzinski unveiled it with the Panthers leading Houston 14–0. There was a lengthy setup first. With a first down at the Houston 11, "Chud" sent in a personnel group that included running back DeAngelo Williams, wide receiver Steve Smith, and little-used fullback/tight end Richie Brockel, who was typically a blocker.

On first down, Cam Newton threw a safe four-yard pass to Brockel. Then the entire team hurried to the line. The offensive linemen stood up, as if they were discussing whom to block. Then center Ryan Kalil quickly bent down and snapped the ball to Newton, who was in the shotgun formation.

With the defense's view partially blocked and Brockel crouching in the backfield without moving, as if he were waiting to block somebody himself, it was natural for the Texans to all follow Newton when he spun right and started to run on what looked like an option play.

But Newton had already reached between Brockel's legs and slipped the football to him. Brockel waited for the Texans defense to sprint after Newton, then ran around left end, untouched, for a seven-yard touchdown. Brockel, an undrafted rookie free agent Newton had nicknamed "the Mauler" for his punishing style of football, had his first Panthers TD.

Fortunately, Brockel was wearing a helmet, so he didn't have to worry too much about keeping a straight face when the play call came into the huddle. "The level of excitement definitely goes up," said Brockel, who went to college at Boise State, where trick plays were a part of the repertoire. "The fact [that] coach calls a trick play, that takes a little bit of guts. When they call it, you know you have to execute it and make it work so they'll call stuff like that again."

If you've never seen Brockel's touchdown, you can find it pretty easily online. It's worth looking up. It certainly flummoxed the Texans. J. J. Watt, the Texans defensive lineman and one of the best defenders in the NFL at the time, understood the movie reference himself. Said Watt after the game, "It's almost like the annexation of Puerto Rico, I think, and we clearly didn't defend it well. We're going to be ready for that in the future."

The Fan Who Guaranteed a Butt-Kicking

Like Forrest Gump and his box of chocolates, you never know what you're going to get when you go to a home Panthers game. But you rarely get anything quite as weird as what happened on November 9, 2003, when one of the Panthers' most visible fans inserted himself into the game's narrative flow.

This sort of thing happens occasionally—the streaker who delayed the second-half kickoff of the Panthers' Super Bowl by cavorting in front of John Kasay, for instance. But I've never seen it happen before or since in quite this way.

The fan was named Joe Muscarello, and he billed himself as the "Carolina Prowler." Muscarello liked to wear a furry black outfit to Panthers home games—it included huge black paws and a miniature panther perched on each shoulder like parrots. Although not as well-known as "Catman," the most famous Panthers fan, in the early years of the franchise Muscarello did show up in a lot of pictures and videos whenever the cameras would cut to the stands. He was even part of an exhibit in the Pro Football Hall of Fame about NFL fans.

The Panthers used to select a "Fan of the Game"—they don't do this anymore—and let the guy say something short on a microphone held by a member of the Panthers staff during a break in the action on the field. You may see where this is going already.

The Panthers and Tampa Bay have had a long and heated rivalry, and Carolina was playing Tampa Bay at home in 2003 when Muscarello was selected as the Fan of the Game. The Panthers led 20–14 at the time and had the ball. Muscarello was well aware that Tampa Bay defensive end Simeon Rice had publicly guaranteed a Buccaneers win earlier in the week.

The Panthers fan with the microphone generally said something akin to "Go Panthers" and left it at that. Not Muscarello. He yelled, "Let me tell you something, Warren Sapp and Simeon Rice. You *guaranteed* a win. We *guarantee* we're going to kick your butt."

Panthers fans roared in support. But the taunt—heard by everyone in the stadium—fired up the Bucs defense. Both Sapp and Rice gleefully pointed to the scoreboard, where Muscarello's picture had just been shown, and then Rice quickly sacked Jake Delhomme twice in the next three plays. It was as if the taunts had given the Bucs a sudden dose of 5-hour Energy.

Panthers defensive tackle Brentson Buckner would say later of the fan's comments, "It was good that he thought that, but he needed to say it with 30 seconds on the clock when we're up by 10!"

Before long, Carolina had fallen behind 24–20 late in the fourth quarter as Tampa Bay scored 10 more points in a row. And Muscarello—a banking loan specialist during the week—had left his seat. Although he hadn't been threatened, he had heard some grumbling about "firing up the other team" and feared for his own safety and that of his nine-year-old son, who was with him, if the Panthers lost.

Then Delhomme and the offense saved the day with a last-minute touchdown drive. And afterward, since it had all worked out all right, everyone had fun with Muscarello's taunt.

"I don't know who he is, but my God!" Delhomme said, laughing. "We have racehorses back home. Maybe I can order a muzzle."

Quipped Panthers center Jeff Mitchell, "That guy, we need to seek him out and revoke his season-ticket privileges."

Buckner, however, thought Muscarello's comments were right on the money. "That's what you want from your fans, really," Buckner said. "You put a mic in front of somebody in the stands and ask that question in Philly or Tampa or Pittsburgh and you'd get the same reaction."

Muscarello knew he had escaped by a hair becoming the Panthers' answer to notorious Chicago Cubs fan Steve Bartman. He felt bad about the whole thing. So a few days later, Muscarello came by a Panthers practice to personally apologize to coach John Fox.

"Don't sweat that," Fox told the fan. "You were fired up. I like people who get fired up. We just need to keep you off the big screen."

96 Anthony Johnson

His Panthers teammates called him "A. J.," which were his initials but could have just as easily stood for "Average Joe."

Anthony Johnson was just that on an NFL level—an average player by NFL standards who was versatile enough to make one pro roster after another, but not a star. He knew it too. He drove a 1990 Toyota Supra for much of his time as a Panther—the same car he had when he entered the league in 1990.

But for one season, A. J. was not average; he was awesome. In 1996, he rushed for 1,120 yards, got another 104 in the playoff win over Dallas, and still played on all the special-teams squads—a true rarity for a starting NFL running back.

He still acted like an average guy in that charmed season, which is what teammates loved about him. "I'm not real flashy, but I definitely get the job done," Johnson said once.

Johnson; his wife, Shelley; and their four children (at the time—they later had a fifth) spent that season in Charlotte in a 1,400-square-foot apartment instead of buying a second house to go along with the one they owned in South Bend, Indiana. They were conservative both in their money and their values. Johnson didn't like R-rated movies as an adult because of, as he said, "the blood, gore, and sex."

It seemed only fitting that after an 11-year NFL career he would join the Christian organization Athletes in Action. He ended up being assigned to the Jacksonville Jaguars as the team chaplain in 2003, counseling players on all manner of subjects. He has stayed in that job ever since, saying his call to ministry was ultimately far more significant than anything he did on a football field.

Johnson spent five of his 11 years in the NFL with the Panthers, usually platooning with either Tshimanga Biakabutuka or Fred Lane at running back. Dom Capers loved him, in part because of his attitude and in part because he was so versatile. Johnson was one of those guys who did whatever he was told. In college at Notre Dame, he had 32 rushing TDs but never ran for 100 yards in a game. He could cover a kick, catch the ball out of the backfield, block as a fullback, or get a hard yard up the middle.

"The more you can do, the longer you stick around," he would say.

For the Panthers, his big break came when Biakabutuka got a season-ending knee injury four games into the 1996 season. Johnson became the every-down back and had his lone 1,000-yard season and six 100-yard rushing games including the postseason. The Panthers never played Johnson as much after the 1996 season, but his versatility kept him employed until August 2000, when the team finally released him.

In a heated team meeting midway through the 1996 season, the Panthers' offensive linemen came under fire for not doing their job well enough. Johnson was the only player other than the linemen themselves who defended the group, which endeared him to his linemen forever. Perhaps the best tribute ever given to Johnson during his Panthers years came from Greg Skrepenak, the offensive tackle who made approximately seven times Johnson's salary of $275,000 in 1996.

While well-paid running backs have sometimes been known in the NFL to give their offensive linemen a present when they go over 1,000 yards, Skrepenak decided it should be the other way around this time, since Johnson was so poorly compensated by NFL standards that year. He talked the other offensive linemen on the 1996 team into buying Johnson a Rolex watch and presented it to him in another team meeting.

In that meeting, Skrepenak would later recall saying, "I have one son, and another one to be born in a month. As I am raising my sons, I can tell you that I would want them to grow up to be like A. J. That's because of his work ethic, his character, and his belief in God. He is everything I wish my sons could be. Honestly, I wish I could be more like him."

97 Watch the Panthers' Commercials

If you have access to a computer, tablet, or a smart phone and need a laugh, here's a quick way to get one. The Panthers have made some funny commercials over the years—some intentionally hilarious, some unintentionally hilarious—and they are all easily found on YouTube.com. Just search "Carolina Panthers commercial" and you'll have more than a dozen choices.

Most Panthers fans seem to get the biggest kick out of the Cam Newton Play 60 ad, promoting the NFL's efforts for all children to get at least 60 minutes of exercise per day. Even easier, search "Cam Newton commercial with kid" on YouTube and it pops right up.

In the commercial, Newton is talking with a young boy on the playground following an appearance at the kid's school. The kid starts asking Newton a rapid-fire series of questions about what exercise can do for him, starting with easy ones like "Will I get big and strong like you?" and progressing to more and more outlandish ideas, such as the kid replacing Newton as the Panthers' starter.

"You can be my backup?" the boy asks. As Newton stutters out an answer, the boy hypothesizes that he will "become your Mom's favorite player."

Newton—one of the most charismatic Panthers ever—plays the straight man perfectly. This is the closest thing the Panthers have ever had to the "Mean" Joe Greene Coke ad from so many years ago.

There have been other good ones too. Another Play 60 ad—featuring most of the Panthers team taking a Play 60 bus to another school appearance—has several nice touches, including team owner Jerry Richardson as a well-dressed bus driver.

Newton and wide receiver Steve Smith both filmed *SportsCenter* promos for ESPN, each in their Panthers uniforms. Neither ad is incredibly inspired from a comedic viewpoint, but they both received heavy airplay. Newton has also done an ad for Windows Phone ("Pound cake! French fries!") in which Jonathan Stewart shows up, as well as spots for Under Armour and Gatorade.

Smith and former Panthers quarterback Jake Delhomme both have done several ads for Bojangles, the popular chicken-and-biscuits restaurant franchise. One in which Smith tries to fit a biscuit through his helmet so he can eat it is pretty good. Another, with Delhomme and a genie who will grant Delhomme three wishes—only to see the quarterback use them all on Bojangles food—is decent.

CPI Security has used several of the bigger, more menacing Panthers players—mostly offensive linemen—in its ads to represent safety for its clients. And running back DeAngelo Williams did a couple of ads with Morris-Jenkins, a regional heating and air conditioning company, that look very "local."

Probably the most sustained laughs come from an ad that wasn't Panthers-related at the time. Prior to the 2007 NFL Draft, Southern Cal center Ryan Kalil filmed some extended spots with comedian Will Ferrell for NFL Network (the Panthers would eventually draft Kalil in the second round of that draft). Ferrell played a fictional trainer who was preparing Kalil for the draft with a number of unusual techniques, including substituting a Twinkie in for a quarterback and making Kalil protect it while Ferrell tried to do a "swim technique" so he could eat it.

Kalil is a natural—his gift for the dramatic would be made more evident by his full-page ad in the *Charlotte Observer* in 2012 predicting a Super Bowl for the team. Ferrell, in a huge Afro wig and short shorts, is great.

As a side note, Ferrell also has one other Panthers connection worth mentioning. He visited the Carolina locker room in 2005, while he was in town filming *Talladega Nights*, in which he plays a NASCAR driver named Ricky Bobby. Ferrell was the guest of Panthers coach John Fox and his wife, Robin. I had never seen the Panthers players as starstruck as the day Ferrell walked into the locker room—especially quarterback Jake Delhomme. It was cool to see them react to a celebrity in the way that a lot of Carolina fans often react to them.

98 Dave Gettleman

While the Carolina Panthers have had four head coaches during their existence, they have only employed three men as dedicated general managers since the franchise started playing games in 1995.

The third and most recent is Dave Gettleman, who got the job at age 61 in January 2013, after former GM Marty Hurney was fired in midseason.

At his first press conference, Gettleman said he felt as if he had "won the lottery." He had been passed over for possible GM jobs many times before and had worried that his age was working against him.

"I just needed someone who was looking for an older, more mature guy," Gettleman said. "That's really what it came down to. Our culture is the next whiz-bang is the next great thing....It was one of those deals where, 'Oh, he's an old dinosaur. He's probably cranky.'"

Panthers owner Jerry Richardson, who was 76 at the time, thought bringing in an older GM might help head coach Ron Rivera, who at that time was entering only his third NFL season as head coach.

Charming and gruff, Gettleman had a 25-year NFL background before joining the Panthers. It included scouting and personnel stints with six different teams that went to the Super Bowl, including three winners. He wore his most recent Super Bowl ring—from a trip with the New York Giants—to his opening press conference. At their first breakfast together, he told Rivera, "If we do this right, you and I are holding up the [Super Bowl] trophy with Mr. Richardson."

He also got choked up the first time he met the media when he talked about his late mother-in-law. This was considered a good sign by a number of Panthers officials—that Gettleman was so passionate he would get teary-eyed not about his mother, but about his mother-in-law, for gosh sakes.

Gettleman inherited a Carolina team that was already $16 million over the salary cap, so his first job was cutting the fat and restructuring contracts rather than adding players for Rivera. He had to preach patience to Panthers fans during his first free-agency signing period. As for his style, Gettleman said he was nothing fancy.

"I'm pretty simple. My wife will vouch for that," said Gettleman, who was accompanied at the press conference by his wife and their three children. "I believe in faith, family, and football. Those are my priorities. I'm called a grinder and I think that's a compliment."

Hurney served in the job for a decade—throughout the John Fox era and for part of Rivera's, too. The Panthers' first real GM, Bill Polian, built the club in the mid-1990s into a team that could make the NFC Championship Game in only its second season, but then departed for Indianapolis. Head coaches Dom Capers and George Seifert then basically assumed the GM's duties as well as their own in the period from 1998 to 2001, which did not work out well.

It's impossible to thoroughly evaluate a GM until he has a couple of years on the job—enough time to get through at least two drafts and off-season signing periods. Gettleman said he's most comfortable in a dark room watching film and evaluating players. That's the kind of guy the Panthers would appear to need—but the proof will be in the pudding.

The Panthers' 2013 Free-Agent Class

When Dave Gettleman took over as the Panthers general manager in early 2013, he inherited a spot in salary-cap jail.

Gettleman's first task was to whittle his way out of that sentence, one contract at a time. He started by releasing cornerback Chris Gamble and defensive tackle Ron Edwards—two decent starters in 2012 but also two players whose salary-cap hit was too large to bear given their production. Gamble then said he was going to retire, although team observers still wonder if that will really stick.

The team also released starting linebacker James Anderson, who had set a franchise record for tackles only two years before. Anderson quickly signed with Chicago. By releasing Anderson, they put their faith in Jon Beason and Thomas Davis, who are more spectacular players than Anderson when healthy but who had not been as durable in recent years.

Those hard choices—along with convincing tackle Jordan Gross and safety Haruki Nakamura to take pay cuts so they could remain with the team—cleared a path for Gettleman to improve the team's secondary, which he deemed one of their biggest needs after arriving. He signed veteran cornerbacks Drayton Florence and D.J. Moore and veteran safety Mike Mitchell. He also re-signed nickel cornerback Captain Munnerlyn, a fan favorite, and defensive tackle Dwan Edwards.

Gettleman also signed two players he was familiar with from his time with the New York Giants—wide receiver Domenik Hixon and linebacker Chase Blackburn. He called them "pros who have been there, know how to prepare, and have jewelry," referencing the two Super Bowl rings each of them won with the Giants. Hixon and the Panthers' Louis Murphy basically were a swap—Murphy went to the Giants and Hixon to the Panthers, and it seemed likely that each would play a backup receiving role with their new team.

Most of those deals were one-year moves and came cheap by NFL standards. In a relatively soft free-agent market, more players than usual were willing to take less money in return for having their freedom to again negotiate with teams in 2014.

Gettleman's most intriguing off-season free-agent signing during his first few months on the job, however, was Ted Ginn Jr. A wide receiver and kick returner, the Panthers signed Ginn mostly because they want to upgrade a return game that has been mostly blasé ever since Michael Bates and Steve Smith were returning kicks more than a decade ago. Ginn, who last played for San Francisco, has six career returns for touchdowns.

After only three months—and even before he conducted his first draft with the Panthers—Gettleman seemed excited about the roster. He told a roomful of reporters in mid-April 2013, "Maybe you guys think I'm Pollyanna, but I don't see any major hole here."

Noting the Panthers had gone 5–1 in their last six, Gettleman said: "You have to be careful you're not looking at fool's gold. They won five of their last six… Is it real? Is it a mirage? After watching the tape and given the circumstance that team was in, for them to finish like that... I don't think it's fool's gold. I really don't."

100 The Panthers' 2013 Draft Class

There was nothing subtle about the Panthers' 2013 draft class, the first under new general manager Dave Gettleman. The Panthers went for steamrollers instead of speed. They picked three 300-plus-pound linemen with their first three choices, trying to add beef up front and undoubtedly increasing their food bill for training camp.

Gettleman likes to quote Tom Coughlin, the New York Giants' Super Bowl-winning coach, and one of his favorites is this: "Big men allow you to compete." Coughlin was talking about linemen there—the players that Gettleman calls "hog mollies."

Gettleman's primary hog mollies for 2013 included Utah defensive tackle Star Lotulelei in the first round, Purdue defensive tackle Kawann Short in the second, and Valdosta State offensive guard Edmund Kugbila in the fourth (the Panthers didn't have a third-round pick). Both defensive tackles should play right away, with Lotulelei as more of a space-eater and run-stopper and Short more of a pass rusher. Kugbila will compete for a starting job at right guard.

Lotulelei, selected No. 14 by the Panthers, was once considered a possible top-three pick. But he had a heart scare during the run-up to the NFL Draft. And, even though doctors cleared him, it dropped his draft stock.

"What Star does is he impacts the game on every snap," Gettleman said enthusiastically the night be drafted Lotulelei. "The other huge thing he does is he's going to occupy two [blockers] quite often, which is going to keep Luke [Kuechly] free. So it gives Luke more protection, which makes our defense better."

Lotulelei became the first top-50 draft choice the Panthers have used on a defensive tackle since Kris Jenkins in 2001. Only one

Is this the face of the future? New GM Dave Gettleman seems to think so. Defensive tackle Star Lotulelei meets the press in April 2013.

night later, the Panthers did it again, selecting Short in the second round (No. 44 overall). Short was a more effective pass rusher in college than Lotulelei was, but Lotulelei was superb at the point of attack.

"We got another hog molly," Panthers coach Ron Rivera said that night, speaking of Short. On the personal side, Short is louder, more demonstrative and nicknamed "K. K." Lotulelei is more soft-spoken.

On the third and final day of the 2013 draft, the Panthers selected three more players—Kugbila, as well as Iowa State linebacker A. J. Klein and Oregon running back Kenjon Barner. Klein should help on special teams right away while learning behind the veterans. Barner is a scatback type with great speed, but he will need an impressive training camp to make the veteran roster because the Panthers are so well stocked at his position. Kugbila is a 317-pounder who played at a small school but has fine potential.

The player Gettleman seemed most excited about initially, though, was Lotulelei—the rare NFL rookie who is already married and has two small daughters with his wife. The GM believes that his first-ever first-round Panthers draft choice will solidify the defensive line and allow Charles Johnson and Greg Hardy to have a few more special seasons together.

"The guy's a player," Gettleman said of Lotulelei. "He fits what we do. He's very talented. He's mature. And it gives us a chance. You look historically at the Super Bowl champions, and you show me one that's had a bad defensive front. Doesn't happen—I'm telling you."

Does that mean Gettleman plans on constructing a team that will get to the Super Bowl? Can he actually do that? As Gettleman likes to say, stay tuned.

Sources

This book is primarily based on the author's interviews and informal conversations with all its subjects over the past 20 years. It also includes information from the following sources:

Wire services
Associated Press

Periodicals
Charlotte Observer
Carolina Panthers media guides and "Year in Review" annual guides, 1995–2013

Websites
www.CharlotteObserver.com
www.ESPN.com
www.NFL.com
www.Panthers.com
www.ProFootballHOF.com

Books
Tales from the Carolina Panthers Sideline by Scott Fowler (Sports Publishing, 2004)
Year of the Cat by Scott Fowler and Charles Chandler (Simon & Schuster, 1997)
The Ultimate Super Bowl Book by Bob McGinn (MVP Books, 2012)
The Carolina Panthers: The First Season of the Most Successful Expansion Team in NFL History by Joe Menzer and Bob Condor (Macmillan, 1996)

SCOTT FOWLER

Cardiac Cats: Carolina Panthers' Unforgettable Super Bowl Season by the *Charlotte Observer* (Triumph Books, 2004)